THE INNER PLACE

Tom Gunning

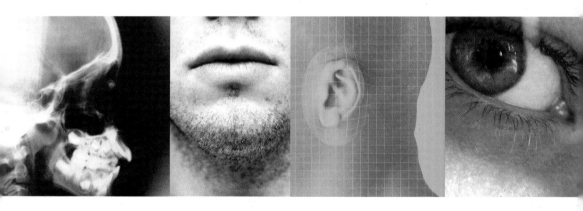

Senior Cycle Religious Education

A Curriculum Framework for Senior Cycle

VERITAS

Published 2006 by Veritas Publications
7–8 Lower Abbey Street, Dublin 1

ISBN 1 85390 958 0
978 1 85390 958 0 (from January 2007)
Copyright © 2006 Irish Episcopal Commission on Catechetics
Printed with Eccelesiastical Approval

Theological Adviser:
Patrick Mullins OCarm, STD
Consultant to the Programme: Maura Hyland
Designer: Niamh McGarry
Text Editor: Elaine Campion
Copyright Research: Ruth Garvey and Caitriona Clarke
Origination: Digital Prepress Imaging
Printed in the Republic of Ireland by Lithographic Web Press Ltd,
Dublin

Text and picture copyright acknowledgements
may be found on pages 363–4.

CONTENTS

SECTION A: THE SEARCH FOR MEANING

SECTION B: CHRISTIANITY

SECTION C: MORALITY

SECTION A

THE SEARCH
FOR MEANING

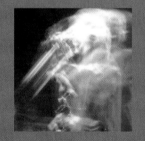

Chapter One

AN INTRODUCTION

The following is a story about three secondary-school students.

The first student was Mary Bourke. She was from Mayo, which is way off over there, unless you're reading this in Mayo, in which case it's right here. Mary was a good student and did very well at sports. In fact, she could be described as a very good all-rounder. In any given year, she could have been placed in the top three of her class. She went to Mount Anville boarding school in Dundrum, Dublin. There was nothing in particular that stood out about her. Yet there was a teacher, a Sr Joan, who commented that she 'followed her own mind to an exceptional degree'. Mary managed to have a good attendance record right through secondary school.

Paul didn't. Paul didn't like school that much. Not at first anyway. Much of the time he spent on the hop from St Patrick's Secondary School. Instead of class, he opted to have a little wander around the streets and go for coffee on Grafton Street. (Don't try this during school hours!) He just didn't fit in and constantly got in trouble. He wasn't bothered. Once he threw something at the Spanish teacher – from behind a bush. Unsurprisingly, it impressed nobody. So his father decided to send him to Mount Temple High School in Artane. He settled down. He was good at history, drama and art.

The final student, Robert, went to school in Blackrock College. He was OK at school and got some good results, but he was fairly useless at maths. Three per cent in one exam – better than two per cent. Once he got into serious trouble over his dinner money. A massive bill went home to his da. A teacher had to take matters into his own hands and so he introduced Robert to the 'biffer'. Biffer was a thick flexible rubber strap. It hurt like hell.

Robert remembers that event. He remembers it with a deep sense of shame and rage.

These three students have something in common with you. Like you, they sat for hours on end in classrooms in secondary schools. Like you, they daydreamed and looked out the windows at grey cold skies. Irish skies. Like you, at some stage, they wondered what would ever become of them. Where would they fit in? What would happen after Leaving Cert?

This is what happened.

Mary Bourke got married and became Mary Robinson. After she left school, she became President of Ireland. Not immediately, obviously, but within time. She was President for fourteen years. During that time, she focused world attention on those in the developing world who suffered poverty, famine and a denial of their basic human rights. After being President, she got another job – she became the United Nations High Commissioner for Human Rights (2001–2002). She wasn't afraid to stand up to powerful governments to challenge their record on human rights. She described herself as having an 'awkward voice'. Or, as Sr Joan might say, 'She followed her own mind to an exceptional degree.'

Paul's second name is Hewson – but he is better known as Bono. A mega-successful rock star, he could have just kept the money and said nothing. Instead, Bono believed he could make a difference – a difference that mattered. Bono believed that he could give something back. The world didn't exist to make him wealthy or famous. As one biographer commented:

 Whether we bought a U2 record or not, we all want to believe in Bono, or at least in someone like him. Someone straight with you, who doesn't just take the money and run, but really does give something back; something more precious than money: his time.

After secondary school, Robert became better known as Bob – Bob Geldof. An accomplished rock star with the Boomtown Rats, he was watching the six o'clock News one evening and was silenced by the images of famine, hunger and death that appeared

the
inner
place

on the screen. Haunted by these images, he embarrassed, harassed and cajoled his fellow rock stars to do something. Something had to be done. They formed Band Aid and released the chart-topping single 'Do they know it's Christmas?' By the following year, Geldof had organised Live Aid. On 18 July 1985, Geldof stood in front of an audience of 80,000 in London's Wembley Stadium with a simple message: 'And the lesson today is how to die.' It reached a televised audience of millions. It was a message born in rage. Rage at the injustice of it all.

Geldof has spoken about that moment:

> All my life I had been waiting. For what I was unsure. Things felt good or bad, but never complete. There was always something else – something unspecific. Not today. Had all the waiting been for this?

Mary Robinson, Bono and Bob Geldof have been, and continue to be, outspoken voices on a world stage. They have championed the cause of the underprivileged and the forgotten. All, independently wealthy, could have pursued their own interests, but they stand out for one striking reason: they believe that the world does not exist to serve their needs; the world does not exist simply to furnish them with luxury, recognition or privilege; the world exists to be challenged, served and healed.

All of Geldof's life led to one moment. It was not a moment of excess, fame or wealth, but a moment of service to a broken, hungry and forgotten humanity.

the inner place

Look around your classroom now, and remember that these three people were all Irish secondary-school students just like you. They sat in seats, just like you, wondering what lay ahead. They could never have imagined. Nobody could have imagined.

When they sat in seats, just like you, there was nothing exceptional about them. On the outside, they were the same as everyone else. But on the inside, in some inner place, a seed had been planted.

The world will continue to yearn for people like these. Perhaps you will not be the next President of Ireland or the next global champion for the underprivileged and abandoned. But some day, you will have your own story to tell, your own purpose to reveal. The journey begins now and you have a great start. You are sitting in a classroom, and it's an Irish secondary school. The lesson today is how to live.

> **'Glory be to him whose power working**
> **in us can do infinitely more**
> **than we can ask or imagine.'**
> (Ephesians 3:20)

the
inner
place

1 Look around your classroom. As a single group, try to make a list of each student's unique talent at this stage in your lives. Look at each person. Are there any signs of voices/gifts that might emerge later on? What makes each of you unique in a special way? Are there people in your midst who are already emerging as voices that could make a real difference for the better on a local or global level?

2 Are there any amongst you who would admit to having no interest in making a difference for others and who believe the world exists to get what you can out of it? How do you justify such a stance?

3 Are there any amongst you who rage against what you perceive to be injustice at different levels of society or throughout the world? Check the roll. They may be absent. They may have been suspended recently for a misplaced rage against the system. They may be in the school Justice and Peace Group. They may be fundraising down at SuperValu for the Chernobyl Children's Project. Teenagers with an innate sense of injustice are everywhere.

4 Is there anyone who believes that it is their purpose to give something back? Do some of you feel that there is something that you have to give in service to others? You might be the quiet one who has nothing much to say now, but you have a sense that there is more to life than the adverts on TV and the general chit-chat of your age-group would have you believe (hair extensions, binge drinking, who scored, etc.).

5 What would signify accomplishment in your life ... now...in ten years...in twenty years?

the
inner
place

Chapter Two

THE SEARCH FOR MEANING

The meaning of life differs from person to person and from moment to moment. It is up to each individual to define the meaning of their own life, in their own particular moment.

The average lifespan is 25,550 days. You will have used up around six thousand by the time you read this. The meaning of your life right now is for you to decide. It is your story. You may have around 19,550 days to go. During their lifetime, many people search for meaning in their lives. What the meaning of your life will ultimately be is your story to tell. Until then, here are some stories to help you on your way.

Paul Auster

In October 1999, Paul Auster and the hosts of National Public's radio *Weekend* asked the listeners to send in true stories of American life. The following story, 'A Failed Execution', is about a renowned photo-journalist, one of those people who risk their lives to visit battle zones and natural disaster areas.

This story seems to raise more questions about the meaning of life than it answers.

A Failed Execution

It is 1994 and Thomas travels to South Africa to cover the election of Nelson Mandela. Upheaval reigns throughout the country; he and several other journalists travel to a poverty-stricken region where white supremacist rebels are preparing to confront the black population, which is agitating to gain voting rights.

As Thomas and his colleagues enter the region, they inadvertently drive into a convoy of white rebels. Bullets fly past their vehicle, but no one is injured. Suddenly the motorcade jerks to a stop. Black soldiers are attacking white rebels. A gunfight ensues. The terrified photographers scramble out and hide behind a car.

Slowly the soldiers gain a bloody upper hand. Most of the rebels have now fled or have been killed. Those that have survived lie injured and indignant, cursing and insulting those they had come to kill. Thomas emerges from the powdery dirt of his hiding place. He hurriedly snaps photos of the eerie surrender that has unfolded. Nobody knows what will happen next.

A black soldier, rifle aloft, approaches the rebels.

A shot rings out and a listless white body drops to the dry ground. With another shot the soldier kills a second rebel. Thomas, in a daze, can only observe and record the terrifying scene. There can be no intervention. The executions continue; the chaos deepens. The photographers eventually flee, terrified of what might occur next.

the
inner
place

Several days later, the photographers receive a call from a news cameraman who had been at the scene of the executions.

'Come over here,' they are told, 'there's something you should see.'

As Thomas enters the editing room, the tape rolls. The battle scene slowly replays. He sees the rebels and the soldiers. But then he sees someone else – himself.

He and a fellow photographer can be seen to one side as they capture image after image of the bloody executions. Then a figure appears above them, a black soldier. His weapon is pointing not at the rebels but at the oblivious photographers. He shakily rises his weapon, squeezes the trigger and ... click. Nothing happens.

The soldier hesitates and examines his weapon. It has jammed. A sharp whack ejects the bullet. The soldier reloads. Click. Again nothing. Another whack, another ejected bullet, and another reload. Click. Nothing again.

Then, outside the field of vision, a distraction occurs. The soldier flees the scene, leaving the photographers to complete their work.

Thomas slumps in the edit booth. He has just seen his own death.

(Paul Auster, *True Tales of American Life*)

the

inner

place

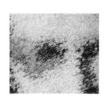  

The Search for Meaning

1 Why do you think Thomas might live his life differently after this experience?

2 In your opinion, why was his life spared? Was it just a coincidence or was there some other reason?

3 Why might an experience like this make a person think that life is meaningful?

4 Do you have a story like this that you could share with the class?

A student, upon hearing the story above, related the following story from her own experience.

It was this summer and my cousin called over. He and some friends were taking a trip into town and he wanted to know if I was interested in going along. I was quite happy to go because it was my granny's first anniversary. She had died the previous summer. Excuse the expression but the house was like a morgue all day. I felt like getting out.

My cousin was on a high because he had been driving for only a few months and he was telling us how to save on insurance and how driving a car was a real plus with the girls. We were discussing this girl he was after, when a thought came into my head in the back of the car. I don't know why, but this bend was coming up and I thought I might as well put on my seat belt. I'm a bit of a nervous type anyway. It was an old car, so I wasn't sure if there were any, but I found some ould yoke and wrapped it around myself. Next thing I remember was the car was on its roof and everyone was cursing. Some lad had taken the bend wide and

the inner place

my cousin had to go up on the ditch. There were four of us in the car, which was now a complete wreck. Everyone was OK though, because all four of us were strapped into our belts.

,

(Elaine Dunne, 17)

The above two stories seem to suggest that there might be a greater force looking out for us. Then again, they might just suggest the power of coincidence. Either way, the questions that they force us to ask set us on our search for meaning.

DISCUSS

1 How do you feel about the incidents described above? Do you view such things as involving chance, coincidence or some power looking out for us?
2 Do some people in your class have stories about how they believe their religious faith has helped them to avoid harm? How does this affect their view on the meaning of life?

ASIDE

A teacher told her class about a St Christopher medal her mother gave her when she bought her first car. She described all the mad near misses she had, but she'd never had an accident. She said she believed the medal had protected her; but then she said 'touch wood'. When the class asked her why she did that, a student explained that it was a pagan superstition. The teacher said it was just a habit. The class had a huge discussion about that.

the

inner

place

'Teenage angst has paid off well.'
(Nirvana, 'Serve the Servants', *In Utero*)

Kurt Cobain

When Kurt Cobain, lead singer with the band Nirvana, died in 1994, many young people felt that they had lost a spokesperson for their generation. Cobain screamed out the loud and sometimes chaotic lyrics of his age. His music was a symbol of freedom and independence. He represented a lost and confused generation. But this generation, like any other, was used to losing its heroes. Everything changes and nothing stays the same. Bands come and go, fashion by definition must constantly change, and whatever is hi-tech today is obsolete tomorrow. The generation that Cobain spoke to are known as 'Generation X', a people who struggled to find meaning in their lives. They listened to his music so as not to feel alone. They could leave their own despair and enter his.

This despair or lack of anything to believe in can also be interpreted as an experience that life appears meaningless. If life appears meaningless, it begs the question: Is life meaningful? This question in itself is a starting point for the search for meaning.

'The Scream' by Edvard Munch

the
inner
place

The Search for MEANING -
What's it all about?

I'm not sure anyone really knows what the meaning of life is but I think finding the meaning in your own life is important! 💡 For me it's important to just accept yourself for who you really are. We all want to fit in - we all feel we need to be part of a group. Friends and family help us achieve this. 😊

But sometimes it's like we have to be someone else to be accepted. We have to put on this image. We have to drink and party. We have to wear the right thing. We have to be rich - we have to be beautiful - like the people on TV. If you do, you're in! But this is kinda stupid I think. If you live your life to impress others or fit in, then it's not really you or your life, in fact!

I think the MEANING OF LIFE is relationships with people. It's the most important thing. People talk about the meaning of life as being rich or famous or successful. All they really want is to be known. But in life the only way you'll ever be remembered is by the positive effect on other people. Having a big car or lots of money isn't going to make a

difference - like being a nice person to someone
or encouraging them to do something that will
have a positive effect on other people. I don't
think people will remember you for the money, the
cars or the house but for the person you were.
Were you decent? Did you care about
just yourself or did you care about your friends?

Some people know there's something but are not
sure what it is. The search for meaning -
until you find it there's this space or void. I
think some people shop to fill the void.
This is fun at the time - there's a buzz - but then
the void soon returns.

You have to enjoy yourself too though. That's
where your friends come in. And you have to aim
in life and try to achieve goals for yourself.
Try to get the job you really want + not the
job you think people will be impressed with. You
have to be content with what you're doing +
where you're going.

I think we were all put here for a reason.
Religion has something to do with it. It kinda
shows us how to see things. In my opinion,
Religion shows us that the meaning of life is
to care for those around you. The people less
fortunate in the world present a challenge for those
around them. WE HAVE BEEN PUT HERE FOR A
REASON but you do have to have fun on the way.
Making people feel better is a start!!

THE END

the

inner

place

> 'At different times as individuals, we may be exposed to illness, loneliness, betrayal, disappointment, amongst other experiences, and these may raise basic doubts for us as to whether life can have any meaning.'
> (Gordon Lynch, *After Religion: Generation X and the Search for Meaning*)

MEANINGFUL EXPERIENCES

It is usually particular experiences in life that force us to search for meaning. Consider the following examples.

1   LONELINESS/ISOLATION

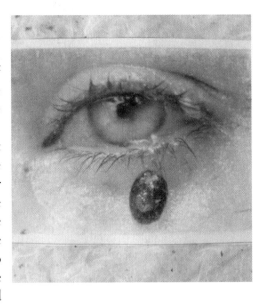

The philosopher Jean Paul Sartre said: 'Hell is other people.' In truth, the feeling of loneliness can be one of the most oppressive of experiences in life. We believe that someone out there should accept us for who we are. We believe that everyone should have some friends or family to call their own. We need to feel accepted by someone, as this makes life meaningful. The experience of loneliness raises difficult questions: Why am I not accepted? Why do I not belong?

the inner place

Over the past few years, the Russians have been conducting experiments at their Institute for Medical and Biological Problems (IMBP). In order to prepare future cosmonauts for a long-haul flight and mission to Mars, they are locking people into steel capsules for 500 days (with food and water obviously). They want to know the effects of isolation on humans. It is thought that it might create feelings of deep depression and anxiety, and they want to know how to avoid that for actual missions.

Consider this dilemma: in an imaginary horrible world, which would you least prefer of the following?

a   You go into school and get in trouble in every class and spend the best part of the afternoon in the principal's office.

b   You go into school and all your friends ignore you for the whole day.

Why does friendship and the company of others make life meaningful? Or do you belong to the Jean Paul Sartre school of thought?

the

inner

place

2   POPULARITY/APPROVAL

Look at any class group in school and it's obvious that some students are more popular than others. Why are some people more popular than others? The difficult question can sometimes be: Why am I not popular? Popularity can give us meaning because we feel that it's a way of gaining other people's approval.

Consider this dilemma: why is it that the more I seek other people's approval, the less I get; the more I try to be popular, the less popular I seem to be?

the inner place

DISCUSS

1   Do people get meaning out of being popular? Do you think that popularity should be the basis of a meaningful life? Why?/Why not?
2   Why is it so important for teenagers to fit in?

Sometimes to be popular we can create an outward appearance that gets us accepted. Yet hidden behind this appearance is the reality of who we really are. Diana Wilson, a student at Loreto, Wexford, created the following project, called 'Appearance versus Reality'. The person is represented as a book. The outer cover represents the appearance, while the inside represents who a person really is.

The inside reads: 'Outer beauty versus inner thoughts, feelings, emotions…scared to speak…tell someone…suffer in silence… instead alone. Everything looks so beautiful on the outside…no one knows what's really going on inside. Outer beauty doesn't tell us everything. We have to search to find the real person on the inside.'

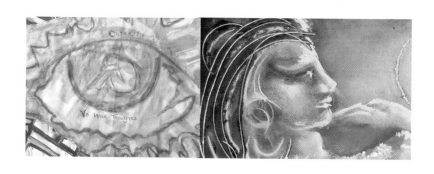

1 In what way might the search for meaning in life be connected to the search for the real person on the inside?
2 Why do we tend to hide the 'real' person? In what way are friends important in discovering who we really are?
3 Do you think it's important to look beautiful/handsome on the outside? Give reasons for your answer.

ASSIGNMENT

POSTERS/MUSIC

Do some research in groups on the different sources in the media and elsewhere that try to convince us that looking beautiful is important. You could create a poster or book, as above. Present your findings to the class. Which songs tell us we need to be beautiful/handsome?

Alternatively, look at the sources in contemporary society that tell us that inner beauty is more important. Are there any songs you know that carry that message? Play them for the class and share your thoughts on the lyrics.

the

inner

place

3   FAILURE/SUCCESS

Life can appear meaningless when it seems that we have been given no talents or that the talents we have aren't very useful. The school system seems to reward those who are intellectually capable. Why are there no rewards for being responsible, good or caring? If I continually fail to meet other people's standards, does that mean my life has little meaning? Has life in some way betrayed me?

Consider the following story, where a student feels a failure but ultimately finds meaning.

A Moment of Inspiration

A girl sits on her own at the back of the classroom. She sits alone because she has just been moved. She has been moved because she was talking. Of course she was talking – it's Monday afternoon and there is the whole weekend to talk about. Last warning, according to the teacher, then it's a note home. Trouble on all fronts then. She sits there, gazing out the window at a grey wall. She's not happy, but restless, and feeling a bit down. Sadness like a cloak seems to wrap itself around her since this morning.

Perhaps it is the thought of the meeting with her career-guidance teacher that afternoon that has her in a spin. Her grades were never brilliant. Failed a few at Christmas. In trouble a lot. What are her career options? Not that many coming to mind. All she can do is talk... 'If you talk again, Catherine Bennet, you'll be out of this classroom. Look at me when I'm speaking to you...'

the

inner

place

In fact, now that she thinks about it, she could probably talk for Ireland in a Talking Olympics. Then, in a moment of pure inspiration, she realises that that is it – her talent is in communicating. Later, the meeting with the careers teacher goes well. She explains what she has just discovered about herself, and the teacher gives her the number of the producer of a local youth-radio programme. It looks like the world of communications is where she will find her niche. Life isn't so bad after all.

DISCUSS

Do you think society rewards people for the wrong reasons? Do you think some people are made to feel like they are failures, even though they are not? Why does life seem meaningless when we fail?

ASIDE

One day, a partially deaf boy, named Tom, was sent home from school because he was deemed to be too slow and was holding up the rest of the class. His mother resolved to teach him herself. Many years later, the United States would mark his death in a very special way. At exactly 9.59 p.m., every home in the United States turned off its lights for one minute to honour the man who had invented those same lights.

Thomas Eddison not only invented the electric light, but also the film-projector and the record-player. The same boy who was too slow for school had over a thousand patents to his credit at the time of his death. According to Eddison, many of life's failures are people who do not realise how close they are to success when they give up.

Thomas Eddison

the inner place

4   DEATH

Story has it that when Pope John XXIII was dying, he said: 'My bags are packed, and I am waiting for her.' There is a sense in his words of fulfilment and promise, of expectation and anticipation. His sentiments seem to contrast with the wake-room and tragic graveside scenes of anger and incomprehensibility which many of us witness. In the latter, death can be perceived as that which makes all of living and loving absurd. Why invest so much energy and intimacy in life when it can be wrenched away so easily, so futilely or with no word of warning? Life may be perceived as a venture bereft of meaning, lacking in value and worth.

Pope John XXIII

Now we will consider the following extract, where a young man tries to come to terms with his father's death.

One day there is life. A man, for example, in the best of health, not even old, with no history of illness. Everything is as it was, as it will always be. He goes from one day to the next, minding his own business, dreaming only of the life that lies before him. And then, suddenly, it happens: there is death. A man lets out a little sigh, he slumps down in his chair and it is death. The suddenness of it leaves no room for thought, gives the mind no chance to seek out a word that might comfort it. We are left with nothing but death, the irreducible fact of our own mortality... Death without warning. Which is to say: life stops. And it can stop at any moment.

(Paul Auster, *The Invention of Solitude*)

the

inner

place

DISCUSS

Why do some people think that death makes life seem meaningless? Is it pointless to invest so much into a life for it all just to end?

One student who read the previous extract told the following story because she felt it showed how death can sometimes have meaning behind it.

> A man had a custom of giving his wife a single red rose every year on their anniversary. He then died very tragically and his wife was devastated. She dreaded in particular their anniversary, which was only a few weeks away. But on the day of the anniversary, a single red rose arrived from the florist. The woman rang up to tell them that there was some mistake. The lady answered that it was from her husband. She explained that her husband was dead and that that was impossible. The lady explained that the husband had left instructions with the florists to send a rose to his wife on the date of their anniversary, even if he had died. He said that he wanted his wife to know that he was thinking about her even after death. The last thing he told the florist was to continue to send the red roses.

the

inner

place

1   How do you think the above story might show that
    there can be meaning even in death?
2   In what way can the Christian belief in the afterlife
    make death seem less meaningless?

A WORLD FULL OF FEAR

World Trade Center,
11 September 2001

Death can make life seem meaningless because it annihilates life. However, in recent times an even greater threat has presented itself to humanity: the annihilation of not one life but thousands of lives in a given moment. In the final years of the twentieth century, there were predictions that a 'millennium bug' hardwired into most computer systems would wreak havoc and bring with it catastrophe come the new millennium. It didn't happen, but the possibility was there. It seems there may be a darker side to technological progress, and a price to be paid for it.

Then on 11 September 2001, a new century of fear really began with the terrorist attacks in New York. In 2004, a gigantic tsunami washed away thousands of homes and thousands of lives. In 2005, there were terrorist attacks on the London Underground, and fifty-two people were killed. In the same year, Hurricane Katrina destroyed cities along the Gulf coast of America, and again, without warning, thousands died. We live in a time of fear, where the lives of many can be wiped out, without warning, in the course of a morning or an afternoon. Many of

the

inner

place

those who live in the twenty-first century are obsessed by a fear of technology, global warming, natural disasters and terrorism. A world of fear is a world that struggles to find meaning.

DISCUSS

1 Does it appear to you that the world is becoming more threatening to human life and survival?
2 Why does a world with an unpredictable future seem meaningless?

ASSIGNMENT

FILM

Do you know of any current films that present the world as a hostile and fearful place? Are there films that predict the annihilation of the planet and the human race? You could look at a section of a film in class and discuss the message that the film is portraying.

If life appears meaningless, there are two options. The first option is to give up and give in to despair, pull the curtains and start listening to depressing music. The second option is to refuse to accept that life is absurd and meaningless, and instead begin the search for meaning. It is to that search that we will now turn.

the

inner

place

THE SEARCH FOR MEANING

Humans have been searching for a long time. It would appear that we are hardwired with a restlessness and a drive to question and search for alternative ways of viewing our lives. In ancient Greece, wise thinkers began to ask serious questions about the meaning of life. They were called philosophers because of their love of wisdom. They grappled with the big questions about life and death: What is the goal and purpose of life? What is truth? What is the nature of good and evil? What is justice?

Cave paintings at Lascaux

Over fifty thousand years ago, our ancestors were venturing deep into dark caves to paint images on the walls with specially prepared mixtures. These, they believed, would dissolve the rock face, allowing them to enter a completely different world, the world of the spirits. The spirits would put things right for them, put meaning and order on their primitive and chaotic world.

In the last century, our search has brought us out to the vastness of space. It is the final frontier. Humankind believes that somewhere in space may lie the answers to the origins of the universe. Space might answer that great question: Why are we here? Science is trying hard to come up with the answers, but, as we will see later in this course, perhaps religion has known the answer for a very long time.

the
inner
place

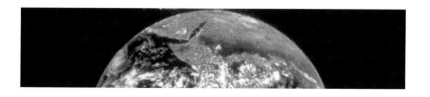

MY MIND FULL OF QUESTIONS

Any search begins with a question. How do I get there? Why am I going there? I wonder should I be doing a different course? Is there a better job out there for me?

What kind of questions do you ask about your life? What questions do you think are linked to the search for meaning? Check from the list below. Do you ask these questions: rarely, sometimes, all the time, or never?

Break into groups and discuss these questions quietly.

1. Why do people expect so much from me?
2. Will I go to college straight after school or will I take a year out?
3. If there was one thing I could change with my life, what would it be?
4. Why are the youngest always spoilt?
5. Why can't I have more freedom at home?
6. Why are there so many rules in school?
7. Can I trust my friends to keep a secret?
8. I wonder do my friends accept me for who I really am?
9. When I look in the mirror, am I happy with what I see?
10. Why do I get a spot just before a night out?
11. Who will I bring to my Grad?
12. Why do good people suffer?
13. Is there really a God?
14. What happens after we die?
15. Are there really such things as ghosts?
16. Will I ever get married?
17. How many children would I like when I get married?
18. Will I ever take drugs?
19. I wonder was I sent here for a purpose?

the inner place

20 Will Ireland ever win the World Cup?

21 Why, after Mass, will no one ever let you out of the car-park?

22 How did Munster manage to beat the All Blacks?

23 How will I get money for credit for my phone?

24 Do people like me?

25 I wonder will my parents insure me on their car?

26 Should I give some of my money to charity or volunteer to do charity work?

27 Why is there so much evil in the world?

28 Is there a meaning to coincidences or are they just ... coincidences?

29 What would make me really happy?

30 What would I do if I won the lottery?

CONTEMPORARY EXPRESSIONS OF THE SEARCH FOR MEANING

The search for meaning is an expression of our belief that the world and our lives are not meaningless. This search refuses to accept that life is absurd. Those who search for meaning refuse to live their lives in fear and doubt. They believe that their lives have a purpose and a meaning. The search to belong, for purpose and identity, for truth and goodness, is found all around us in our culture. Consider these examples.

1   SPORT

A contemporary expression of meaninglessness is the feeling that I am alone. Yet sport has the ability to transcend all boundaries and provide meaning in people's lives. Consider All-Ireland day in Croke Park. It doesn't matter

the inner place

Munster captain Anthony Foley holds the Heineken Cup European final trophy aloft at the Millennium Stadium in Cardiff, 20 May 2006

where you sit or whom you sit with – just get a ticket. If your team wins and the celebrations begin, it doesn't matter what your postal address is or your income. It doesn't matter how smart or successful you are. For that one glorious moment, everyone, no matter who they are, is rapt in a delirious joy. Everyone belongs to the team of supporters. Strangers embrace strangers and fans from rival clubs dance and sing and roar out their tribal songs together. Sport unites people, and, for that one moment, everyone belongs, everyone is accepted.

In 1978, a rugby touring party set out from New Zealand to take on teams from the northern hemisphere. No one gave their opposition any chance, and all fell in their wake, amongst them Wales and a star-studded Barbarians XV. But things were to change when they arrived in Munster. Sometimes sport can act as a mirror-image of life. Those problems that seem overwhelming and impossible to overcome can be taken down on a good day – just like the All Blacks. The following is an account by the referee of one of the most famous tackles in the game.

the inner place

    It was the most incredible tackle I ever saw in seventeen years as a referee. Stuart Wilson (All Blacks) came through at a hundred miles an hour on a switch ball and it was literally as if he had run into a brick wall and just slid down it. He collapsed in a heap. He didn't go backwards. He just crumbled. I looked around and every Munster player had grown twelve inches. You could sense it, you really could. I'm not being romantically reflective; it was a hard-nosed observation I made at the time. I thought, "These guys are bigger than when they ran on a few minutes ago." It happened in the middle of the park and of course the crowd reacted, but it wasn't a wild cheer. It was like, "Phwooah!" Gasps really.

    With a collision like that, you expect both players to go off. You stand nearby and try to avert your

gaze if there's blood. But they got up and carried on. I thought, "Oh my God! We're in for a game here today." In that one tackle, Seamus Dennison confirmed the reality to the Munster team. The reality that they could win.

(Alan English, *Stand Up and Fight*)

DISCUSS

1   Why do you think an experience such as this can give meaning to a fan's life?
2   Do you have a story of a sporting event that almost changed people's lives?

2 MUSIC

Music is another contemporary expression of the search for meaning. Earlier we mentioned how, when Kurt Cobain died, many young people felt they had lost a spokesperson for their generation. If they were angry or confused about the world, they weren't alone – Cobain felt the same way. To listen to his music, for some, was a way of not feeling alone. They might be in despair, but at least they had someone with whom they could share the feeling.

At another level, the music you listen to can help determine the friends you have. Music can be a means of carving out your own identity. If other people listen to the music you listen to, then you feel as if you belong to that group.

Music can inspire people and even change their mood. How often have you felt down or angry, but felt better after you listened to your favourite songs? Music helps us to transcend the limitations of our own here and now. Put on your headphones...close off the world...feel better. The following story illustrates the power of music, even in the most extreme conditions.

the

inner

place

The Search for Meaning   31

In 2005, Louise Woodger and her fiancé Gordon Pratley, two novice divers, had a momentous experience in the waters off Australia. Twenty minutes into a forty-five-minute dive, they resurfaced only to find that the currents had swept them several hundred metres from their boat. They tried swimming back but to no avail. Eventually, they were swept five nautical miles away from their vessel.

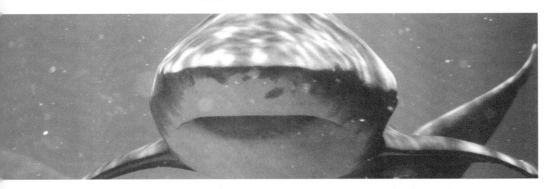

For six hours they sang songs to keep their spirits up. Later, when Louise glanced down into the ocean and saw a shark circling eight feet below, she decided not to tell her partner. Eventually, the reality of their situation hit them both, and worse was to happen when they were separated from each other as the white-tipped reef shark hovered below. They failed to attract the attention of the rescue helicopters and rescue boats due to the choppy seas, and were lucky to be spotted two hours before dark when the waters became calm. Later, when asked how they kept their spirits up, they claimed that they just sang songs to each other. Gordon said: 'At first you think you are going to be fine, and then as it gets later and later you think, well you don't really want to think what might happen, you just stay cool. When we got separated we were just supporting each other, keeping each other's spirits up with a bit of singing.'

(*The Guardian*, 15/9/05)

the

inner

place

DISCUSS

ASSIGNMENT

1 Does music sometimes manage to keep your spirits up during bad times? Share some examples with the class.

2 Would you agree that singing was a good way for the divers to maintain control of their situation? What might be appropriate songs to sing while lost in the ocean with a shark circling eight feet away?

MUSIC

For your next Religion class, bring in some songs that you think deal with the meaning of life. Play them for the class and see if others agree.

You could also break into groups and compile a list of your favourite songs that seem to point towards the search for meaning. Each group could then explain why they picked each song.

the

inner

place

3   LITERATURE

Another way of closing off the world and entering into a different space is through reading. Have you ever had the experience of reading a book and feeling yourself completely closed off from the world around you? That can be a liberating experience. Like music, a good story or book has the ability to inspire and also to help one overcome loneliness. In the film *Shadowlands*, C.S. Lewis, played by Anthony Hopkins, asks a group of students why they read. They offer their own ideas. Lewis says: 'We read to know we are not alone.'

Just like us, people long ago wondered about their place in the world. Why are we here? Where did everything come from? The earliest stories ever told, known today as myths, addressed those big questions and, in offering answers for their own culture and generation, they provided pointers to meaning. Stories today can also act as pointers towards meaning.

ASIDE

The French author Albert Camus expressed his philosophical beliefs through his novels. Camus believed that the world was essentially absurd and he looked for a way to make meaning of such an existence.

One novel, *The Plague,* reveals the absurdity of the world through the theme of the suffering of innocent children. Camus poses the question as to how we can be authentic in a world of absurdity. The novel tells the story of the city of Oran in Algiers, which is attacked by a plague. Thousands of rats come into the open streets and die. As humans begin to die from the infectious plague, a group of citizens get together to fight back.

When a young child dies, the medical doctor asserts that he 'will always refuse to love a creation where children are tortured'. A Jesuit, Fr Paneloux,

Albert Camus

the
inner
place

states: 'Perhaps we should love what we cannot understand.' Eventually the plague recedes and it is never clear whether the resistance has been successful or not.

By the end of the novel, Camus brings the position of the doctor and priest together by showing how both, in their own way, struggle against all forms of evil and suffering. The novel reveals the struggle to lead a meaningful life, and shows that an authentic life can be found in human solidarity against the absurdity of existence.

ASSIGNMENT

Bring in some books or stories that you have read that are concerned with the search for meaning. Share them with the class.

You could produce your own book of short stories and extracts from poems and literature and then sell it in the school for a charity of your choice. The pieces selected would be inspirational and engage your own age-group.

the

inner

place

4　ART

Themes relating to the search for meaning can also be found in modern art. Here we will briefly examine two paintings.

A　*Nighthawks* by Edward Hopper

This picture may be familiar to some already. It is a classic city scene, yet the city is deserted save for the four characters in the painting. Hopper himself explained that he was probably 'painting the loneliness of a large city'. The couple at the bar seem to emphasise the solitariness of the third drinker in the bar. Yet the couple themselves seem strangely unconnected. They seem to be simply sharing the same space, yet it is a space shrouded in shadow and darkness.

DISCUSS

What way does the depiction of loneliness make us feel? In what way does it prompt us to search for meaning?

B　*The Restaurant Window* by George Segal

In this picture, a woman sits on her own at a restaurant window. A man is passing by, but it seems unlikely that he will notice her or see her. There's something strangely disturbing about this picture and it reminds us of *Nighthawks*. There is an overpowering sense of coldness

and isolation about it. One commentator describes it thus: 'The scene sends shivers down one's back. In a single "decisive moment", everything that contradicts the promise of commercial culture that happiness and fulfilment can be had through

the inner place

consumption comes together: the piercing loneliness of the individual in the shadow of the world of glamour and glitter.'

DISCUSS

1 This picture seems a contradiction. Are we conditioned to think that buying and being a consumer should give us comfort?

2 Is it true that people can be incredibly lonely when they go out to socialise?

5 FILM

Many films carry the theme of the search for meaning, and you can identify some in class discussions, and even bring in clips to view the relevant scenes. Here we will briefly treat one film that deals with the theme: *Dead Poets Society*. The students in a boarding school discover an old cave, once used by past students to read poetry and suck the marrow out of life. They were romantics who let poetry work its magic, as in the darkness spirits soared and gods were made.

The central character is the new English teacher, Mr Keating. One particular scene early on in the film stands out with regard to the theme of the search for meaning. You can watch this clip in class yourselves.

In the scene, Mr Keating brings the boys down to the hallway where, along the walls, there are pictures of students long dead and gone. Keating asks the boys to study the images on the walls. Those students are now dead, pushing up daisies. Keating encourages the boys to listen to the silent faces and see if they can hear the legacy of those gone before them. What do they whisper to the faces of the present? As the boys lean in closer, Keating whispers 'Carpe diem, seize the day...'

the

inner

place

The faces that peered out from beneath the veil of the past felt they were once invincible, just like the present boys. They felt they were destined for great things. The world was their oyster, their eyes are full of hope.

Those boys, who are now fertilising daffodils, pose a question to the younger ones. Mr Keating poses it for them: did these boys wait until it was too late to make from their lives one iota of what they were capable of? And now, the young boys peering in, would they wait until it was too late?

6 SPIRITUALITY, PRAYER AND RITUAL

In recent years, there has been an upsurge of interest in different forms of spirituality and prayer. Recent surveys show that organised religion is in decline in Ireland. Yet this trend is matched by a growing interest in Eastern forms of prayer and meditation. Go into any bookshop and there will be a significant section devoted to Body, Mind and Spirit. The interest in this type of literature points to a search for something deeper in life.

Spirituality may be defined as our ability to transcend or go beyond ourselves. The interest in spirituality points to the contemporary belief that there is more to life than what can be got from the material world. The many modern spiritual practices currently gaining popularity in Ireland include yoga, meditation, aromatherapy and integrated energy therapy.

Later we will examine in detail how religion can express the search for meaning in a person's life. Yet for the moment it is interesting to note how many young people in Ireland have adopted traditional religious rituals into their own lives. An

the
inner
place

example of this is pilgrimage. A pilgrimage is a journey to a place that is regarded as sacred because it is associated with a person or event of religious significance.

The continuing popularity of pilgrimages in Ireland is a distinctive feature of the impact of religion in this country. People go in their thousands to places like Lough Derg and Croagh Patrick every year, and the number of young people visiting these sites has continued to increase. Today, almost 25,000 visitors make their way to the top of Croagh Patrick on the last Sunday of every July, and many of these are young people. Most walk up the 2510-foot-high mountain, while some who are really penitent go up on their knees.

DISCUSS

1 Why do you think people express their search for meaning through spirituality and prayer?

2 Why do you think young people are attracted to the hardships of pilgrimage?

the

inner

place

Chapter Three

THE GREAT QUESTIONS ABOUT THE MEANING OF LIFE

In Douglas Adams' trilogy *A Hitchhiker's Guide to the Galaxy*, there was a race of people somewhere out there in the galaxy who created a special and incredibly powerful computer called Deep Thought. When the computer was ready, they gathered around it during a special ceremony. Not completely sure what to do with the computer, they decided to ask it the ultimate question: what is the meaning of everything – life, the universe, the whole lot? Deep Thought was lost in deep thought for a while.

The computer then responded that that was a very challenging question and it would take some time to come up with an answer. A few generations later, the grandchildren of the original creators were summoned to the computer. All gathered round the computer expectantly and waited. Deep Thought had come up with an answer to the question. The answer was forty-two.

After a pause and some silence, those gathered conveyed to Deep Thought their disappointment regarding the answer. Forty-two didn't exactly excite them to further discussion and exploration. Deep Thought responded that the problem was with the question in the first place. They needed a better question, but Deep Thought wasn't capable of formulating such a question. A new, more powerful computer would have to be created, which would have the ability to come up with the right question. And so a new computer was created and it was given a special name: Earth.

42

In chapter 2, we noted how the need to ask questions about ourselves and life is an inherent part of being human. The message imparted in Douglas Adams' trilogy is that the answer to the ultimate question about the meaning of life is to be found here, on this very planet. In this chapter, we will continue to ask questions to uncover something of the meaning of life. For many generations, people have wondered about the goal and purpose of life and the problem of evil and suffering. It is to those questions that we will now turn.

> **DISCUSS** According to Douglas Adams' trilogy, the answer to the ultimate question about the meaning of life is to be found here, on earth. Does this mean that you are part of the answer to the ultimate questions? What in your opinion are the ultimate questions about the meaning of life? In what way might earth and you be part of the answer?

THE GOAL AND PURPOSE OF LIFE

In the previous chapter, we examined the different experiences that can cause a sense of meaninglessness. One of these was a lack of purpose in a person's life. We looked at the example of the girl in the classroom who was anxious and troubled because she didn't know if she had any talents, and she was very unsure of what future path her life would take. Once she realised that her place was in the world of communications, her sadness lifted. She now had a goal and purpose to pursue.

The following example, from the autobiography of Irish soccer international Roy Keane, illustrates how the purpose of a person's life can be revealed at the least expected moment. Keane is playing for the under-eighteen Cobh Rambler team, and they're about to be hammered:

> On the day of the replay, 18 February 1990, everything went wrong from the start. The bus was

The Great Questions about
the Meaning of Life

late picking us up in Cobh. The traffic was heavy. Most of the journey was spent looking anxiously at clocks and watches. Would we make it by kick-off time? We got to Fairview Park, an open, windswept public park, with only minutes to spare. We were knackered, beaten before we began. Belvedere hammered us 4-0.

Afterwards we went across the road to a pub for a glass of orange and a sandwich. John O'Rourke, the Ramblers' vice-chairman, came and sat beside me: 'Roy, there was a scout from Nottingham Forest over there. He said they'd like you to go over for a trial…'

Considering where I had come from, this to me was heaven: the uncertainty, the perpetual feeling of drift, the rumours of scouts supposed to be interested, trials that never materialised, the odd jobs, one step away from the dole…worrying where the next 'fiver' would come from. Compared to my recent existence this was fabulous. In those first few weeks of proper full-time training I felt a buzz every morning. I celebrated my nineteenth birthday on 10 August feeling for the first time really that I had a real life.

(Roy Keane, *Keane: The Autobiography*)

the

inner

place

DISCUSS

1 Why do you think Keane reckoned he had a 'real life' when he joined Nottingham Forest?

2 Why would you think life is just 'a perpetual feeling of drift' when there is no purpose to it?

3 Why is it important to feel that there is a goal and a purpose to your life?

4 Give examples of what the goal and purpose of a person's life might be like.

The Great Questions about the Meaning of Life

In response to the above piece about Roy Keane, the following student offered her own account of finding the purpose of her life.

❝ I think it was only in October '05 in Kinsale when I realised that playing music is definitely what I want to do in my life. We were at the Jazz fringe festival in Cork and the buzz in the place was amazing! There were bands playing in every pub and hotel and there were musicians everywhere.

On the first night we arrived in Kinsale, we went to a venue called "Muddy Maher's" and there was a deadly blues band playing. The band was really burning and the energy in the room was electric. The players were so into it and the crowd was loving it! People were dancing and going crazy for the band. I just thought it was the coolest thing – these musicians were really enjoying themselves and this was their job!

The next few days were just unreal. The atmosphere was really breathtaking and I was so inspired by all the players and the bands. I met loads of musicians and jammed with some bands on my sax. It was such a brilliant laugh!

Loose Change

the

inner

place

The Great Questions about the Meaning of Life

The highlight of the weekend was definitely playing with a band called 'Loose Change' from Kent. I've now played with them every time they come to play here in Ireland.

It's such an amazing feeling. It's hard to explain what it's like to play with a group with so much energy and to a crowd that's so enthusiastic. All I know is that it feels right for me and makes me happy. I want to keep doing it – to keep getting that buzz from the crowd.

(Rachel Clancy, 17)

DISCUSS

1 Do you believe that we all have a purpose in life? How do you think we find it?

2 The purpose for the student above seems to be connected in some way with the relationship between the band and the crowd. Do you think our purpose in life is in some way tied to our relationship with other people?

3 How many people in your class believe that ultimately their purpose has to do with other people, and not just themselves?

the

inner

place

The Great Questions about the Meaning of Life

THE ROLE OF SERVICE

**'The only ones among you who will be really happy are those
who have sought and found how to serve.'**
(Albert Schweitzer)

The story about Roy Keane makes no specific reference to happiness, but Rachel's story did. Yet it is clear enough that when people decide on their purpose in life, this brings with it a certain amount of happiness. Universally, happiness is what everyone wants from life. Do you know of anyone who would say: 'Well, my goal and purpose in life is to be totally miserable'? If someone did say that, and mean it, they would rightly be called sad. If our goal in life is to be happy, then we should take the above quote by Albert Schweitzer seriously. Yet, in what way is service or helping others linked to happiness?

Consider the following passage by the psychologist Dr Wayne Dyer, who writes about the power of purpose in a person's life:

One of the reasons for so much contemporary depression is the inability to see ourselves connected to something greater and more important than our own egos. Young people whose primary focus is on their possessions, their appearance, their reputations with their peers – in short, their own egos – have very little sense of humility. If you want to feel connected to your own purpose, know this for certain: Your purpose will only be found in service to others, and in being connected to something far greater than your body/mind/ego.

(Wayne Dyer, *The Power of Intention*)

the

inner

place

There are two things worthy of examination here. Firstly, that we should be connected with 'something far greater', and secondly 'your purpose will only be found in service'. The results might surprise you.

1 BEING CONNECTED TO SOMETHING FAR GREATER

We noted already that a contemporary expression of the search for meaning could be found in modern forms of spirituality, prayer and ritual. Here it is suggested that people can find meaning by being connected to something 'far greater' than themselves. In the Christian tradition, we refer to that which is 'far greater' as God.

Why does a sense of being connected to something far greater than ourselves, or God, have such a significant effect on people? Consider the following reasons.

Personal Purpose
The belief that they are connected to a greater power makes people feel that they have been created for a purpose. There is a meaning to their existence, because it did not happen simply by some biological chance. People sometimes say that they feel they have been 'put here for a reason'.

The World has a Purpose
The sense of being connected to a greater power makes a person feel that there is a purpose and meaning to the world. Despite all the occurrences that make us fearful of the world, such as terrorism and natural disasters, the world is not spinning out of control, because there is a greater power in control.

The Great Questions about
the Meaning of Life

Source of Comfort

In times of personal sadness or loneliness, a belief in a greater power can be a source of comfort and meaning because the person does not feel alone. The person who believes in the power of prayer might also believe that they have some control over their situation. If I pray to God, perhaps God will help me.

Studies also show that belief in God can have a positive effect on patients' health. In 1995, Dr Thomas E. Oxman and his colleagues at Dartmouth Medical school reported that heart-disease patients over the age of fifty-five who had had open-heart surgery for either coronary artery or aortic valve disease, and who had received solace and comfort from their religious beliefs, were three times more likely to survive than those who did not.

(Herbert Benson, *Timeless Healing*)

Sense of Community

Those who believe in a greater power, or in the Christian tradition what we would term God, often belong to an organised religion. People can get a great sense of meaning from the formal rites of worship, prayer and ritual in a worshipping community.

> **DISCUSS**
>
> 1 Why do you think that people who pray and feel connected to God have a greater sense of purpose in their lives? How might they express that sense of purpose?
> 2 Does the existence of God give a sense of purpose to the world? Does it seem safer if God exists?
> 3 Do you know of any stories of people who seemed to have recovered better from illness due to their religious beliefs?

the

inner

place

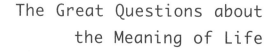

2   SERVICE TO OTHERS

It has been suggested above that purpose and meaning can be derived from service to others. The strange thing about doing something for others is that it seems to benefit the doer as much as the person on the receiving end. Young people particularly seem to respond to the needs of those less well off, as can be seen in the following examples.

Dozens Join School Head in Sleep-out to Aid the Homeless

Seventy past and present pupils of Belvedere College began braving the elements, and the Christmas revellers, yesterday as part of a 48-hour fast and 'sleep-out' to raise money for the homeless. The group hopes to break last year's record of 105,000 euro raised over the two days. Sixteen pupils, plus the school's headmaster Gerard Foley and a couple of other teachers, slept rough outside the GPO last night and will do so again tonight.

(*Irish Independent*, 23/12/04)

The Children of Kosovo

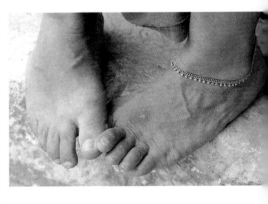

In 2006, a sixteen-year-old student in Presentation School, Kilkenny read about refugees who had to walk many miles to escape the war and devastation in Kosovo. She was particularly moved by the descriptions of the young kids who had no shoes and had to walk barefoot, and so she decided to raise money to buy them shoes. Here is a copy of the e-mail she sent to explain the fundraising venture, along with the reply she received.

The Great Questions about
the Meaning of Life

From: kilkenny@presentation.ie
Subject: Sponsored Walk
Date: 7 June 2006
To: valdet@kosovo.com

Dear Valdet,

We are a small group of sixteen-year-old girls who live in Kilkenny, Ireland. Recently, we did a sponsored walk to raise money for the innocent people who are suffering in Kosovo. We raised 469 euro, which we are now giving to you.

We know that the refugees there walked very far - that is why we were glad to walk too.

We finished our walk in the church, where we prayed silently for all those who suffer. We continue to think of and feel the pain of these people. We will keep in touch.

Fourth Year Girls

From: valdet@kosovo.com
Subject: Sponsored Walk
Date: 16 June 2006
To: kilkenny@presentation.ie

Dear girls,

I'm so touched and impressed by your message. I'm forwarding it to all of our board members. I'm so happy that you feel close to the tragedy of Kosovo children. This helps me believe that your generation will give an end to all inhuman situations and actions that the world is unfortunately repeating even in our times. I promise to translate your message and distribute to the kids in those refugee camps your funds. We are developing many projects based on the money Irish people are sending over.

Valdet

the

inner

place

DISCUSS

Why do you think the students undertook a forty-eight-hour fast or went on a sponsored walk? Do you think they would have felt good after it was over? Did you ever do anything like this yourself? What did you do and how did you feel afterwards?

Presentation Secondary School, Kilkenny

Our own experience tells us that doing something good for someone feels good somehow. So in what way is service and care of others beneficial? Consider the following reasons.

- There is scientific evidence that acts of service and kindness are actually beneficial for us. Dr Wayne Dyer explains it as follows:

  The positive effect on the immune system and on the increased production of serotonin in the brain has been proven in research studies. Serotonin is a naturally occurring substance in the body that makes us feel more comfortable, peaceful and even blissful. In fact, the role of most antidepressants is to increase the production of serotonin chemically, helping to ease depression. Research has shown that a simple act of kindness directed toward another improves the functioning of the immune system and stimulates the production of serotonin in both the recipient of the kindness and the person extending the kindness. Even more amazing is that persons observing the act

the
inner
place

The Great Questions about
the Meaning of Life

of kindness have similar beneficial results. Imagine this! Kindness extended, received or observed beneficially impacts the physical health and feelings of everyone involved.

(Wayne Dyer, *The Power of Intention*)

- If our brains reward us with serotonin when we think of others, it suggests that humans have evolved in such a way that we are hardwired to think about other people. But could you imagine a society where everybody just thought about themselves? The result would probably be anarchy and chaos. A society functions on the basis that we all think about others. We care for those who are less well off or who are unable to think for 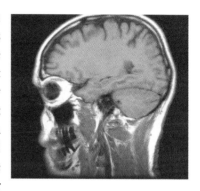 themselves. Otherwise there would be deep and radical divisions within the group, and conflict would be inevitable.

- In our search for meaning, we have noted the different ways that people strive not to feel alone or isolated. Friendship is one of the most important ways to overcome isolation, but friendship would be impossible without acts of kindness or thinking about the other person. A totally selfish person would most likely find it hard to maintain true and lasting friendships (unless of course all the totally selfish people decided to hang around with one another).

- In the Judaeo-Christian tradition, the 'something far greater' is called God. According to the book of Genesis, God created the world and all that is in it. Viewed in another way, we could say that at the heart of God lies the process of giving, creation and expansion. If at the beginning God had simply sat

the inner place

there thinking about how great God was, there would have been nothing else.

- Probably the most compelling evidence for service as a source of meaning is your own lived experience of giving, kindness and thinking of others. At Christmas time, when the presents are being given out, which is the better feeling – to receive a present, or to give one and see the appreciation in another person's face? Each one of us will answer that question for ourselves.

ASSIGNMENT Examine the following account and ask yourself what you would have done in this situation.

At 9.00 a.m. a group of science students were about to begin their final exam of four years' work. Pass this one and they could graduate. For over two hours, people scribbled furiously, doodled dementedly, scratched their heads, examined the ceiling looking for answers (why do people do that?), and regurgitated the previous night's crammed study. With half an hour to go, an elderly student let out a sigh, grabbed his chest and fell to the floor in agony.

Everyone stopped and stared. Everyone looked at the clock. Half an hour to go. Only two students left their seats and began to help the stricken student. One had a vague idea of CPR. The other just thought she should help. The medics eventually arrived. They arrived ten minutes before the end of the exam. When the bell sounded for the exam to end, the two students were ordered to stop writing or they would invalidate their entire exam.

the
inner
place

The Great Questions about
the Meaning of Life

TO HELP OR NOT TO HELP

An act of service or kindness to someone is often preceded by some form of dilemma. Should I or shouldn't I help? Such a dilemma played itself out with disastrous consequences for the following young woman.

The Story of the Toyota Land-cruiser

Having recently moved to Africa, a young woman was driving along the road one day in her extremely big 4x4 Toyota Land-cruiser. Her husband gave it to her to keep her safe, along with the instruction never to stop for anyone or anything while out on her own. One day, while driving along a dirt road, she came across a man lying out in front of her. Her immediate reaction was to stop and get out and offer some help, but she remembered her husband's advice. Unfamiliar with

her surroundings, she decided to mount a bush embankment in her 4x4 and go to the next town as speedily as possible to summon some help for the man.

In the next town, she went straight to the police station and immediately reported her story. She was asked to wait while a policeman went out and checked the man. After some time he returned to the young woman looking ashen-faced. 'Was he OK, I hope he wasn't too badly injured?' the woman enquired. The policeman looked at her searchingly and delivered her the news, 'The guy on the road is OK, but his two friends who were waiting in the bushes are dead. You drove over them.'

the

inner

place

GOOD AND EVIL AND THE EXPERIENCE OF SUFFERING

Thus far, we have examined the search for meaning from the perspective of our own experiences. We have seen how life can appear meaningless in the face of particular experiences such as isolation, failure, death and fear. We have looked at ways in which people search for meaning in the context of their own lives, through friendship, belonging, sport, music and by discovering their own purpose in life. Yet the experience of evil and suffering poses a particular challenge to the search for meaning. Put simply, can meaning be found in the midst of suffering and in the presence of evil?

Inmates at Omarska

In his book *The Tenth Circle of Hell*, Rezak Hukanovic gives a first-hand account of life in the Serb concentration camp at Omarska. In his foreword to the book, Elie Wiesel, himself a survivor of the Nazi concentration camps, explains the title: 'Dante was wrong. Hell consists not of nine circles, but of ten. Rezak takes you to the latest one, the most dreadful and the most heartbreaking.'

Rezak tells the story in the third person, but it is his own story. He witnessed horrific tortures, among them that of a man who had a piece of timber nailed to his heel. Nobody was allowed remove it, and after a deadly infection he died in absolute agony. In the following extract, he recounts the torture received at the hands of the drunken guards. It is an account of a raw and brutal evil. The question to consider as you read this text is: how could anyone find meaning in the midst of such horror?

the inner place

'Dying was easy at Omarska, but living was hard.'

Wednesday, June 10, early evening. The interrogators had already left for the day, in the van that took them back and forth from Prijedor. One of the guards, drunker than usual, stuck his unkempt head through the door of the dorm and called for Djemo. The same deathly silence that accompanied night calls descended on the dorm. Djemo felt a booming in his head, as if hundreds of hammers were pounding at his temples, at the top of his skull and the nape of his neck. His heart started pounding wildly; he could feel it beating in every part of his body. His blood pulsed through the labyrinth of capillaries across his face. He turned to his son and began to speak, his voice breaking: 'Don't be scared, son, nothing will happen to me.' Djemo hugged Ari tightly, feeling the delicate rhythmic trembling of his fragile body.

'Ari, son, Daddy will be back, believe me.' Timidly he took his son's arms off his shoulders, turned aside so that Ari wouldn't see the tears trickling down his cheeks, and started to walk away, not believing his own words. Somewhere at the back of his head he could almost feel the eyes of the poor souls whose silence spoke so eloquently. Gasps and deep sobs began from where he had been sitting, first softly, then louder and louder. Ari was weeping as the weak arms of those nearby reached out to keep him from going after his father. 'Daddy, come back, please!' Djemo stopped for a second as his eyes tracked his son's voice. Something big and heavy, like a cannonball, lodged in his throat. He could hardly breathe. The tears that had trickled down his cheeks now flowed freely.

Trying to flee such a merciless fate, he forced himself to utter: 'I'll be back son, I'll be back.'

Then he stepped forward past the guard, whose

the

inner

place

The Great Questions about
the Meaning of Life

bearded face was flush and whose eye transmitted only darkness. 'In front of me,' the guard ordered, pointing to the white house. On the way over he ranted and raved, cursing and occasionally pounding Djemo on the back with his truncheon.

The hot, heavy air made everything even more unbearable. Djemo cast one more dull look backward, into the distance, almost stopping. The guard pushed the barrel of his rifle hard into Djemo's back, until he felt a sharp pain and beads of sweat gathered across his face.

An overwhelming desire came over Djemo. He was on the verge of turning to spit into the bearded creature's face and punch him right in the middle of his ugly, drunken snout. But no – the voice of his son resounded in his ears like a seal ripped open in his torn heart.

Something flashed across his eyes, and everything became blurry. Blistering heat scorched his face and neck. He couldn't open his eyes. Half-conscious, sensing that he had to fight to survive, he whipped the blood from his eyes and forehead and raised his head. He saw four creatures completely drunk, like a pack of starving wolves, with clubs in their hands and unadorned hatred in their eyes. Among them was the frenzied leader of the bloodthirsty pack, Zoran Zigic, the infamous Ziga whose soul, if he had one at all, was spattered with blood.

'Now, then, let me show you how Ziga does it,' he said…

His recovery lasted twenty days. During that time he couldn't even move. Ari and some other prisoners

the inner place

The Great Questions about the Meaning of Life

had to carry him to the toilet. It didn't make Djemo feel very good, having everyone else do things for him. When Djemo looked at himself in the mirror for the first time, he started crying. His face was covered with black contusions and bruises. Where his nose had been, there was only a huge swelling that almost shut his eyes. Several of his front teeth were broken. His whole back was black and blue.

While recovering from Ziga's beating, a hajji [Muslim pilgrim] from Bosanka Kostajnica helped Djemo a lot. Hajji Ramiz slept by Djemo's side, offering his part of the blanket, while he himself lay on a ragged leather jacket...

(Rezak Hukanovic, *The Tenth Circle of Hell*)

DISCUSS Was there anything in this account of the camp at Omarska that would have given Djemo some sense of meaning to his life? In your opinion, was there something to live for, something to keep him going?

SUFFERING AND THE SEARCH FOR MEANING

Victor Frankl and the Search for Meaning in Suffering and Evil

Victor Frankl provides an answer to the great question of whether meaning can be found in the midst of suffering and evil. Frankl was a survivor of the Nazi concentration camp at Auschwitz. In his book *Man's Search for Meaning*, he recounts the horrors of the concentration camps. His story of brutality and torture mirrors the more contemporary stories from the Serb camps.

Victor Frankl

the inner place

Yet Frankl insists that it was possible to overcome the sense of meaninglessness of Auschwitz. Obviously many gave into despair and despised their existence in the camps. As Frankl puts it: 'They preferred to close their eyes and to live in the past. Life for such people became meaningless... Woe to him who saw no more sense in his life, no aim, no purpose, and therefore no point in carrying on. He was soon lost.'

According to Frankl, any suffering can be endured once there is a meaning to it. Even the hell of Auschwitz could be tolerated once there was a purpose.

Usually, those who gave into despair found it very difficult to survive the camps, but those who found a purpose or future goal managed to overcome the horrific truth of their existence.

When Life Asks Questions of Us

'Sometimes, it is not we who ask questions of life. Instead, it is life that asks questions of us.'

When we read the horrific accounts of the camps at Omarska or Auschwitz, we might be tempted to despair and blame God and everyone else for such happenings. That might seem the natural

The Great Questions about
the Meaning of Life

option. But some of those who survived Auschwitz revealed a startling mechanism for survival. In Auschwitz, there were two choices: fall into despair, or search for some meaning. Frankl believed that what was needed to survive such an ordeal was a radical change in one's attitude to life. He explains:

It did not really matter what we expected from life, but rather what life expected from us.

We needed to stop asking about the meaning of life, and instead think of ourselves as those who were being questioned by life – daily and hourly. Our answer must consist, not in talk and meditation, but in right action and right conduct. Life ultimately means taking the responsibility to find the right answer to its problems and to fulfil the tasks which it constantly sets for each individual.

Frankl gives an example of what he means. As a doctor, he describes how two men were close to giving in to their desperate situation. Both were completely hopeless. He describes the efforts to get the men to see that they still had a purpose to their lives.

In both cases it was a question of getting them to realise that life was still expecting something from them; something in the future was expected of them. We found, in fact, that for one it was his child whom he adored and who was waiting for him in a foreign country. For the other it was a thing, not a person. This man was a scientist who had written a series of books which still needed to be finished. His work could not be done by anyone else, any more than another person could ever take the place of the father in his child's affections.

the
inner
place

These passages are very challenging but worth thinking about because they offer insights into the meaning of life. Even in suffering and bad times, meaning is possible once a person realises the responsibilities they have. These responsibilities concern the goal and purpose of their lives. There is something they must do, and towards that end they must endure the difficult times.

Example 1

Take a student. Though capable of doing much better, he's getting on very badly in his exams at school. His parents get on to him and his teachers get on to him. Why? Because they get a secret and sadistic pleasure from annoying him, or because they know what he's capable of achieving for the future?

Answer that yourself. But the student can respond in two ways.

a   He moans, whinges, complains, blames everyone else, drinks more, smokes more, gets an attitude about life, becomes paranoid. Not only that, but he brings everyone around him down as well.

b   He accepts there is a problem, his problem. He swallows his pride and admits he might need a bit of help. He realises his responsibilities for his future career. He experiences humility and asks people to help him. Yet people admire his 'get up and go' attitude and his ability to turn things around. In future life, people admire him

the

inner

place

The Great Questions about
the Meaning of Life

because of his 'never say die' attitude. In short, you want him beside you on the battlefield.

ASIDE 'When a man finds that it is his destiny to suffer, he will have to accept his suffering as his task; his single and unique task. He will have to acknowledge the fact that even in suffering he is unique and alone in the universe. No one can relieve him of his suffering or suffer in his place. His unique opportunity lies in the way in which he bears his burden.'

(Victor Frankl, *Man's Search for Meaning*)

Example 2

When Hurricane Katrina struck the Gulf States of America, it brought suffering to thousands. People reacted differently to their plight. When the flood-waters came, some saw it as an opportunity, and looted, stole and raped. Others charged $700 to ferry people to safety on their private boats. Lovely. One teenager saw things differently, accepted his suffering, discovered his responsibilities, and acted accordingly.

Teenager Snatches Bus to Save Dozens

A New Orleans teenager saved dozens of people from the stricken city after commandeering a 70-seat school bus and driving it on a harrowing 300-mile journey to Houston. Jabbar Gibson, who was reported by an American television channel to be just fifteen, was determined to leave New Orleans after two days wading alone through the filthy waters of the former red-light district of Storyville. Although he had never driven a bus in his life, he broke into a school and made off with the bright yellow vehicle. What began as an act of sheer panic turned into what has been called 'a magnificent journey' that placed Gibson among the heroes emerging from the horrors of Hurricane Katrina. 'I

Floods in New Orleans

knew how to get over the fence, and where the keys were, so I felt it was worth the chance,' said Gibson. Although he had only eight passengers on board when he set off on route towards Texas, Gibson picked up many more, young and old, stranded beside the road during the eight-hour journey. 'By the time we gotten here we had all kinds of folk on board, from mothers with young babies to people in their seventies and eighties,' said Gibson, speaking from Houston. 'And when we ran out of gas we had a whip-around and everyone gave me enough cents to fill up and get here.' The young driver, who was still looking for some of his family and friends, said he was not worried about the legal repercussions of driving without a licence.

(*The Sunday Times*, 4/9/05)

the

inner

place

DISCUSS

1 Do you think Gibson was a hero? Why do you admire his attitude to the terrifying situation that he found himself in?
2 Is it possible that another person might have taken the bus and just saved themselves? Why do you think Gibson tried to save others?
3 What would you have done in that situation?

The Great Questions about the Meaning of Life

Think of examples of people who have responded to difficult situations by becoming responsible and acting in such a way as to put the needs of others first. You could take your examples from real life, literature, film or drama.

the

inner

place

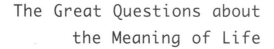

Chapter Four

SYMBOL

Read the following story about one of the first public performances by the band Nirvana, as described in Kurt Cobain's biography, *Heavier than Heaven*. It's in a dingy little club, before they were famous. They prepare their set-piece by pouring fake blood on their necks.

When Nirvana finally took to the stage, or more accurately moved to the corner of the room acting as the stage, they played only a twenty-five-minute set… He had, surprisingly, a confidence now in front of the microphone that he had nowhere else in his life. Kurt's increased energy seemed to egg on Krist, who bounced around so much that he smacked several members of the crowd with his bass.

But the *coup de grâce* was to come. At the end of their short set, right after they played 'Love Buzz', Kurt lifted his relatively new guitar and brought it down with such violence that pieces shot through the room like projectiles from a cannon. He poised for five seconds, hoisted the remnants into the air, and held it there while eyeing the crowd. Kurt's face appeared serene and spooky…The guitar went up into the air, and smash, it hit the floor once more. Kurt dropped it and walked out of the room.

He had never smashed a guitar before, probably never even thought about such an act, since guitars were expensive. 'He never explained why he freaked out,' recalled John Purkey, 'but he was smiling. There was a finality to it – it was like his own private little celebration. No one got hurt, but when he smashed the guitar, it was as if he really didn't care if he hit anyone. It was completely out of the blue. I was talking to him after the show, and the guitar was lying

there on the floor, and people kept grabbing pieces of it.' The Greeners now couldn't get enough of Nirvana.

(Charles R Cross, *Heavier than Heaven*)

The above extract raises certain questions. Nirvana wasn't famous or rich at the time, so Cobain could ill afford to smash a guitar. We need to figure out what was going on. You might take time to discuss the following two questions in class.

DISCUSS

1 Why do you think Kurt Cobain smashed the guitar?

2 Why did the band members begin by pouring fake blood on themselves?

the

inner

place

SYMBOLIC ACTIONS

We get an insight into Cobain's behaviour in a following extract from the same publication.

> When the band came back for the next number it was all about catharsis. They played…against their producer's wishes, and ended with the destruction of their instruments. Kurt began the assault by puncturing a speaker with his guitar; Grohl knocked his drum set off the riser, and Krist threw the drums in the air. It was certainly calculated, but the anger and frustration weren't faked.

The interesting word in this extract is the term 'catharsis'. The Greek word *katharsis* meant a cleansing or a purification, but we use it today to refer to a dramatic release of emotion. The emotions in the extract above are anger and frustration. These raw emotions were released through the smashing of the instruments.

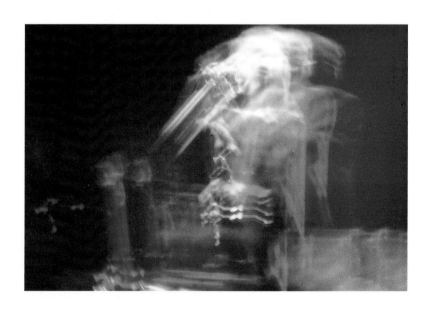

the

inner

place

DISCUSS

The young audience that witnessed the destruction of the guitar were greatly impressed by the action. What was it about the act that so impressed them? Did they somehow identify with the energy of the act?

This account of a crazed band can also be explained in terms of symbols. The destruction of the guitar can be understood as a symbolic action. If we examine the action, we see that it highlights some of the characteristics of symbols. Let's look now at three of these.

1 SYMBOLS HAVE MANY MEANINGS

When you were asked the question as to why Cobain smashed the guitar, there were probably many different answers. Cobain had his own reasons, because he was angry about something or everything. Perhaps it was a publicity stunt. The audience went wild after it, but what did it mean to them? For some, it connected with their own anger. Others may have been spellbound just by the theatrics of the whole thing... 'Entertain us.' Yet others might view the spectacle as reckless, self-indulgent behaviour, pitiful and sad. Either way, the action was symbolic of something, and meant different things to different people.

2 SYMBOLS CAN AFFECT US IN MANY WAYS

Unlike signs, which only relate information, symbols can affect our emotions. This ability means that symbols are very powerful. Cobain's act was highly emotive, and it also evoked emotions from the audience. The act was full of anger and rage, and those who witnessed it in some way responded to that anger. The act was also disturbing in so far as it was an act of destruction. Was the act in some way symbolic of Cobain's life, a life destroyed and abused by drug addiction?

3   SYMBOLS CAN TRANSCEND LANGUAGE

This sounds more complicated than it is. It happens that in life we experience things that are very difficult to put into language or words. For example, it's often difficult to put words on experiences such as death or love. Often in the face of terrible tragedy, people are literally 'lost for words'.

When Cobain smashed the guitar, it was obviously an act of destruction. Yet many would claim that the whole thing was actually very creative. While language has no words to describe something that is both creative and destructive, a symbolic act can capture both realities and therefore can go beyond language. The young audience might not be able to express in words their own feelings of anger or whatever, but the symbolic action on stage somehow captures it. This is the power of symbols.

GROUP WORK

Break up into groups and discuss the following points.

1   Unlike signs, symbols have many different meanings for different people. For example, fire can mean warmth or destruction. Wearing particular clothes can be a way of belonging to a group, or it could be a way of rebelling against another group. Can you think of other examples of symbols that have many different meanings?

2   Symbols can affect our emotions. On 30 November 2005, six days after George Best died, 50,000 posters of the football legend were held aloft in Old Trafford for a symbolic minute's silence. Many men and women were moved to tears. When boyfriends and girlfriends buy presents to mark an anniversary, the gifts can take on a symbolic value and affect the

the inner place

emotions of the individuals concerned. Can you think of other examples of symbols that affect our emotions?

3   Symbols can transcend language.

We find it difficult to talk about things that affect us deeply, like love and death. Often symbols take over around these two human experiences. If a guy really loves a girl and wants to be with her forever, he might find it difficult to put into words. Instead, he might buy her a ring, and it will act as a symbol of his love. When someone dies, people hug one another for comfort because there are no words to express how they feel. Can you think of other examples of how symbols transcend language?

DIFFERENT TYPES OF SYMBOL

Here we will examine two types of symbol: personal and group. If you reflect on your own life, there are some things that are personal to you that nobody knows about. There are also parts of your personality that you share with your friends, family, club or even country. As we try to identify different kinds of symbol, remember that they usually affect our emotions and can have many meanings.

1   PERSONAL SYMBOLS

Personal symbols are characterised by their relevance to you and nobody else. Nobody can fully understand the impact of another's personal symbols. They are unique to each individual. Consider the following story, where a man goes to his father's house shortly after his death to sort everything out. The passage identifies the symbolic moment when the finality of his father's death actually hits him.

the

inner

place

"If there was a single worst moment for me in those days, it came when I walked across the front lawn in the pouring rain to dump an armful of my father's ties into the back of a Good Will mission truck. There must have been more than a hundred ties, and many of them I remember from my childhood: the patterns, the colours, the shapes that had been embedded in my earliest consciousness, as clearly as my father's face had been. To see myself throwing them away like so much junk was intolerable to me, and it was then, at the precise moment I tossed them into the truck, that I came closest to tears. More than seeing the coffin itself being lowered into the ground, the act of throwing away these ties seemed to embody for me the idea of burial. I finally understood that my father was dead."

(Paul Auster, *The Invention of Solitude*)

DISCUSS

1 In your opinion, in what way did the ties act symbolically for the son?
2 How does this story capture the power of symbols?
3 Why might we describe the ties as personal symbols?

Symbols usually fill us with emotions and energy. They might mean different things to you at different times and they are often almost impossible to explain using words. That's the nature of symbols. They go beyond words and help us to go beyond ourselves. Read the following examples of people's personal symbols and then complete the assignment.

the

inner

place

'There's a ticket to Old Trafford on me bedroom wall. Amazing experience. Manchester United won 2-0 that day and hammered Liverpool. It was one of me happiest days. It was a present from me da. We had a great day. We met Uncle Seán who lives in Manchester and he explained all the songs that the United supporters were singing. Some fun that day and me da is a Liverpool fan! Made it even more special. If the ticket is a symbol, then it's probably of a really happy time.'

'There's this ring in my jewellery box that Mum gave me. It's gold with a blue gemstone. Her mum gave it to her and told her to give it to me. The ring makes me feel special but it also makes me think of if I ever have a little girl… It's funny 'coz it makes me think about the past and the future. I know the ring is a symbol for me because it's a very special thing I own.'

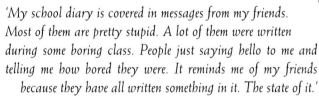

'On my shelf is the complete collection of Beatles' CDs. I love their music and I identify with so many of the songs and lyrics. When I feel down I usually put on my headphones and listen to one of their CDs. I know the collection is a symbol for me, except I don't know how to put it into words.'

'My school diary is covered in messages from my friends. Most of them are pretty stupid. A lot of them were written during some boring class. People just saying hello to me and telling me how bored they were. It reminds me of my friends because they have all written something in it. The state of it.'

'There's this lad I saw in a film the other night. The way he dressed was really cool. I'd love to be able to dress like that. The clothes he wore were him. I think if I wore the clothes I really wanted to wear, people might laugh at me. But the clothes would be me.'

the
inner
place

Examine the following list and identify which of the items could be personal symbols for you.

1 Posters on my bedroom wall.
2 Banging my bedroom door.
3 My CD collection and/or the selection of music on my iPod.
4 A prayer.
5 My bike.
6 My school journal/diary.
7 Doodles I do on my copies all the time.
8 Books/magazines I read.
9 Make-up I wear.
10 My wardrobe and the clothes I wear.
11 The wardrobe I'd like to have/the clothes I'd like to wear.
12 Photos in my bedroom.
13 My mobile phone and/or the names and phone numbers on my mobile.
14 A sacred object in my home.
15 My group of friends.
16 The people who are definitely not my friends.
17 Medals I own.
18 My personal idols.
19 My favourite TV programmes.
20 My favourite colours.
21 A certain place.
22 A certain day in the year.
23 My girlfriend/boyfriend.
24 A church/sacred place.
25 Where I live.
26 A certain object in the house.
27 My favourite car.
28 My dream holiday.
29 My favourite place to go when I go out.
30 A memory or anniversary card.

the

inner

place

2   GROUP SYMBOLS

Unlike personal symbols, two or more people share group symbols. The meaning of the symbol is not confined to the experiences of one individual. Group symbols are many and varied. The group could be just a group of friends with no set, structured or agreed symbols. Alternatively, the group could be a club, a school or a sports team with set symbols, such as team shirts, emblems and mottoes.

In friendship, symbols emerge because it's a way of creating an identity for the group. A group of friends don't usually sit around a table and decide to be a group of friends. It just happens, and the symbols of that group emerge also. Having shared symbols doesn't mean that the individuals in the group are clones or sheep, all following one another. It simply points to the fact that friendships are important and they save us from isolation and boredom.

Example of a group symbol

The term 'Goth' comes from the word 'Gothic', which in turn refers to gloomy or dark literature. Goths are a particular group or sub-culture. In the words of one Goth, it is '…the ability to find the art where art seems lacking; to find the light in the darkness and embrace it for all it's worth'. Because Goths have a particular view of the world, it is not surprising that they have their own symbols to forge and display their identity.

Fashion: Goths adopt an unusual fashion to separate themselves from other youth. Whilst they would prefer to be left alone, they also want to be seen. They wear black clothing and unusual hairstyles. One Goth explains: 'My black clothing and dark music aptly reflect my feelings…'

Music: Goth music is dark, with its own particular mood and view of the world. It includes groups such as Korn, Pantera, Slip Knot, and individuals such as Marilyn Manson.

the

inner

place

Jewellery: The Christian cross, an Egyptian ankh or 'Eye of Ra' and body-piercing are symbols that are often worn very visibly. As one Goth noted: 'I want to be left alone but I want to be seen.'

ASSIGNMENT

Think of a group you belong to/used to belong to. Try to figure out some symbols that defined/defines the group.

Music

Fashion/clothes

Symbols/Jewellery

THE IMPORTANCE AND POWER OF THE SYMBOLIC IN THE SECULAR WORLD

the

inner

place

Later in this chapter, we will examine the power and function of religious symbols. Basically, religious symbols reveal spiritual realities, but symbols function differently in contemporary secular society. Secular symbols operate outside of a specific religious framework and are encountered in many facets of modern life.

Some secular symbols are easily recognisable and affect entire nations, such as a national flag or national anthem. Like religious symbols, secular symbols function in different ways, depending on their contexts. A national flag rouses feelings of pride and national identity at sporting occasions, whereas it is more likely to cause feelings of nostalgia for those away from home. Societies can have symbolic places, such as war memorials or other places of historical significance. These might remind people of sacrifices made in the past, as soldiers gave their lives to fight for freedom and independence. Such places can forge a nation's identity and define the characteristics of a nation.

Other symbols operative in society may not be so obvious but remain laden with powerful meanings. In contemporary society, fashion, music and sport have become highly symbolic for various reasons.

Clothes can be viewed simply as a means of dressing and keeping warm, but they can also have a symbolic value. For example, one way for teenagers to rebel against their parents or school is by wearing clothes that challenge a particular mindset and make a definite statement of independence. As we saw when we examined Goth culture, clothes demand an emotional response and may lead to many and various consequences for the wearer.

THE AUTOMOBILE AS A SECULAR SYMBOL

One of the most powerful symbols of the modern age is the motor car. Cars are functional in so far as they get people from A to B, but there's much more to cars than that. Cars have the ability to stir our emotions, to set the pulse racing. For some, the type of car they own is a symbol of their own power and prestige. For teenagers, cars almost act as a rite of passage into the adult

inner

place

world. For example, the first time a teenager gets the car keys, learns how to drive and eventually passes the car test, they may feel they have entered the adult world. Such experiences can release great energy in us and almost transform our understanding of who we are. The car can be symbolic of individual freedom, and the open road sparks the imagination to think of endless possibilities, as captured through the years in a succession of road movies.

> **ASIDE**
>
> A 1975 Ford Escort that once belonged to Pope John Paul II was sold in Las Vegas to a Houston multimillionaire for $690,000. If you think your parish priest may one day be Pope, consider buying his car from him as an investment!

The Bugatti Veyron

In 2005, Bugatti produced a car that could boast to be the fastest car in the world.

Environmentalists were outraged at what seemed to be the idiocy of the project. Why produce a car that has 1001 bhp (brake horsepower), a car that can accelerate from 0 to 60 mph in 2.5 seconds and that has a top speed of 253 mph? They argued that given the threat of climate change, nobody needed a car that could travel at more than four times the speed limit. Car manufacturers should, they said, be producing greener cars.

While their argument was certainly valid, they had forgotten the symbolic value of cars. Bugatti was originally founded in 1909 by Ettore Bugatti, whose motto was: 'Nothing is too beautiful, nothing is too expensive.' The Bugatti Veyron was never intended to be a functional car that got people from A to B. An ordinary family saloon will do that with an engine one-fifth the size of the Bugatti. Instead, the Veyron is a symbol of beauty, and proof of this is the fact that pictures of it adorn the bedroom walls of teenagers throughout the globe. Right up there beside the most beautiful actors and pop stars. The Veyron is also symbolic of human progress. The fact that we can actually produce a car that can travel faster than a Formula One car and

the

inner

place

still manage to stop itself is a testament to the human ability to continue to seek ways to transcend ourselves. This car can go so fast that its body shape has to change at high speeds to prevent it from taking off. It can cover the length of a football pitch in one second.

Probably the most interesting aspect of a car like the Bugatti Veyron is its religious qualities. This may seem strange, but for decades super cars have been shrouded with religious imagery. Perhaps this is because they go so far beyond the realm of ordinary experience that they are symbolic of the extraordinary. They transcend or go beyond what we can adequately explain. The Veyron was described by commentators as 'the ultimate one' and driving it was to 'give the driver a sense of awe'. Unlike other prestige cars, the Veyron has 'a soul'. When the accelerator is pressed to the floor, the sound that emerges from the engine could only be described as 'the voice of God'. This car is 'all powerful'.

ASIDE

Symbols Transcending Language: **When Jeremy Clarkson drove the Veyron through France, he described the experience, or rather didn't, as follows: 'I cannot tell you how fast I crossed it the other day. Because you simply wouldn't believe me. I also cannot tell you how good this car is. I just don't have the vocabulary. I just end up stammering and dribbling and talking wide-eyed nonsense.'**

(*The Sunday Times*, 27/11/05)

How would you describe the following cars in terms of their symbolic value?

- Range Rover 4x4
- Bentley/Rolls Royce
- Ferrari Enzo
- Ford Mustang
- VW Beetle
- Mini Cooper

THE AUTOMOBILE AS A SYMBOL OF TRANSFORMATION

There is one final reason why the car has become such an important symbol in contemporary culture. Since the dawn of the combustible engine, very little has actually changed in the mechanical workings of the car, yet cars themselves have been transformed into even more modern and stylish forms. There is very little real difference between a saloon car now and ten years ago, except in styling. Yet every three or four years, the industry produces a new version, with a more modern and sleek look. Every few years, cars are transformed, and the consumer is seduced through advertising and marketing to buy the 'latest model'. The strange thing is that when most people change their car, there's absolutely nothing wrong with it. What's wrong is that it is not the transformed version.

A businessman in Dusseldorf, Germany took his new company Ferrari for a test drive. Unused to such power from the 400bhp F360, he lost control and crashed into three parked cars, knocked over a street lamp, a set of traffic lights, a billboard, a set of signal boxes and two trees. A number of houses were left without power. Witnesses said it looked as if a bomb had exploded. There was debris everywhere. The driver was investigated for speeding and dangerous driving. When he emerged from the wreck, he said, 'There was a problem with the gears.' No one was injured. (We were going to show a picture of the smashed Ferrari but it's too upsetting for car enthusiasts.)

OTHER SECULAR SYMBOLS OF TRANSFORMATION

MY NEW FACE!

The Make-Over Culture

In recent years, culture has become obsessed with transformation, and this has taken different symbolic forms. TV shows regularly feature the transformation of the interior of a house or garden. Yet some shows have put a more radical twist on the process of transformation by literally transforming the person themselves. In recent years, plastic surgery has lost its socially embarrassing baggage. Now teenagers and adults alike admit to some day hoping to fix something at odds with the perfect body. One of the most extreme versions of plastic surgery on TV was a show called *The Swan*, where women subjected themselves to radical surgical procedures so as to create the perfect figure and face.

the inner place

The show culminated with the woman standing in front of a concealed mirror and, as the curtain went back, the 'new' her was revealed to gasps of amazement. David Lyle, the producer of *The Swan*, explained it thus:

> 'I defy you not to watch that moment when the curtain goes back, and the person sees what's happened to them. Let's face it – slapping a new coat of paint on is not as dramatic as having someone carve your face off.'
>
> (*The Guardian*, 14/09/05)

The Cult of the Celebrity

Since the advent of the big screen, there have always been celebrities, but a recent phenomenon shows how many people are not satisfied to adore celebrities but want to become one themselves, and in so doing completely transform their lives. Reality TV shows such as *Big Brother* display the extent that people will go to in order to be famous, if only for a very short time. Some want to be celebrities even if it's only on the 'Z-list'. Another expression of the cult of celebrity may be found in competitions such as *Pop Idol* or *The X-Factor*. Here young and old audition, hoping that they will be the next big thing. They are further drawn into the celebrity world by spending time in the producers' lavish apartments in exotic places, so as to taste more of the allure and riches of celebrity. Failure to achieve on these shows or failure to completely transform their lives overnight is often met with agonising cries and a deluge of tears.

the inner place

DISCUSS

1 Why do you think people are attracted to shows that deal with physical transformation?

2 Why do you think some people are so desperate to look different?

3 Are young people pressurised to look a certain way?

4 Who in contemporary culture symbolises the perfect look?

5 Why do some people seem addicted to celebrity and fame?

6 Do you think fame can really change a person's life for the better?

7 Do you think most people would like to transform their lives in some radical manner?

THE IMPORTANCE AND POWER OF THE SYMBOLIC IN THE SACRED WORLD

In our discussions and explorations of symbol so far, one thing is evident: symbols tap into experiences or emotions that are powerful, transforming and difficult to put into words. Symbols cope with, and are found clustered around, those experiences in life that we might term mysterious, if only for the fact that we find it difficult to talk about them, like death, love, friendship. Yet symbols have an extraordinary power to connect us with mystery. Symbols can act as a bridge between one realm of experience and another.

SYMBOLS AND MYSTERY

At its heart, religion is a very mysterious phenomenon, and this is exactly why symbols are found in religion. Symbols cope with mystery. If you're unconvinced of the mysterious nature of religion and the spiritual world, consider the following accounts.

the
inner
place

St Teresa of Avila and her Mystical Experiences

St Teresa wrote about encountering her deceased parents during one of her mystical experiences.

> I thought I was being carried up to heaven; the first persons I saw were my mother and father...such great things happened in so short a time... While the light we see here and the light we see there are both light, there is no comparison between the two, and the brightness of the sun seems quite dull if compared with the other. Afterwards I was...left with very little fear of death, of which previously I had been very much afraid.

On another occasion, St Teresa wrote about having a near-death experience.

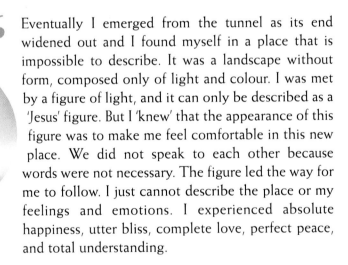

> Eventually I emerged from the tunnel as its end widened out and I found myself in a place that is impossible to describe. It was a landscape without form, composed only of light and colour. I was met by a figure of light, and it can only be described as a 'Jesus' figure. But I 'knew' that the appearance of this figure was to make me feel comfortable in this new place. We did not speak to each other because words were not necessary. The figure led the way for me to follow. I just cannot describe the place or my feelings and emotions. I experienced absolute happiness, utter bliss, complete love, perfect peace, and total understanding.

Apparitions in Medjugorje

The journalist John Cornwell went to Medjugorje to witness for himself the reported apparitions to some children there.

> It was at this point that I witnessed something truly astonishing, and for which, in principle, I could find no ready explanation. For about three minutes, I saw

the inner place

Jakov, Marija and Vicka speaking silently and in turn to the invisible figment that hovered in front of them. The extraordinary fact was that when one of them stopped 'speaking', the other, in that same split second, would begin. Yet they were not uttering a sound, nor were they capable of observing each other's lips; I could see no bodily movement whatsoever by which they could cue each other in order to achieve such a feat.

Marija, on whom I now began to concentrate, did not appear ecstatic in any melodramatic or histrionic way, but her face radiated a striking loveliness, innocence and wonder. Her gaze was steady, unblinking, tender; the whites of her eyes seemed to shine with an unearthly light.

'Transfiguration' was a word that came at once to mind. And when I focused my attention on Jakov I saw that same transfiguring quality in his face, made all the more poignant because of his adolescence.

(Powers of Darkness, Powers of Light)

A Dead Friend

I recently lost my best friend and I was quite upset. It hadn't been expected, he had a heart attack. I didn't know what to do. I went to see him waked out at the house. He looked as he always had done. I found it so hard to say goodbye to him. It just wasn't fair. A while after I went to his grave, the gravestone was up for the first time. It was a cross with his name on it.

Just after that, I was on my own, walking up the hallway, and standing in front of me was my best

the
inner
place

friend. He smiled at me. We just stood there smiling at each other. It was lovely to see him, he looked so happy. I then heard my name being called and I turned around. When I looked back, he was gone. I don't really understand what happened but I think he was telling me that everything is OK and that he will always be with me. I will miss him.

(Female student, 16)

DISCUSS

1 In what way might you describe the above experiences as mysterious?
2 Do the above accounts have anything in common?
3 Do you think the people were adequately able to describe their experiences?
4 Do you know of anyone who has had similar experiences? Tell the story to the class.

SACRED SYMBOLS

the

inner

place

The spiritual world is mysterious for many reasons. In the Creed we say: 'We believe in all that is, seen and unseen.' The spiritual world is part of that invisible realm, which in many ways fascinates us.

Another reason that the spiritual is mysterious is because we don't have adequate words to capture it or clearly describe it. Yet sacred symbols act as a powerful bridge between both worlds.

These symbols communicate the mysterious spiritual realm of the supernatural world. Though sometimes difficult to recognise, the spiritual world is all around us; in our relationships, in nature and in our innermost being. It is a world that has the ability to fascinate, energise and transform.

In this section, we will concentrate on how symbols of initiation from the Christian tradition communicate the spiritual realities of what it means to become a Christian.

CHRISTIAN SYMBOLS OF INITIATION

Water: Symbol of Transformation

The search for water in our solar system is tantamount to establishing the possibility of other life forms. Because water is equated with life, it is one of the most powerful of the sacred symbols. The early Christians adopted the symbol of water, or aquatic symbolism, from other mystery religions, and so it was used as a symbol of initiation long before Christianity.

The meaning behind aquatic symbolism is not what one might expect. Though we equate water with life, in the Christian tradition the waters of baptism are as much about dying as they are about life. Back in the early centuries of the Church, John Chrysostom had this to say about the water of baptism: 'It represents death and burial, life and resurrection... When we plunge our heads into the water as into a sepulchre, the old man is immersed, buried wholly; when we come out of the water, the new man appears at the same time.'

the inner place

According to the most ancient Christian traditions, to be immersed in the waters of baptism is to enter the tomb with Christ, only to emerge with him in his resurrection. Earlier we examined how contemporary culture is in some ways obsessed with symbols of transformation. Yet, fundamentally, Christian initiation is also about transformation, a deep and spiritual transformation. People might yearn for transformation in contemporary culture, but Christians have been transformed in the waters of baptism.

The waters of our baptism point to a radical inner transformation into Christian life. As the following account from England illustrates, our Christian identity can transform us at any time.

Things Fall Apart

‘ When I left school back in the nineties, I really thought I had it all going for me. I was so confident and felt so invincible. I decided to skip college for a while and just hang around. Life would wait and I really wanted just to have lots of fun. Parents went ballistic that their little girl was heading into big bad world. It happens. Anyway things would have been OK except I kinda got in with the wrong crowd. Everything you're not supposed to do – I did it. For a while it was a complete blast, but then everything started to unravel.

Everything just fell apart. One night I had absolutely nothing. I mean it. Nothing. I was on the street and I was a complete mess. I just sat there watching people go by with their lives still intact. I had been taking lots of stuff. I was down there and I

the

inner

place

was not coming back up. I had no money for food or a fix. Then – it was funny – but this old dear came up to me. She spoke with an Irish accent and was really kind. She gave me some cash and a rosary beads. Thing is, it was at that moment that I broke down and fell apart. The tears started and they didn't stop. But way back from the sodden mess that was my brain came this voice saying that God loved me. Over and over. The more I seemed to crack and strain, the stronger the voice was.

Nothing could have saved me from oblivion that night. But something did. I cry even now when I think of it. I have two kids now. I have my life back and someone gave it back to me that night. I know it was God, though I'm still not madly religious.

My mum and I are friends again. My grandparents were dead way before I was born.

One night my mum told me her mum kinda lost it in her last few years. Bit like me I guess, except I was younger! She became a sort of religious fanatic. She prayed the whole time and when anyone came to visit she would always give them a rosary beads.

DISCUSS

1 A person is changed in the waters of baptism. Do you think water is a good symbol of transformation? Can you think of ways that water transforms and energises people in everyday life?

2 In the above story of transformation, why do you think the girl had such a meaningful religious experience when she was at her lowest ebb?

Oil: Symbol of New Identity

Oil is used in many Christian sacraments. It is used to ordain priests, to anoint the sick, and in Baptism the infant is anointed with the oil of catechumens and the oil of chrism. We saw earlier how culture seems obsessed with TV shows that offer a celebrity

status, which can make a person feel incredibly special. Yet during the rites of Christian initiation, the person receives a very special spiritual identity. In the sacrament of Baptism, the person is anointed with oil and told that they are 'anointed like Christ as priest, prophet and king'. It doesn't confer a celebrity status, but neither is it a 'Z-list' spiritual identity.

Unlike celebrity status, which can often disappear as quickly as it begins, the spiritual identity conferred during the rites of initiation can never be removed or taken away. The person who is anointed is especially marked to be a prophet and work to help build up the kingdom of God on earth.

ASSIGNMENT

According to Christian tradition, the oil of Confirmation is also used to strengthen the person for adult Christian life.

Read the following account of the stresses of being a teenager, written by a sixteen-year-old female. Then read the Prayer of Confirmation.

In the light of what the teenager says, in what way do you think the Prayer of Confirmation might be relevant to a young person's life? Would you agree that teenagers do have these stresses, or are things different for you?

the
inner
place

Stressed

"There are loads of pressures in school. There's the uniform and all the rules about that. I don't feel free. But worse are the tests. There are so many tests and teachers are telling you how you have to work hard and then your parents are also telling you how hard you've to work. There are so many expectations to know everything. Then I've to work at weekends to get money but I'm also supposed to be studying... Parents can't give you money because  'it doesn't grow on trees' but then they don't want me to work either... Life is too busy because you've to study, work, go to school and have a social life... Then there's relationships and trying not to fight with friends because fights with girls are terrible. You're always trying to keep people happy – boyfriends, friends, family, teachers. Also you've to make decisions about sex, drink and drugs. I was having to make decisions about those things when I was only fourteen."

the
inner
place

THE TREE CLIMBER AND THE INNER PLACE

**'Nothing is holier, nothing more exemplary,
than a beautiful strong tree.'**
(Herman Hesse)

Did you ever climb trees? Have you ever built a tree-house or fort in a tree? There's something about a tree that comes across as a challenge or an invitation. If it can be climbed, then it should be.

Jim Cogley grew up on a farm in County Wexford, and due to an abundance of mature and ageing trees, he spent much of his youth up in trees and swinging out of branches. The seeds of our purpose in life are often planted in childhood, and though Jim wanted to pursue a career in wood, he opted instead for the priesthood.

Thirty-five years later, he was giving a sermon at Christmastime about the 'Birth of Possibilities', when his old fascination for trees came back to him. It came as a sentence that formed in his mind and wouldn't go away: 'Go to the wood.' So, as a Christmas present to himself, he bought a Polewood 2000 lathe (a machine for shaping wood) and some chisels. Everything was thrown out of the garage to make way for the arrival, and so began one of the most fascinating journeys of his life. He immersed himself in the ancient art of wood-turning.

the
inner
place

Jim is a trained counsellor and, familiar with the psychology of Carl Jung, he soon began to see patterns in his wooden pieces that reflected psychological realities of the inner personality. As he chiselled the fast-spinning timbers, shapes emerged that seemed to him to be highly symbolic of the inner spirituality and psychology of the human being. Here is one example.

'The Embrace'

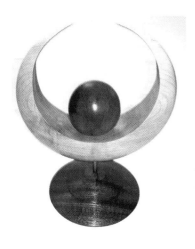

This piece is called 'The Embrace'. Before any piece is created, it must first be accepted from the pile of other timbers by the wood-turner. Yet the acceptance of yourself at the psychological level is the starting point of maturity and growth.

This piece acts as a symbol because different people see different things in it. Some see the enfolding arms as embracing and accepting the inner self or the 'real' you. Often the 'real' you is not accepted by others. Do you do the same and reject yourself or, as this piece suggests, do you embrace the core of who you are?

At a spiritual level, others see this piece as a symbol of God embracing humanity in the Incarnation, when God became human in Jesus.

What do you see in this piece?

the

inner

place

We will now look at some pieces that Jim has created. He believes that all the pieces are symbolic of spiritual and psychological truths about ourselves. Because these pieces act as symbols, different people will see different things.

Below are the titles and description of each piece. What you are asked to do is to break up into groups and see if you can match each title and description with the right piece of wood.

So, which of the following titles would you match with each piece?

'Accepting the Inner Defect' Accepting what seems to be an inner defect makes us more interesting. Often the wood-turner is tempted to discard a piece that turns out to have an inner defect, but often it is this feature that people find most interesting about the piece. Is it the same with the way we view ourselves?

'It's all about Perspective' There are often two ways of looking at your life.

'Mistakes and Remakes' – What initially seemed like a mistake can lead to an imaginative and innovative finish. What should we do with the mistakes we make in our lives – reject them and ourselves, or accept who we are and redesign our self-image?

'The Suffering Self' – Sometimes a nail or piece of wire can poison the inner wood. Yet when accepted by the wood-turner, it can turn out to be the most striking piece. Is it the same with our inner selves? If our suffering is accepted as part of who we are and of our life story, are we better for that?

'Getting a Balance' – There are many aspects to our lives – family, school, work, etc. What's

the
inner
place

needed in life is a healthy balance between all our different energies and relationships. Otherwise we might just be going around in circles.

'Passive–Assertive–Aggressive' Some people are passive when hurt by others. They retreat into themselves, only to cause inward pain. Assertive people respect themselves and others. Their boundary wall is firm, but not destructive or damaging to others or to themselves. Others are simply aggressive. They demand immediate attention, but due to their psychological make-up are incapable of forming close and meaningful relationships.

'Bird or Dinosaur – Don't Label Me' Sometimes people will view us from one angle only, and come to a hasty decision or label. Similarly, as with these sculptures, we can be viewed from many angles, and accordingly people will find that there are different aspects to us.

Chapter Five

RELIGION AS A RESPONSE TO THE SEARCH FOR MEANING

THE IMPORTANCE OF BELIEF IN HUMAN LIFE

'He who has courage and faith will never perish in misery.'
(Anne Frank)

There are particular experiences in life that call into question what beliefs we hold. A girl looks in the mirror (for one, two or maybe three hours) before she goes out for the night. She examines her features, and some nights she decides that she looks absolutely fantastic, drop-dead gorgeous. Other nights she believes that she looks like something that was dragged up from the deep. Tonight she decides she looks awful, drab and boring. She goes out and meets two guys who say, 'You look great tonight!'

DISCUSS

What do you think this girl really feels about her appearance?

Another girl goes out and decides that she looks fabulous. She meets two guys who reckon she doesn't look too good. They lower their gazes. 'Wow,' she thinks, 'I'm so fabulous, I've intimidated them. They know they don't have a chance.'

DISCUSS

In fact, she's having a bad hair day, but what do you think she believes: that she looks wonderful or terrible?

Our beliefs are important as they shape the way we view the world and interpret our own experiences. How many times have you heard of two teams who meet in the final, and when one wins, the captain puts it down to the fact that they had more belief?

BELIEF AND THE CHAMPIONS LEAGUE FINAL

When Liverpool FC began their Champions League campaign in 2004-2005, they were rank outsiders to lift the trophy. Incredibly, however, they beat some of the finest teams in European club football to reach the final. Their opponents – the Italian giants, AC Milan – were the favourites to win the cup. Few gave Liverpool a chance, and fear and cynicism weighed heavy on the players' shoulders. When the match started, they were 3-0 down by the half-time whistle. Fink Tank is a statistical model for European football, and at half-time Liverpool had a statistical chance of winning of 0.2 per cent.

Djimi Traore, the Liverpool full-back, described what happened at half-time: 'Honestly, when I sat listening to the manager at half-time, I didn't really believe we could do it. But the Milan players were outside already celebrating that they were champions, celebrating the victory. That really got to us and

the

inner

place

gave us the hunger to come back. The manager told us we could do it if we scored in the first five minutes. He said if we did that, we could keep scoring.' When the teams went out for the second half, Steven Gerrard scored and then set up the second. They scored a third goal, and that was all in the space of six minutes, '360 seconds of nuclear fission'.

Liverpool went on to win the trophy on penalties. Journalists and critics alike later looked to the inspirational captain, Steven Gerrard, for an explanation of the incredible turnaround:

Steven Gerrard

'Back in December he was condemned for his honesty when he said Liverpool had no chance of being European champions. Fans doubted his commitment but on Wednesday, even when Carragher lost faith, Gerrard still believed. Running back after scoring, he pumped his arms to exhort colleagues and the crowd.'

(*The Sunday Times*, 29/5/05)

the

inner

place

DISCUSS

1   Do you think belief can play such a transformative role in sport? Can you think of other examples from sport?

2   Our beliefs determine our attitudes. Consider the following:
   ● How do our beliefs affect the way we approach study? 'I'm good at business but useless at Maths...' What do you think this student's maths grades will look like, and why?

Religion as a Response to
the Search for Meaning

- How do our beliefs affect our self-esteem? 'I look terrible in this...' 'I'm no good at...' 'I just know she doesn't like me...' 'I'd never be able to do that.' If you believe you're no good at something, what are your chances of being good at it?
- How do our beliefs affect our judgement of others? 'Did you hear about Suzie? Well I believe that over the weekend...blaa blaa blaa...' Do our beliefs about people affect the way we treat them? Do our beliefs always correspond to the reality of what people are like?

BELIEF IN THE FACE OF DEATH

At one stage in his career, the famous cyclist Lance Armstrong faced his own death. Armstrong had cancerous tumours on his brain, and on the night before surgery to remove them, he asked himself the question: how do you confront your own death? The surgeons shaved him and placed coloured dots all over his head to mark out the incisions for the following morning, and as he lay there he asked himself another question: what do I believe in? He admitted that he had never prayed a lot but 'I felt I had the capacity to be a spiritual person, and to hold some fervent beliefs'.

Armstrong outlines in his autobiography how belief became the thing that meant most to him as he thought about dying:

> I knew this much: I believed in belief, for its own shining sake. To believe in the face of utter hopelessness, every article of evidence to the contrary, to ignore apparent catastrophe – what other choice was there? We do it every day, I realised. We are so much stronger than we imagine, and belief is one of the most valiant and long-lived human characteristics... Without belief, we would

the

inner

place

be left with nothing but an overwhelming doom every single day. And it will beat you. I didn't fully see, until the cancer, how we fight every day against the creeping negatives of the world, how we struggle daily against the slow lapping of cynicism. Dispiritedness and disappointment, these are the real perils of life.

DISCUSS

1 Why do you think beliefs are important for people when they confront their own death?
2 Why do people turn to their religious beliefs when they confront death?

THE ORIGINS OF RELIGIOUS BELIEF: ARCHAEOLOGICAL AND SCIENTIFIC EVIDENCE

As you read this sentence, it is being processed by three pounds of grey matter locked inside your skull. It's your brain. The brain is shaped like a walnut and has the consistency of butter. It's very important, so important that we will return to it again and again throughout this course. It's important because most people, when asked, would reckon that it's where they live or where their 'I-ness' is to be found. People believe that their personality etc. is to be found in this mass of tissue and blood that could fit in a shoebox.

ASIDE

Ask people to point to themselves. What do they point at? You should try it now in class. As you'll see, people, without exception, point to their hearts and not to their brains. Why do you think that is?

When we search for the origins of religious belief, it appears that it evolved some time around 60,000 years ago inside the heads of our ancestors – Neanderthal hominids. They were a more primitive form of what we are now – Homo Sapiens.

Archaeological evidence has uncovered something startling happening around this time. Neanderthals began, for the first time, to care for one another and also to display a type of behaviour that suggests spiritual beliefs. For the first time, our ancestors, the Neanderthals, were beginning to bury their dead.

Shanidar Caves

It could be argued that they only buried their dead for hygienic reasons, but the crucial piece of evidence is that they placed weapons and food beside the corpses. This has been interpreted to mean that they believed that the dead would use these items in their next existence. Clearly, they believed in some sort of non-physical or spiritual realm. Other evidence, from the Shanidar caves in Iraq, of two men who were kept alive by their companions despite severe physical disability – one had a spear wound in his ribs and the other was crippled with arthritis – is also indicative of a deeper, caring, more spiritual nature.

THE 'GOD SPOT'

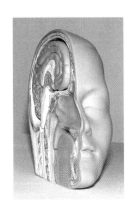

The archaeological evidence also points to some astonishing development in the structure of the human brain. Around this time, humans were beginning to develop a region of the brain known as the frontal lobes. The frontal lobes are located just behind the forehead. However, in recent years, scientists have located what they refer to as the 'God Spot' in this region of the brain. In response to religious imagery, a part of the frontal lobe of the brain became more active than usual. It would appear that our ability to process religious thoughts, images and feelings can be located in a particular part of the brain. The development of this region is accompanied by archaeological evidence of the first signs of spiritual beliefs.

the
inner
place

The discovery of a 'God Spot' does not mean that religion or God is simply a result of our brain chemistry. The research team from the University of California, San Diego said: 'These studies do not in any way negate the validity of religious experience or God.' In other words, the 'God Spot' is simply the region of our brains given over to religious thinking and feeling.

DISCUSS

1 Why do you think the earliest religious activity seems to be around the care of the dead? Could it be said that, even today, much of our religious activity is concerned with how we care for the dead?

2 Sometimes young people slag one another for showing an interest in religion. How do you react to the scientific evidence that being religious is actually related to our brain structure?

THE ORIGINS OF RELIGIOUS BELIEF AND THE SEARCH FOR MEANING

Psychologists, theologians and anthropologists have long wondered at the origins of religious belief and behaviour. Here we will examine four theories that reveal a relationship between religious belief and the search for meaning.

1   A SENSE OF A HIGHER POWER

the
inner
place

According to studies carried out across many different cultures, the origins of religious belief seem to be linked to human beings having an in-built sense of a higher meaning. Almost all cultures and groups on this planet worship some higher power, a power that gives purpose and meaning to their lives. This sense of higher meaning is evident in the spiritual practices of different cultures. Practices such as fasting, self-sacrifice, even martyrdom, suggest that humans have a sense of a mysterious higher power

Religion as a Response to the Search for Meaning

operative in their lives. For some, this power provides such a sense of meaning that they are willing even to give their lives for it.

ASIDE Recent surveys point to the fact that over eighty per cent of Europeans believe in a force called God.

DISCUSS What experiences do people have that give them the feeling that there is a higher power?

2 RELIGION PROVIDES EXPLANATIONS

We established earlier on that to ask questions is part of what it means to be human. Our primitive forebears were presented with many strange phenomena that needed explaining. The first major question addressed the issue of where everything came from – the origins of things. Different traditions answered this by formulating their own creation myths. Natural phenomena such as lightning, thunder, lunar cycles, and growth and disease, would also have intrigued our early ancestors. Other strange phenomena may have induced fear, such as dreams, precognition and ghosts – what we might term today as paranormal phenomena.

ASIDE A young woman in Washington state, whom I will call Amanda, woke up at 2.30 a.m. so upset by a terrifying dream that she had to wake her husband to tell him about it. She had dreamed that the large chandelier that hung over their baby's bed in the next room had fallen into the crib and crushed the baby. In the dream, Amanda could see herself and her husband standing amid the wreckage. The clock on the baby's dresser read 4:35 a.m. In the dream, she could hear the rain on the windowpane and the

wind howling outside. When she told her husband of the dream, he just laughed at her. He said it was a silly dream and she should forget it and go back to sleep. In a matter of a moment, he did just that, but Amanda could not sleep. The dream was too frightening. Finally, she got out of bed and went to the baby's room, picked her up, and brought her back to her bed. She looked out the window and saw a full moon. The weather was calm. Feeling foolish, she got back into her bed with the baby. About two hours later, they were awakened by a resounding crash. She jumped up, followed by her husband, and ran to the nursery. There, where the baby would have been lying, was the chandelier in the smashed crib. They looked at each other in amazement, then at the clock by the crib. It was 4:35 a.m. Stunned, they listened to the sound of rain on the windowpane and the wind howling outside.

DISCUSS

1 In what way might a person's religious beliefs explain the above story?

2 What is your explanation of the events?

3   RELIGION AS COMFORT

Today, many believe that religion provides comfort in a world that doesn't always make sense. As we shall see later, religious traditions try to make sense of the problem of good and evil, and why bad things happen to good people. In olden times, people worried about disease, famine and drought. They believed that if they could contact the gods and make sacrifices to them, then perhaps the gods might offer protection. Today, many turn to prayer when they need comfort. Many believe that prayer really works and that God does intervene in their lives. Religion gives meaning and comfort in what appears sometimes to be a hostile world.

Religion as a Response to the Search for Meaning

4 RELIGION, SUFFERING AND DEATH

The psychologist Carl Jung commented on the many who have turned away from their religion: 'Such people do not understand their religion any longer. While life runs smoothly without religion, the loss remains as good as unnoticed. But when suffering comes, it is another matter. That is when people begin to seek a way out and to reflect about the meaning of life and its bewildering and painful experiences... People feel that it makes, or would make, a great difference if only they had a positive

Carl Jung

belief in a meaningful way of life, or in God and immortality. The spectre of approaching death often gives a powerful incentive to such thoughts.' (Carl Jung, *Man and his Symbols*)

the
inner
place

THE MEANING OF SUFFERING: A RELIGIOUS PERSPECTIVE

THE PROBLEM OF SUFFERING

One of the biggest challenges to a sense of meaning in a person's life is the experience of suffering. Suffering stands in the way of happiness and challenges the notion that life has a purpose. We will examine the problem of suffering using the following questions.

1   Does everybody experience suffering or is it just me?
The following is an extract from the diary of 'Clinton X', outlining his experience of suffering:

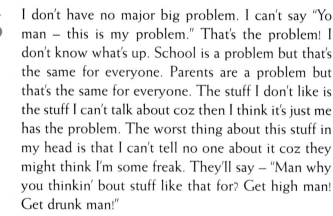

> I don't have no major big problem. I can't say "Yo man – this is my problem." That's the problem! I don't know what's up. School is a problem but that's the same for everyone. Parents are a problem but that's the same for everyone. The stuff I don't like is the stuff I can't talk about coz then I think it's just me has the problem. The worst thing about this stuff in my head is that I can't tell no one about it coz they might think I'm some freak. They'll say – "Man why you thinkin' bout stuff like that for? Get high man! Get drunk man!"
>
> Sure I can drink and forget but for like, how long? A day? An hour? Do you ever really forget? I see all these freaks drunk out of their little minds pretendin' like everything is ok, "look at me I'm so happy!" Oh yeah? So why do I see you pukin' your ring up and cryin' baby? Don't look so good now. Not from where I'm standin'. I see my friends rat-faced in the toilet and they is like lookin' in the mirror and sayin' to themselves "Yo buddy how are you?" And then they wink at themselves. I'm thinking it's like they get drunk coz they need a break from their own heads, their own lives. Did you ever see a drunk

person wink at themselves in a mirror? How many people is livin' inside those heads? Why is it people has to get drunk before they like themselves?

But the mirror is where my problems start. I don't like that face that looks back at me. I'm thinkin – who would want to go out with that face? Man you is ugly! I look at my head and I think – man you ain't never gonna be a brain surgeon or rocket scientist. You ain't ever gonna drive a flash car. I'm lookin' at that head and I'm sayin' – you ain't ever gonna pick up a pretty lady. In my worst moments I'm thinkin' – Buddy you're nobody.

I wanna make my folks proud but I ain't good at nothin'. Sure I made the team but what's that? So I just hang out. I'm a child again. I'm sitting on the side of the street and everyone is just passing by. Nobody notices the kid playin' on his own. That's my life man. Everybody is just passin' by and nobody notices a damn thing.

DISCUSS

1 Do you agree with Clinton X that most teenagers have the same problems around school and family? What kind of problems are they?
2 What do you think is the root of his suffering?
3 Is there a sense from this piece that part of his problem is that he can't fit in?
4 Why can't he talk to anybody?
5 Should teenagers feel ashamed of their own suffering, their own sadness?
6 Do girls deal with suffering in a different way than boys? If so, how and why?

2   Do we sometimes inflict suffering on ourselves?
To answer the question, 'why suffering?', it is sometimes necessary to admit that at times our suffering is to a large part self-inflicted, due to the way we deal with life. In the following extract, the author, Koren Zailckas, reveals how her unhappiness

as a teenager led to an even far greater amount of suffering because of the way she handled it through alcohol abuse.

> Girls don't drink in the name of women's liberation, for the sake of proving we can go drink for drink with the boys. We don't drink to affirm that we are "sassy" or "self-confident", which newsweeklies have lately suggested. Nor is our drinking a manifestation of "girl power" or "gender freedom" or any of the other phrases so many sociologists interchange with happiness. On the contrary, almost every girl I've known drank as an expression of her unhappiness. I too drank in no small part because I felt shamed, self-conscious, and small.

> For many girls, alcohol abuse may be a stage that tapers off after the quarter-life mark. Many will be spared arrests, accidents, alcoholism, overdoses and sexual assaults. A whole lot of them will have close calls, incidents they will recount with self-mocking at dinner parties some fifteen years later. Some of them will have darker stories, memories or half-memories or full-out blackouts, that they will store in the farthest corners of their mental histories and never disclose to their families or lovers. But I fear that women who escape the physical consequences of drinking, won't escape the emotional ones. I fear some sliver of panic, sadness or self-loathing will always stay with us.

(Koren Zailckas, *Smashed: Growing Up a Drunk Girl*)

the

inner

place

Religion as a Response to the Search for Meaning

DISCUSS

1 In your opinion, does drinking lead to suffering for young people? What kind of suffering might it lead to?

2 Sometimes people drink and bring suffering on themselves because of an underlying unhappiness. Why do you think people drink to cope with unhappiness?

3   Why does God allow people to suffer?

Often when there are major natural disasters, people ask why God can let such things happen. Why does God allow hurricanes and earthquakes? The first thing to note is that, ultimately, God remains a mystery and we can never fully answer questions about the nature of God. Sometimes when these disasters occur, people blame God and decry God as some sadistic ruler. Sometimes while people are at this, they're too busy to take down the phone number of the charity that urgently needs hard cash. The real problem about natural disasters is that it is we who are asked the questions. It is we who are asked 'what will you do about this?'

Yet this is also where God comes in, because the gospels make it clear that you should help those in need. It's there in the parable of the Good Samaritan and in Jesus' teachings about the kingdom of God. When Jesus told the story about the man being beaten and robbed, he didn't say, 'Well now, isn't God terrible to let that happen?' The story was firmly directed towards us. What will you do now? Do you help the person who suffers? Do you ignore the person, or do you take advantage of the person who suffers and make it even worse?

In the aftermath of the hurricanes that hit America in 2005, thousands perished in the flooded area. People needed others to help them. Some helped. Some didn't.

the inner place

❝ One old lady was found lying on the pavement at dawn yesterday in downtown New Orleans. She had been tipped from her mobile stretcher during the night and left on the ground. "Someone stole her

stretcher," said Bruce Lizalde, an airman who had helped to carry the dying woman to a small first-aid tent set up by the US Air Force's 149th medical team. "They just dumped her on the ground and left."

DISCUSS

1 Why do you think people might blame God in times of hardship, instead of doing something to help?

2 In your opinion, are young people generally good at responding to people in need of help, especially after natural disasters? Give reasons for your answer.

4   If God can't be blamed for suffering, does that mean God doesn't care about it?

People often ask why God allows suffering to take place. Why doesn't God do something about it? The story of Adam and Eve goes some way to answer this. Basically, we were created with free will. It was men like Hitler, not God, who caused the Holocaust. If God were to intervene in every morally evil act, there would no longer be choice or freedom, and we would be little more than robots.

We could shout and scream at God in the face of suffering and holler: 'It's OK for you, you're God – you don't have to suffer, suffering doesn't matter to you.' Yet such an accusation goes to the very heart of the mystery of who God is. Far from being removed from our suffering, God is intimately involved in it. The following story from Elie Wiesel challenges the notion that God doesn't care in the face of human suffering.

the inner place

One day, the electric power station at Buna was blown up. The Gestapo, summoned to the spot, suspected sabotage. They found a trail. It eventually led to the Dutch Oberkapo. And there, after a search, they found an important stock of arms.

The Oberkapo was arrested immediately. He was tortured for a period of weeks, but in vain. He would not give a single name. He was transferred to Auschwitz. We never heard of him again.

But this little servant had been left behind in the camp in prison. Also put to torture, he too would not speak. Then the SS sentenced him to death, with two other prisoners who had been discovered with arms.

Holocaust memorial in Berlin

One day when we came back from work, we saw three gallows rearing up in the assembly place, three black crows. Roll call. SS all around us, machine guns trained: the traditional ceremony. Three victims in chains – and one of them, the little servant, the sad-eyed angel.

The SS seemed more preoccupied, more disturbed than usual. To hang a young boy in front of thousands of spectators was no light matter. The head of the camp read the verdict. All eyes were on the child. He was lividly pale, almost calm, biting his lips. The gallows threw its shadow over him.

This time the Lagerkapo refused to act as executioner. Three SS replaced him.

The three victims mounted together onto the chairs.

The three necks were placed at the same moment within the nooses.

the

inner

place

Elie Wiesel

'Long live liberty!' cried the two adults.

But the child was silent.

'Where is God? Where is He?' someone behind me asked.

At a sign from the head of the camp, the three chairs tipped over.

Total silence throughout the camp. On the horizon, the sun was settling.

'Bear your heads!' yelled the head of the camp.

His voice was raucous. We were weeping.

'Cover your heads!'

Then the march past began. The two adults were no longer alive. Their tongues hung swollen, blue-tinged. But the third rope was still moving; being so light, the child was still alive...

For more than half an hour he stayed there, struggling between life and death, dying in slow agony under our eyes. And we had to look at him full in the face. He was still alive when I passed in front of him. His tongue was still red, his eyes not yet glazed.

Behind me, I heard the same man asking:

'Where is God now?'

And I heard a voice within me answer him:

'Where is He? Here He is – He is hanging here on this gallows...'

That night the soup tasted of corpses.

(Elie Wiesel, *Night*)

the

inner

place

DISCUSS

1 How does this harrowing story illustrate how God is involved in our suffering?

2 Do you have any stories that illustrate how God was present with you or somebody else in the midst of suffering?

Religion as a Response to
the Search for Meaning

Karen's Story

Karen discovered she was sick in July 1992. She was six years of age.

The doctors thought it was chickenpox that had caused a build up of fluid in her ears, and this was causing her imbalance. Over a short period of time she got worse and the doctors decided to send her to Dublin for a CT scan. This showed that she had a malignant (cancerous) brain tumour. It was based at the back of her brain stem, and because it was malignant it could travel anywhere in the body at any time. Karen had surgery to remove her tumour in August 1992, but only a percentage could be removed because it was too deep. If they went any deeper, it could have caused permanent brain damage.

Karen came out of the operation, but was unable to move because she had paralysis of the left-hand side. She had to learn how to do everything again. She had to learn how to talk and walk, how to feed herself and how to grip and write. It was like she was a baby again. She was in a wheelchair for over three years and used a walking frame. Her walking will never come back fully again. She lost her hair through chemotherapy and radiotherapy, but she would never wear a wig. According to her carer: 'What you see now will always be it. It will never

come back, but she does not let it get her down. She always wears a baseball cap. She has loads of colours.'

Karen had quite a few surgeries. She also had surgery to remove her thyroid gland because she had a tumour. Again, Karen's carer describes the type of person she is: 'She never complains and she'll always tell you that she's fine.

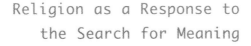

inner

place

She may not be able to do the same things as us, but she never lets it get her down. She has a very bubbly personality and always makes us laugh. She always gets on with it and lets nothing stand in her way. We will never know why it happened. There is no explanation. She feels fine most days, but because of all the surgery to her head she has epilepsy, but again it doesn't get her down. It can sometimes take a lot out of her and make her very tired.'

She goes on to tell how Karen has always prayed to God. 'When she was in hospital, if she was up to it, she would go to the hospital chapel and pray or just sit quietly. When she was in hospital, she met a Franciscan monk who came to see her every morning and told her he was with Padre Pio when he died. He left her prayers to keep by her at all times. She always prays. That's what keeps her safe.'

DISCUSS

1 How would you describe Karen's approach to her suffering?
2 Why do you think her religious beliefs have helped her through her difficult times?
3 Do you think Karen's story has anything to teach us about our approach to our own lives?

the

inner

place

Religion as a Response to the Search for Meaning

Chapter Six

SPIRITUALITY AND THE SPIRITUAL WORLD

'For in him
all things in heaven and on earth were created,
things visible and invisible.'
(Colossians 1:16)

As you sit in the classroom, take a look around you. Most likely, you can see the back of someone's head in front of you, and there is probably someone sitting beside you. There are four walls, a door, one or more windows and lots of really interested students, happy to be in school. It's Ireland, so it's probably raining outside. You're probably feeling hungry. All around you is the real world, one that you can touch, taste, hear, see and smell. Yet religion makes an extraordinary claim. It believes that there is another world, the spiritual realm, which exists all around us – even in the classroom you are now sitting in. In other words, right at this moment you are not alone. All around you is a spiritual world. Unlike the classroom and the people in it, the spiritual world is non-physical and invisible. Spirituality can be broadly understood as the way we relate to the spiritual world around us. Our spirituality allows us to become available and receptive to the spiritual dimension of life.

Padre Pio

Many people claim to have had an experience of the spiritual world, but obviously the type and intensity of the experience varies from person to person. Intense mystical experiences include levitations and out-of-body experiences. For example, Joseph of Copertino wasn't allowed to serve in the monastery kitchen for fear that he would break too much crockery as he levitated about the place. There is evidence that

Padre Pio could bilocate. While his physical body was in one location, his spiritual body was elsewhere. You can try this out at home, but it probably won't work. If it does, make sure to tell the class all about it the next day.

Most of us don't have such intense mystical experiences, but a survey carried out in the UK revealed that many ordinary people do have spiritual experiences. It revealed the following:

Type of Experience	Percentage reporting the experience
God's presence	27
Help received in response to prayer	25
A guiding presence not called God	22
Presence of someone who has died	18
A sacred presence in nature	16
An evil presence	12
The unity of all things	2

(David Fontana, *Psychology, Religion and Spirituality*)

DISCUSS Have you ever had any of the above experiences or do you know stories about people who have had such experiences? Share them with the class.

the
inner
place

Spirituality and the Spiritual World

SPIRITUALITY AND THE MIND–BRAIN RELATIONSHIP

Talk of spirituality and spiritual experiences is based on the assumption that we can have experiences of the spiritual world or the non-physical realm. For example, if there is an afterlife, then there must be some part of us that is not physical, there must be some part of us that doesn't die, that isn't dependent upon our physical bodies for its continued existence. This, in turn, means that there must be a part of us that is spiritual; in other words, there must exist a part of us that no surgeon could find. Is there really a part of us that is non-physical? There are many ways to answer this question, but we will take the scientific route and examine the relationship between our mind and our brain.

DISCUSS

1 Is your mind and your brain the same thing? Can you examine your brain under a microscope? Can you examine your mind under a microscope? If not, why not?

2 Do you think your mind, your 'I-ness', is completely dependent for its existence upon a mass of blood and tissue called your brain? Give reasons for your answer.

When it comes to figuring out the relationship between the mind and the brain, one particular theory has very serious consequences for the student of religion. This theory suggests that the mind is simply created by the electrochemical activity within the brain. If we accept this theory, which states that the mind is completely dependent on the physical brain, it means that when the brain dies, the mind does too. If the mind dies with the brain, then your 'I-ness' dies too, as in,

the

inner

place

ceases to exist. This would effectively be the end to any notions of an afterlife and our existence as spiritual beings after we die. Yet there is another theory.

According to Sir John Eccles, an expert in neurophysiology, or brain science, there is no method or model to explain how the grey matter in the brain can produce thoughts or ideas or what we understand as the human mind. Scientists can't explain it. He believes, however, that the mind can have a non-physical or non-material existence. As he puts it: 'The "self-conscious mind" must have some non-material existence' (David Fontana, *Psychology, Religion and Spirituality*). What this basically means is that there are two types of reality: physical matter that you can see and touch, for example, the classroom around you, and also a non-material realm, that of mind, consciousness and, of course, the spiritual or supernatural.

Yet is there any scientific evidence that the mind can actually be non-physical, and therefore can exist outside the brain or even, ultimately, after death? Is there evidence that a person's mind could continue to survive after their brain has ceased to function? In fact, there is.

The following account is related by Dr Michael Sabom in his book *Light and Death*, where he recalls some incidents from The Atlanta Study into near-death experiences.

> **Code Blue in Room 314**
> 'Code Blue, Room 314! Code Blue, Room 314!' bellowed a voice over the hospital intercom. When the responding cardiologist arrived at Room 314, CPR was already in progress. To his surprise, the cardiac-arrested patient was Gene, a close friend and fellow physician.
>
> The cardiologist immediately grabbed the defibrillator paddles and began shocking Gene's heart with a maximum output of 360 joules. An anaesthesiologist arrived to begin artificial ventilation, while nurses continued pushing powerful IV cardiac drugs. Gene would later recall the early moments of this procedure as a 'terrifying experience' that he 'blocked' out of his head.

Spirituality and the
Spiritual World

According to the medical record, Gene showed no response after fifteen full minutes of full CPR and ten to fifteen electrical shots. The code team wanted to stop. Gene's cardiologist friend, however, could not let him go and sent for a special high-output defibrillator kept in his electrophysiology lab two floors below.

Amazingly, one super-charged shock of 500 joules from this defibrillator restored normal sinus rhythm. By this time, however, Gene's pupils were 'fixed, dilated, and unresponsive', a clinical sign of brain death. It was during this time, Gene later told me, that he, 'was out in infinity space…What it felt like was that I didn't really have a body. It was like a mind and soul. From a very far distance I could see a light. I started approaching this light. Then, as I got closer and closer, it seemed that I was picking up speed. The intensity of the light was like a beam that got brighter and brighter and brighter as I approached it. It was incredible how intense that light was.'

DISCUSS

1 Why do you think the above incident might provide evidence that a part of us is non-material?

2 Do you believe that you have a non-material part to you that you could identify as spiritual? Is this spiritual part of you important? Give reasons for your answer.

So scientific evidence suggests that the mind can exist independent of the brain in a non-physical realm. If the mind can operate in a non-physical realm and if the spiritual realm is non-physical, then it is entirely possible that people do have very real spiritual experiences, as outlined above. It also helps us to understand how we can have a spiritual side to us, along with our own distinctive spirituality.

the

inner

place

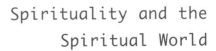

Spirituality and the
Spiritual World

SPIRITUALITY AND SELF-TRANSCENDENCE

Our lives are full of everyday and ordinary experiences. We sleep, eat, shop, text, talk, play, study, sleep, eat, shop, text, talk, play, study, sleep, eat, shop, text, talk, play, study. On and on life goes. But, every once in a while, something different happens. We do something extraordinary, something that goes beyond the ordinary and the routine. We do something that goes beyond ourselves and what we consider to be our own limitations. We transcend ourselves. Some of our best stories are about people who go beyond themselves and create a world where, what was once thought impossible, becomes possible.

Borderlands 1996: A Story of Transcendence
In 1995, Liam Griffin took over as manager of the Wexford senior hurling team. It was a team that hadn't won an All-Ireland in twenty-seven years. Nothing hurt Wexford people so much. In 1995, they didn't win it either. In 1996, Griffin got them to the Leinster final against Offaly. On the Friday before the match, Griffin was watching the television, and Brian Cowen the Fianna Fáil TD was singing 'The Offaly Rover'; the punters were giving Wexford no chance and they were dismissed as a hurling team. There was good reason to write them off, but Griffin's blood began to boil. His mind went into overdrive and he forgot about hurling and realised that this was about Wexford and what Wexford meant to the team.

> Then I started thinking about George O'Connor's father (Griffin's uncle) who was dead and my own father who was dead, and I started thinking about the great Wexford teams that were gone and the way of life I'd grown up with, and that hurling was synonymous with the people I felt we were. I said to myself, 'I'm gonna write this.'
>
> I got up the next morning early and I wrote what I wanted to say because I didn't want to have wasted words. I said to myself, 'We need something monumental, something that's going to be mind-

the
inner
place

Spirituality and the
Spiritual World

blowing, something to raise the whole thing onto a different plane, something that's going to make them believe that this is so important, a level where it's much bigger than the match. It's not just a game, it's about our life, it's about who we are.' I felt, we've got to transcend sport. This thing, 'Ah, it's only a match' – that's for county finals. This was about freedom. This was about striking out from this terrible place where we'd been for so long. So I wrote that speech.

(The Sunday Times, 9/10/05)

Griffin's idea was to stop the bus just before the Wicklow border, and there to deliver his speech about history, place and identity. He would then walk the team over the county bounds. He told no one of his plans in case they thought he was mad.

Supporters' cars flew by blowing their horns, assuming that the bus had broken down. Griffin stuck to his plan. He delivered his speech and finished it thus:

> Today we are playing for a way of life. Breathe in now, long and hard, and as you walk, think of yourself since childhood. All of the matches you played. All of your friends, both alive and gone. And make this promise to yourself: 'Today is the day we will be proud again.' And remember: 'We are the boys of Wexford, who fought with heart and hand.' That's real tradition. Let's go.

He walked the players over the county bounds and the bus drove up to meet them.

> I knew I got through to them. As we got back onto the bus there was hardly a word out of anybody.

Wexford beat Offaly that day and went on to win the All-Ireland, beating Limerick in Croke Park.

DISCUSS

1 What do you think Griffin meant when he said that he had to 'transcend sport'?
2 Why do you think Griffin's speech would have helped Wexford to win the Leinster final?
3 What do you think was so inspirational about Griffin's approach?
4 Do you think winning the match would have given meaning to people's lives?
5 Griffin told his players: 'This was about freedom. This was about striking out from this terrible place where we'd been for so long.' For Wexford supporters, that terrible place was not having won an All-Ireland in so many years. Griffin and his players went beyond that routine of losing finals, of being losers. Can you think of other examples where people go beyond themselves and achieve the impossible?

WHAT IS SPIRITUALITY?

Spirituality is about going beyond ourselves or transcending ourselves. Spirituality refers to that part of a person that relates to or experiences the spiritual world. Spirituality also refers to the way that we express our spiritual beliefs in how we think, feel and act. Religion has always put a structure on the spiritual world. In Christianity, a person's spirituality is based on their belief in God. Their spiritual life is an expression of Christian values and beliefs.

St Paul tells us: 'Glory be to him whose power, working in us, can do infinitely more than we can ask or imagine' (Ephesians 3:20). In Mark's gospel, Jesus tells us: 'For mortals it is impossible, but not for God: for God all things are possible' (Mark 10:27). Our spirituality transforms our lives and the lives of those around us in the best possible way. Spirituality allows us to transcend ourselves to become what we truly can be. The story of the Wexford hurlers is a story of a group of players transcending

the

inner

place

Spirituality and the
Spiritual World

themselves and living their lives in the best possible way. Ultimately, when we embrace our spirituality, it transforms us and gives meaning to our lives.

The process of becoming spiritual in many ways means discovering the spiritual side to our personalities. Many would like to dismiss the notion that there is a spiritual side to them, but as we saw when we considered the mind-brain relationship, there is scientific evidence that there is more to us than just our physical selves. It would appear that we are connected to the non-physical world or what we would term the spiritual world.

The Dark Destroyer

When Nigel Benn was a boxer he was known as 'The Dark Destroyer'. Described as almost primeval, he took a sadistic pleasure in his fights. They often had the characteristics of a street brawl.

The boxer Chris Eubank described him as 'savage…he was strong enough to kill me and I think he desired to'. Elsewhere he was described as having a relentless and destructive aggression.

Yet Benn's life was completely transformed by his own spirituality. He has dedicated himself to charitable causes, has founded his own church, and cooks dinners for pensioners in his neighbourhood. When asked what transformed his life, his reply was: 'My flesh has achieved but what have I done spiritually.'

(*The Sunday Times*, 15/5/05)

The image of 'The Dark Destroyer' cooking Christmas dinners for pensioners can only be put down to the transforming power of his spirituality. Benn transcended his old destructive self-image and embraced Christian spirituality of service to others.

the

inner

place

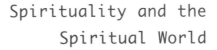

1 What has been your impression of spiritual people? Is there anybody you know of whom you would call spiritual? How would you describe that person?

2 Do you think a person's spirituality could transform their lives? If so, in what way?

3 People rarely talk openly about their own spirituality, their Christian beliefs or values. Why do you think that is? Is spirituality something to be ashamed of, or is it just something very personal?

4 Do you think teenagers have a particular spirituality? If so, what is it like and how would it differ from the spirituality of your grandparents?

5 Would you prefer to have gotten into a fight with Nigel Benn before or after his transformation?

SPIRITUALITY AND THE TEENAGER

Teenagers are very different to other groups of people. Teenagers view the world in a particular away. They understand that they have their own unique role in the world. They are also aware of their own particular needs. Because being a teenager is a distinctive time in a person's life, then we should also find a distinctive spirituality in teenagers.

Christian spirituality is based upon the person of Jesus Christ. As such, Christian spirituality mirrors his life, teachings and ministry. In the gospels, Jesus is constantly reported for sneaking off into the wilderness to be on his own. Perhaps everybody was wrecking his head because often they couldn't follow what he was saying. But we know that he spent much of this time in silent prayer to the Father. Jesus also challenged the systems of the day and he constantly challenged people to transform their lives. He fiercely rejected injustice and hypocrisy. Finally, Jesus saw himself as one who was here to serve others and not to be served.

the inner place

SPIRITUALITY OF PRAYER AND MEDITATION

'But whenever you pray, go into your room and shut the door and pray to your Father who is in secret; and your Father who sees in secret will reward you.'

(Matthew 6:6)

> I don't pray that much, I suppose, but I often say a prayer before I go to sleep. I tend to worry a bit and I usually worry a bit before I fall asleep, 'bout stuff at home and in school. I think praying helps because you feel someone might help you. My granny told me once that we all have an angel to protect us, like a guardian angel. She told me that if you ask for a sign that your guardian angel exists, you'll find a feather the next day. So I did and I found this small white feather on the doorstep. Honest it happened. So I put it under my pillow. When I pray I just talk to God. Sometimes I say prayers. Don't know why. But the talkin' is better. The feather is kind of a sign that there is someone really listening.

(Female, 17)

One important characteristic of being a teenager is that life is changing rapidly. But change is difficult because it means letting go of things and getting used to extra responsibility and independence. Change can sometimes make people feel more vulnerable and they may feel that they need help. As a teenager, you are trying to establish yourself in the world. You have to let go of a childhood identity and adopt an adult identity. This means creating a new identity for yourself, new friends, a new image, the world of work, becoming independent from parents, and socialising. All of this brings its own pressures, and a teenager's spirituality can express itself in praying to God for guidance or help. This is usually a very personal thing.

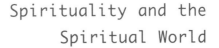

DISCUSS

1. Do you think most teenagers pray and would you agree that they feel they need help and guidance?
2. Do you think teenagers prefer informal prayers, like just talking to God, or do you think teenagers also use traditional prayers like the 'Our Father' and the 'Hail Mary'?
3. Why do you think prayer is such a personal thing?
4. Where do teenagers learn how to pray and who has the most influence over their prayer life: the Church, parents, school or grandparents?
5. If you had children, would you like them to be able to pray? If so, why?

SPIRITUALITY OF ENCOUNTER AND PRESENCE

'And remember, I am with you always, to the end of the age.'
(Matthew 28:20)

the

inner

place

‘ In March of this year my grand-aunt died from cancer. Although I was really upset, I did not stay sad for long because I knew that her pain was over. I knew she was with God. The next three weeks passed and my mother's cousin also died of cancer. I

Spirituality and the
Spiritual World

didn't pray this time as there was nothing I could do. Then in August of this year my other grand-aunt got cancer. My mother was told by doctors that she would die in the next two weeks. She came to live with us but the day she moved in she got very sick and was moved into hospital. I prayed that she would live.

Two weeks after that she was still alive. I continued praying and for the next two weeks she was healthy and she was walking around the place. This is one of the main reasons that I believe in God. Two weeks later she was in a terrible condition, and on the terrible night of August 16 she died. I was devastated.

I went to her funeral and I could not stop crying. I was looking right at the coffin when I remembered all that she had said to me. It was like God was forcing me to remember. I will never forget that day because now I really believe in God. I don't know why but I believe her spirit is still in my bedroom, because when I pray my wishes are granted. Well only small things like good exam results. **,**

(Female, 16)

There are times in every person's life when they have a spiritual experience. These experiences are extraordinarily private and personal to the people involved and are rarely shared. These experiences can often happen during difficult times in a person's life. Perhaps the person can't fully interpret the nature of the spiritual experience but, either through intuition or emotion, they know they have encountered a presence in their lives. Sometimes people feel the loving presence of God in their lives or they feel that someone who has died and who loved them is still present with them in some way. These spiritual experiences often have a very deep effect on people for many years and they help to strengthen their belief in God.

the

inner

place

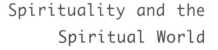

SPIRITUALITY OF CHANGE AND TRANSFORMATION

'What we are waiting for is what he promised: the new heavens and new earth, the place where righteousness will be at home.'
(2 Peter 3:13)

ASIDE

You see things; and you say, 'why?' But I dream things that never were; and I say, 'why not?'
(George Bernard Shaw)

" I remember 2004 because we were in sixth year and the US and George Bush was invading Iraq to topple the dictator Saddam Hussein. A lot of people didn't agree with it. Most of our class were against it because we knew many innocent people would be killed. The US called it "collateral damage". So we had this big class discussion because someone said that the B-52 bombers were flying right over where our school was. Then one student decided we should do something about it. I can't remember who it was. So we talked for ages because, like, what could we do? Then someone suggested what we should do.

Ten minutes before the bell went for afternoon classes we all traipsed down to the hockey pitch. It was a gorgeous sunny day, so the planes would definitely see us. I'd say there were eighty of us. On

the

inner

place

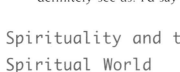

the pitch we organised ourselves into a massive anti-war symbol. Imagine eighty girls sitting on the pitch holding hands waiting for the bombers to fly over. There wasn't much we could do. But that was what we did. To this day I still wonder if any pilot at the time saw us. My boyfriend could make out the sound of the engines and he said one was flying over around that time. That would be cool.

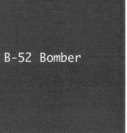
B-52 Bomber

In the film *Dead Poets Society*, the teacher Mr Keating tells the class that the world and life is one big poem. He tells them that their lives can add a verse to that poem, and he puts it to them, 'And what will your verse be?' If there is one thing that characterises the outlook that teenagers have on the world, it is that they want to change and transform it for the better. Many people criticise teenagers, but many teenagers are far from impressed with the world that adults have created for them. They see corruption, greed, prejudice and a lack of concern for the environment. The desire to bring about change for the good is firmly rooted in the Gospel tradition, and it is an energy that teenagers have in abundance. When Jesus threw the money-changers from the Temple, he was attacking greed and corruption and demanding radical change. Throughout his life, Jesus attempted to change how people behaved towards themselves and the world around them.

the
inner
place

DISCUSS

1 Do you agree that teenagers do have a vision for a better world and how to bring that about?

2 If the pilot of a B-52 bomber had seen the girls' symbol, what do you think he or she might have thought? Could it have made a difference?

3   Do you know of any other stories where teenagers tried to change the world in whatever small or big way they could? Share them with the class.
4   Why do you think teenagers are represented too often in a negative way in the media?

SPIRITUALITY OF SERVICE AND ALTRUISM

'We who are strong ought to put up with the failings of the weak, and not to please ourselves.'
(Romans 15:1)

❝ Most of my friends are what society would call "punks". We are the teenagers who hang out at the coffee shops or the movies for lack of anything better to do. But being punks doesn't mean much.

One evening, after a day of not doing much, we were sitting in McDonald's when a guy in our group whom I had just met that day walked in. Brian was the typical punk teenager, dressed in black with the dyed hair. Right before he stepped inside, he yelled something outside to a man walking down the street. I just hoped he wasn't trying to start trouble. He sat down, and a minute later, a burly homeless man stuck his head in and looked at Brian.

the

inner

place

Spirituality and the
Spiritual World

"Did you say something to me?" the man demanded, and I thought I saw a mean glint in his eyes. I shrank back, thinking that if Brian had tried to pick a fight, this was the wrong guy to do it with. I had seen too many places kick teenagers like us out for pulling stuff.

While the rest of us were looking for a place to back into, Brian got up and walked up to him. "Yeah… would you like something to eat?" The relief was almost audible, and the man smiled and walked in.

After a large meal of hamburgers, fries and desert, the man left, and even the staff waved good-bye to him. When we asked Brian about it, he explained how he had money that he didn't need and the man had none, so it was only right.

'

(Shelly Millar, 'McDonald's', from *Chicken Soup for the Teenage Soul*)

It should be no surprise that those who have been baptised into Christ as infants will display Christ-like qualities in their spirituality throughout their lives. Even though Jesus was divine, he did not demand or expect to be waited upon. He constantly looked out for the lost and those made outcast. We will read more about this in Section B.

the inner place

As is evident from the above account, sometimes teenagers have a special ability and courage when it comes to stepping out from the crowd and talking to the one who is less well off. Of course, this is not always the case, but the evidence from second-level schools suggests that when there is a disaster or famine, teenagers are quick to fast, run, walk or do a 'no uniform' day to help victims of suffering.

DISCUSS

1 Do you agree that teenagers have the ability to stand out from the crowd so as to do the right thing?
2 Based on your own experience, are teenagers especially willing to help those who are less fortunate than themselves?

the

inner

place

Spirituality and the Spiritual World

Chapter Seven

DREAMS:
SYMBOLS OF THE UNCONSCIOUS

In chapter 4, we examined the role and function of symbol in human life. In this chapter, we conduct a special report into the role of dreams and the unconscious. As will become apparent, dreams can be best understood as symbols of the unconscious. We can only appreciate dreams and understand them when we approach them symbolically.

Since ancient times, dreams have played an important role in human affairs and can be traced back to the Old and New Testaments in the Bible. In the book of Genesis, Joseph was freed from prison because of his ability to interpret dreams. Samuel, Isaiah and Ezekiel were all called through their dreams in the Old Testament. In the New Testament, the Lord appeared to Joseph in a dream, telling him to take Mary as his wife and to call the child conceived in her womb, Jesus (Matthew 1:20–24). In a later dream, Joseph is warned to flee with his wife to Egypt to escape Herod's murderous intent (Matthew 2:13).

Now after they had left, an angel of the Lord appeared to Joseph in a dream and said, 'Get up, take the child and his mother, and flee to Egypt, and remain there until I tell you; for Herod is about to search for the child to destroy him.' Then Joseph got up, took the child and his mother by night, and went to Egypt, and remained there until the death of Herod. This was to fulfil what had been spoken by the Lord through the prophet, 'Out of Egypt I have called my son.'

(Matthew 2:13–15)

A President's Dream

Abraham Lincoln

In early April 1865, Abraham Lincoln fell asleep in the White House while working late, and had a dream. He later recounted it to his wife, Mary, and to Ward Hill Lamon, his friend and bodyguard. In the dream, Lincoln became aware of the 'deathlike stillness' and the barely audible sound of people crying. He dreamt he left his bed and wandered downstairs in the direction of the noise. All the rooms he passed were lit, but empty. The weeping drew him to the East Room, used for functions, including funerals. Inside he saw a corpse wrapped in funeral vestments, its face covered, atop a platform surrounded by armed guards and mourners. Lincoln asked one, who had died. 'The president,' came the reply. 'He was killed by an assassin.' Soon afterwards, on April 14, he was shot by the actor and southern sympathiser John Wilkes Booth at the theatre, dying the next day. His dream had proved sadly prophetic.

(*The Sunday Times*, 15/5/05)

the inner place

Dreams:
Symbols of the Unconscious

This account of a dream that President Abraham Lincoln is reported to have had raised some interesting questions. Could a dream foresee a future event? Was the dream a warning, like Joseph's dream in the New Testament? But, more importantly, where do dreams come from in the first place? Who or what creates these incredible stories laden with bizarre landscapes, improbable events and sometimes unfamiliar characters? The answer is that our dreams come from our unconscious minds, that part of all of us that acts as creator, producer and director of those internal films we call dreams.

DISCUSS

1 The president's dream suggests that dreams are meaningful. Do you think dreams are meaningful or are they just random images and characters from our sleeping minds?

2 Where do you think dreams come from? What is their purpose?

WHAT IS THE UNCONSCIOUS?

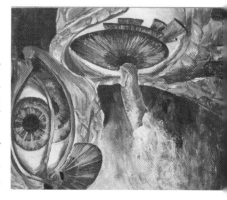

A popular understanding of the term 'unconscious' can refer to the state a person gets in when they have been knocked on the head or have consumed dangerous amounts of drink. In psychology, however, the unconscious refers to a part of our minds. It is only in recent years that Western culture has discovered the riches of the unconscious mind, even though people like Native Americans have constantly been in touch with this realm of human experience.

For many years, dreams were dismissed as irrelevant and superstitious in Western culture. Yet in the middle of the last century, a doctor named Sigmund Freud discovered that many of his patients could be treated for their physical ailments by interpreting their dreams. He discovered a deeper layer of the mind that had a significant role to play in a person's life. It was the realm of the unconscious.

the

inner

place

THE UNCONSCIOUS SLIPS THROUGH

The easiest way to try to understand the unconscious is by identifying the distinction between consciousness and unconsciousness. This is very simple. You will notice that at any given time in class, some people are paying attention and some people aren't. The latter group are off in another place, engaged in what is known as daydreaming. This may have happened to you. One minute you're listening to the teacher, and then, without really noticing the slip, you pass into a different place. No longer are you in the classroom but you're off and immersed in some other experiences. Right at this moment in your classroom, someone is gone. They're no longer with us. Do you remember that moment when you find you have slipped into a different place and suddenly the teacher asks you a question? The panic! That very dilemma is caused by the interplay between the conscious and unconscious minds. In the experience of daydreaming, the unconscious mind has slipped through and taken over your conscious mind. Your conscious mind is that part of you that is awake and aware.

Right at this moment in class, there is someone else who is no longer fully conscious either. Right now, with pen in hand, they are doodling away, happily drawing out faces or squares, flowers, tunnels, etc. Look around, someone is doodling. So what is happening? Basically, the unconscious is a very powerful part of your mind, but the strange thing is that we can never directly access it. That's because our conscious minds are in the way. Once the conscious mind weakens, the unconscious slips through. This weakening is usually caused by sleep or incredible boredom.

Dreams:
Symbols of the Unconscious

ASIDE

Another example of daydreaming involves the conscious mind going on complete walkabout. For example, a person wants to drive from A to C. On the way, they have to pass through B. But something happened at work and the person becomes completely engrossed in an imaginary argument with their boss.

There they are arguing their case and, needless to say, always winning. Suddenly, they become aware of the fact that they are driving the car. They reckon they should soon be in town B, but instead they arrive at town C. So, who drove the car through town B? Luckily the unconscious mind takes over in these situations and guides us safely through traffic lights and around pedestrians. However, it's wise not to try this in your driving test.

When you wake up in the morning and get out of bed and go out into the day, you are more or less in control of your thoughts and actions. You decide what to wear, where to go, whom to talk to and what to say. This is your conscious mind at work. It is awake and full of awareness of all that is around you. But periodically throughout the day, your conscious mind allows your unconscious through. You can never be aware of this; it just happens. For example, everything may seem to be going very well in your life in so far as you are very happy with what's going on, but your unconscious may view things differently, and this might manifest itself in an unexplained mood or temper.

Were you ever really sad or down for no apparent reason? Did anyone ever turn on you and go into a mad rage for no apparent reason? What was all that about? Where did it come from? Chances are it was the unconscious slipping through.

Before we look at some other examples of the unconscious in everyday life, it is important at this stage to try to understand more of what constitutes the unconscious. The first thing to be sure of is that the unconscious is you, but just a part of you that

the

inner

place

is not as obvious as your conscious mind. The unconscious is a marvellous expanse of your entire identity which knows much more about you than your conscious mind does. It is a vast reservoir of thoughts, emotions, aspirations, memories and ideas. It is the best part of you, full of wisdom and insight about you and those around you. It is truthful and never lies. How do we know all of this? It's time to look at dreams, because they act as an incredible window into the unconscious mind.

 Daydreaming and doodling belong to the realm of the unconscious mind, and accordingly the conscious mind finds it difficult to create either activity. You can try this. With your conscious mind, tell yourself to daydream and see what happens. Order yourself to daydream: 'Mind, daydream right now!' What happens? If that doesn't work, tell yourself to doodle. Order your mind to create doodles right now: 'Mind, do doodles right now!' What happens? Can your conscious mind create daydreaming or doodling?

DREAMS AND THE UNCONSCIOUS

Carl Jung remains one of the most significant figures in psychology and dream-analysis. He told the following story regarding a colleague of his and a particular dream he had. This story illustrates how the unconscious mind can be full of wisdom and insight. It can act as a guide to the person. This guidance comes in the form of dreams.

The colleague in question was very successful in life and was blessed with promotion after promotion. He was on the verge of an extremely significant promotion when he referred himself to Dr Jung. He was complaining of mountain sickness, even though he never climbed mountains. But he also told him this particular disturbing dream.

Dreams:

Symbols of the Unconscious

> I am in a great hurry because I am going on a journey. I hunt up my baggage, but cannot find it. Time flies, and the train will soon be leaving. Finally I succeed in getting all my things together. I hurry along the street, discover that I have forgotten a brief-case containing important papers, dash breathlessly back again, find it at last, and then run towards the station, but make hardly any headway. With a final effort I rush onto the platform only to find the train steaming out into the yards. It is very long, and it runs in a curious s-shaped curve.

> It occurs to me that if the driver is not careful, and puts on full steam when he comes to the straight stretch, the rear coaches will still be on the curve and will be thrown over by the speed of the train. As a matter of fact the driver opens the throttle as I shout. The rear coaches rock frightfully, and are actually thrown off the rails. There is a terrible catastrophe. I awake in terror.

(Carl Jung, *The Psyche*)

Jung tried to explain to the man the significance of the dream. He tried to explain that it was a message and advice from the man's own unconscious regarding his conscious life.

the

inner

place

DISCUSS

What do you think that advice was? What message do you think the man's unconscious was giving him?

ASIDE

Often, disturbing dreams can be very important because the unconscious wants to convey an important message. Sometimes our unconscious minds can pick up something during the day that has gone over our heads. For example, a young man dreams that he is driving his car through a decidedly dodgy neighbourhood. He is frightened and fears for his safety. The car speeds up and he begins to lose control. The car is heading for a brick wall when he wakes up. The next morning the young man is still preoccupied by the dream and troubled by the feeling of losing control of the car. As he goes out to drive to work, he checks all round the car, just to be sure. He discovers that one of his tires is dangerously threadbare. He realises that it's something he should have noticed but just didn't.

DISCUSS

What do you think was the meaning or purpose behind this dream?

According to Carl Jung, the man was on the brink of a very big promotion. He was literally rising high in his career, but the mountain sickness seemed to point to the fact that some part of him wasn't too pleased with this ascent. The dream told him in stark imagery that he was going off the rails and losing control of his life. As it happened, the man took the promotion, and with disastrous consequences it didn't work out.

It would appear that the man's unconscious somehow 'knew' the consequences of the promotion and that the man just wasn't up to it. The unconscious then would appear to be full of wisdom, and this can be presented to us in the form of dreams. We will investigate more about dreams later on.

the inner place

Dreams:
Symbols of the Unconscious

Lying and the Unconscious

As noted previously, the unconscious can only tell the truth about who we are and what we're about. Yet it is aware when you are lying, and this creates a tension between the unconscious and consciousness. In the dream above, the man experienced the symptoms of mountain sickness when the unconscious was reacting to his promotion. In the same way, the unconscious will react to a person lying.

Carl Jung was responsible for the theory behind the polygraph or lie-detector test. According to the theory, if a person lies, the tension between the unconscious and conscious mind is expressed in some physical way. This can take the form of an increase in blood pressure or heartbeat. The polygraph can detect this physical reaction, and if it occurs just after the person is asked whether, for example, they ever saw the murder weapon, then it looks like they are lying.

Polygraph test

Sometimes our conscious minds are telling lies without us even knowing it, but our unconscious realises this and can embarrass us big time. It's known as a 'Freudian Slip' and it occurs when we're telling lies. We might be saying one thing but really deep down we're thinking another. For example, a girl meets another girl who is sporting a brilliant tan. She asks where she got it, suspecting it was out of a bottle. The tanned girl replies that she's just back from a foreign holiday. Not satisfied, the other girl wants to know how long she was away. She wants to ask: 'How long did it take?' Instead, though, she blurts: 'How long did it fake?' She then compounds the problem by blabbering on…'Oh sorry, I didn't mean to say…' Maybe she didn't, but her unconscious mind certainly did.

the

inner

place

THE SCIENCE OF DREAMING

Carl Jung once referred to dreams as the 'royal road' to the unconscious, and it is true that we get our best glimpse of what is going on in a person's unconscious in their dreams. In order to experience the unconscious, it is best if consciousness is out of the way, and during sleep that is exactly what happens. In fact, it was through investigating sleep that much of our modern thinking and acceptance of dreams began. As we will see, however, not everyone is convinced that dreams can be meaningful.

THE SLEEP CYCLE

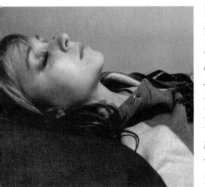

In 1957, researchers Kleitman and Aserinsky, working from Chicago University, discovered Rapid Eye Movement (REM). This means that at a certain time during sleep, your eyes are moving rapidly as if watching a tennis match. Except you're not. Researchers wanted to know what was going on during REM sleep, and this wasn't too difficult. It simply meant getting a few volunteers into a sleep laboratory and waking them up during REM. But the results were fascinating. Each time a volunteer was woken during REM, they were dreaming, and so the connection was made between dreaming and REM. But REM is only a part of your entire sleep cycle, and there are various other stages. You may be interested to know what happens to you as you sleep, and also when you are most likely to dream. The stages are as follows:

the inner place

Stage 1: This only takes a few minutes. As the muscles begin to relax, you 'nod off'. A person can easily be woken during this stage and they may not even be aware that they were asleep. Students are known to enter stage 1 during class.

Dreams:
Symbols of the Unconscious

Stage 2: You are now asleep and are less easily wakened than at stage 1. Stage 2 occupies almost fifty per cent of all sleep-time. It's rare, but some students enter stage 2 during class.

Stage 3: This is deep sleep and lasts for only a few minutes, but during it your muscles are completely relaxed and there is no eye movement. You are completely asleep.

Stage 4: This stage is the deepest form of sleep and you are most difficult to waken. If woken during this stage, you might be completely disorientated, such was the depth of your sleep. The brain shows a decrease of activity in many areas and you have now been asleep for just over an hour. Your brain is sound asleep. But then something strange begins to happen.

Stage 5: Up to now, your brain activity is characterised by the kind of slow electromagnetic waves we would associate with sleep. But then suddenly your brain wakes up. The strange thing is that while your brain has woken up, you haven't. You're still sound asleep but your brain is bursting with activity. It has entered REM.

ASIDE

According to the latest research, we spend approximately twenty per cent of our sleep-time dreaming. We also spend one-third of our lives asleep. Over a seventy-five-year life-span, we will sleep for twenty-five years. Of that twenty-five years, we will dream for five years. If you maintain that you never dream, you're going to miss out on about five years of your life.

the

inner

place

REM SLEEP

REM sleep is fascinating because of what goes on inside your brain. It looks as if your brain is awake, and interestingly there are some parts of your brain that are more active during REM

than when you were awake. In particular, there are parts of your forebrain that seem to be processing information during REM, and this area is associated with memories with an emotional content. It seems that during REM, your brain is being stimulated in the same way as it was when you were awake, except that now all the stimuli are coming from within. Your eyes are moving rapidly, and if you are woken up there's a high probability that you will have been dreaming. Your brain is now being stimulated from the deep reservoir of images, thoughts and feelings in your unconscious mind.

ASIDE

How come we don't act out our dreams?
During REM, the eyes seem to follow the action of our dreams, but the brain has come up with a way of ensuring that the rest of our limbs don't. The brain has developed a way of paralysing the body while the dream takes place, except for the eyes, which are directly linked to the brain. Every other movement is paralysed by the brain stem, which is located at the base of your brain. Experiments on cats showed that the part of the brain that shuts down movement during REM can be shut off. The result was cats who acted out their dreams by chasing mice and jumping at birds, all while soundly asleep. The little paws were going mad while the head was asleep. Some victims of brain damage lose the ability to suppress movement during REM and, like the cats, act out their dreams with their limbs.

the

inner

place

Dreams:
Symbols of the Unconscious

WHAT ARE DREAMS?

There is much debate between scientists and psychologists as to the exact nature and meaning of dreams, and recent research has questioned some of the most basic presumptions about dreaming and sleep.

There is little doubt that dreaming occurs during REM sleep, and recently researchers have discovered what triggers dreaming during this time. Deep in the most primitive part of our brain lies an area known as the pons. REM begins when this area secretes a special messenger-chemical into the brain, which carries messages to other areas, which in turn cause them to become activated. The frontal cortex, along with an area just behind the ears, then becomes involved in synthesising all the information that is created from the different parts of the brain.

WHY DO WE DREAM?

There is much debate around this question, but there seems to be a consensus that dreams are in some way linked to memory and learning. Recently, scientists have established that during dreaming, the area of the brain that is associated with memory is extremely active. According to this theory, for example, something you have read during the day is now processed by the brain during REM sleep. The brain links new information to the information that is already stored in the brain's memory banks. In sleep laboratories, volunteers who were woken constantly during REM sleep found it much more difficult to learn and retain new information during the day.

According to student mythology, if you put a textbook under your pillow at night, you'll remember it the next day. This was always a rather odd belief, but the brain does indeed seem to 'learn' while the person sleeps. You can try it with a book but it doesn't work.

However, as we have already seen, there is another explanation of why we dream. According to this explanation, dreams are meaningful and can be interpreted as messages from our unconscious mind.

DISCUSS

Have you ever had a startling or strange dream that you think had some sort of meaning? Perhaps you could share it with the class.

ASIDE

Teenagers and Sleep

Sleep is a particularly interesting topic for teenagers because they tend to get in trouble over it a lot. Teenagers often sleep when they shouldn't and don't sleep when they should. They go to sleep late and are known to refuse to get out of bed, and when they do they can easily snooze during the school day. The reason is that teenagers actually need more sleep than either children or adults, in fact, over nine hours in total. Basically, if a teenager doesn't get nine hours before they are woken for school, then they are in no way ready to face the day and will find it hard to get out of bed. Insufficient sleep can have significant effects if a teenager is deprived of too much REM sleep, because of its importance for memory and learning. A lack of REM sleep can increase anxiety and can lead to poorer memory and judgement. So, if you're a teenager, it's best to get plenty of sleep.

the

inner

place

DISCUSS

Do you think teenagers need more sleep? Do you think you should go to bed earlier? Would you agree that a lack of sleep seems to affect learning?

Dreams:
Symbols of the Unconscious

THE INTERPRETATION OF DREAM SYMBOLS

'The significance of dream work for spirituality
and personal integration is based on the conviction that every
dream is in the service of wholeness through the integration of
the inner and outer selves.'
(James L. Empereur, *The New Dictionary of Catholic Spirituality*)

We have just examined the scientific understanding of dreams, along with an explanation of what happens inside the brain while it dreams. Yet there are many who believe and insist that dreams are carriers of meaning and are more than just the brain's way of processing new information and organising memory. Many psychologists and others in the academic community believe that dreams reveal important information about a person's inner life, the life of the unconscious. The unconscious is that vast sea of hidden energies, possibilities, memories and abilities that remains hidden for most of our conscious lives. It is the reservoir of your potential in life.

Yet during sleep, the unconscious reveals important meanings for our lives, meanings that can inspire, heal and provide invaluable guidance. To say that dreams can be interpreted is to believe that they are meaningful and useful.

The problem with dream interpretation is that most people find dreams confusing, and it would appear that dreams use strange images, landscapes, characters and stories. Yet this is where we need to appreciate the relationship between dreams and symbols. For example, if you dream about someone you know, you may be inclined to think that the dream is about that person. That might be the case, but more than likely your dream has used that person because of what they symbolise.

the

inner

place

An Example

Let's look at a particular example. A person might be creative and artistic, but those qualities have remained hidden in the unconscious because the person was jeered when they were younger for showing that side of their personality. Later in life, they dream about someone they know who is artistic. The dream may involve that person chasing or following them. If the dream is taken at its face value, it may appear nonsensical, but treated symbolically it can reveal the hidden richness of the dreamer's personality. The artistic person is actually symbolic of the dreamer's own artistic side wanting to be recognised and integrated into conscious life.

Dreams:
Symbols of the Unconscious

There is one crucial difference between our conscious and unconscious selves. Our conscious self has a particular understanding of who we are, but this is often not the whole picture. There may be both positive and negative aspects to our personalities that we would rather not recognise for whatever reason. Often our ego, or conscious self, creates an image of who we are based on other people's expectations. For example, a student might want to be a musician, but her parents are adamant that she goes to medical college. So she studies really hard and gives up on her real interest. Another student wants to be a designer, but his friends think that's off the wall, and so he hides that part of his personality.

The unconscious, however, is more truthful with us and is less likely to allow any aspect of our personalities to remain hidden. Our conscious self might have a limited understanding of who we are, so the unconscious tries to compensate for this imbalance. As in the example above, a person might ignore their artistic side. The unconscious tries to deal with this imbalance in the form of a dream that symbolises the person's artistic side.

HOW TO INTERPRET YOUR DREAMS

The most important thing to remember when attempting to interpret dreams is that the unconscious presents its messages using the language of symbols. Symbols can have many meanings and also mean different things to different people. Therefore, a dream can have different interpretations and, when told, will mean different things to different people. Yet it is only the dreamers themselves who can actually interpret what the dream

means for them. All dreams attempt to offer the dreamer some new information about themselves and their lives. Sometimes dreams even offer guidance and bring the dreamer towards health and wholeness.

the
inner
place

How to set up your Dream Group

1 Sharing your dream with a group of friends can be a good way to interpret your dream. Once you've formed your group, you can tell your dream.

2 Allow the group to ask questions to clarify the details of the dream so it is clear in everyone's mind.

3 Now allow everyone to have time in silence to imagine that it is their own dream and what it would mean if they were in the dream.

4 Then each person should be invited to offer an interpretation of the dream as if it were their own. It is important that the person uses the formula: 'If this were my dream it would be about...' The person should not attempt to interpret the dream for the dreamer, as in, 'I think what this means for you is...' Remember, only the dreamer can interpret their own dream, but listening to other people's ideas can be a big help.

5 The dreamer notes what is being said and sees if any of the interpretations provokes a reaction in them. If they have the 'aha' moment and something really rings true for them, then this is a good way to validate a correct interpretation.

6 This formula protects the dreamer from the group's judgements and misinterpretations. The dreamer must be given the option of whether to reply to an interpretation, so as to allow them their privacy.

BREAKING OPEN A DREAM SYMBOL

The best way to learn how to interpret dreams is to look at a particular dream symbol and see how it can be interpreted. Read the following account of a dream recorded by a young woman.

It is evening time and I am driving along a road but I'm not really sure where I'm going as the road doesn't seem familiar. I don't remember stopping the car but suddenly I am standing beside it. I realise

the

inner

place

Dreams:

Symbols of the Unconscious

that I am also standing on a bridge, and I remember two feelings I had. The first one was when I looked down into the river underneath. It seemed quite turbulent and I realised that I shouldn't stay there for too much longer. Yet when I go to get in my car I don't know which way I should go. I'm completely confused and wake almost immediately.

This dream doesn't really mean much at the moment, but when we add in the details of the dreamer's life, it begins to make more sense. The young woman's place of work is about a three-hour journey from her home. She is happy and content in her job, but recently she got an offer of a job closer to home, with a significant pay rise. She is unsure what to do and the choice is becoming somewhat of a dilemma.

ASSIGNMENT

You should now break into small groups and see if you can offer possible interpretations of this dream. Can you figure out what the dream means?

The following is an account of how the dreamer herself interpreted the dream. As will become apparent, the symbol of the bridge could only have been fully interpreted by the dreamer herself.

I wrote this dream down because I had a hunch it might be something about where I am in life at the moment. I thought about the bridge and I reckoned it was a structure that connected two pieces of land or two different places. I was stuck on the bridge, and so I thought it might be a symbol of the two places or

the inner place

pieces of land I'm preoccupied with here or back home. When I looked into the water it was turbulent, and that was how I feel at the moment – everything is unclear. But in the dream I feel it's not good to be there – that I need to make a decision fast as to which way to go. But which way should I go? I need more help from my dream – there must be some hint as to what to do. I then start to think of the bridge itself. It wasn't in great shape and seemed unsound structurally. So maybe I shouldn't take the crossing then, but stay where I am – stay in my job. I'm still not convinced. So I start to think of "bridges" and what they mean to me personally. I'm racking my brains and then I think of the old bridge at my aunt's that I used to visit back at home. I never liked it because my brothers would play on it even though it just wasn't safe. I never liked that bridge – I never liked that aunt – and all of that was back at home. I think that's it. The bridge reminds me of home, but an aspect of home I never liked. That's it – I'm staying put. **,**

The dreamer in question didn't take the new job and subsequently devoted a new energy to her work. She was soon promoted and also began to date a colleague from the job. Somehow, her unconscious believed that staying was the best option and, in symbolic fashion, it conveyed that to her in her dream. Let's note some important aspects of how she interpreted her dream.

- The dreamer **wrote down her dream** and showed an interest in it because she felt that it might offer advice for her particular situation in life. This is important, because a dream can come alive when we apply it to where we are in life right now.
- She noted **the context of the dream** and its location – above turbulent waters – and the feeling that she should get out of there. So, at the most basic level, the dream is telling her to make up her mind soon, as this dilemma is doing her no good.
- But she believes the dream offers her more. Now she really has to work with the dream and **focus on the**

the

inner

place

symbol of the bridge. It 'seemed unsound structurally', so maybe it's not safe to cross, or needs to be crossed with care. Which is it?

- But then she has her 'aha' moment, when she begins to respond personally to the symbol of 'bridge'. She remembers a bridge from 'home' that she never liked, and so the bridge is focusing her attention on what she doesn't like about home. Advice from the dream now seems clear – don't take the job at home.

- It's very important to note that there were different ways of interpreting this dream. One was 'cross with care'. But it was the 'aha' moment that **verified her interpretation of the dream**, as in 'don't go home'. This moment of insight is very important when verifying an interpretation of a dream.

OTHER COMMON DREAM SYMBOLS

ASIDE

There are many ways of interpreting dreams, but one of the most popular is Carl Jung's theory of archetypes. This sounds complicated, but archetypes can be simply understood as energies that motivate and guide us. According to Carl Jung, the archetypes reveal themselves symbolically in dreams. The archetypes can be revealed as mythical figures, images, or people known or unknown to us.

Carl Jung believed that the archetypes belong to what he termed the collective unconscious. Just as we have inherited genetic material, we have also inherited psychological material deep in our unconscious. But this material is collective or common to all cultures and to humanity as a whole. Therefore, people from all over the world dream about the same archetypes. It doesn't matter whether they are from a primitive tribe in Papua New Guinea or city dwellers in New York.

the

inner

place

Here we will examine some common dream symbols. In each case, you will get the opportunity to try to figure out what they mean first, because this will help you as you try to figure out your own dream symbols.

Teeth Falling Out

>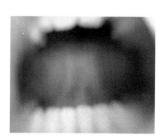
> I am at a night club and there's this guy there that I really fancy. I'm not sure now who he was, maybe I've never met him before. Anyway, I really want to go over to him but he's with some people who are sitting on these big pink chairs that seem to revolve around. My head is in a spin. I decide to go over to him, but then I stall and instead go into the toilet, but my maths teacher is there. I say hello to her and go to the mirror to fix myself. I notice that one of my teeth is loose. I pick at it and it comes out. Then one by one I pick all my teeth out. I'm really sad as I liked my teeth a lot. I go back into the club and the guy is with somebody else. My friends take no notice of my gummy smile.

The background to the dream is that the girl, though quite attractive, is very shy with guys. She is doing OK at school but is not too good at her maths, and her teacher is always telling her she has the ability but that she just needs to work at it, or, as she says, 'get your teeth into it'.

Question: So what do you think the dream is about?

What she needs to do in her maths is get her teeth into the subject. That's what her teacher keeps telling her anyway. But dreams about teeth falling out or becoming loose usually point to an inability to get your teeth into something or an inability to communicate. She is shy with guys and finds it hard to communicate with them. The dream, though, is very positive, because it is telling her to be confident and go for things. The pink chairs may refer to the fact that her friends say she doesn't dress with enough confidence and is too drab. She should be more colourful.

Dreams:
Symbols of the Unconscious

Note: Another common dream symbol is hair. The complete shaving of hair could refer to ancient rites of initiation and to the emergence of a new state in life. Alternatively, hair comes out of your head and so could refer to the thoughts that come out of your head. Thus, if you dreamed of turning up at a party in a mad new hairstyle, that dream might refer to a new way you have of thinking about things, but you're not sure how people will react to your innovative change.

Water Dreams

Water dreams come in many forms and are often archetypal, pointing to deep unconscious energies. They are most often associated with our emotional condition. Consider the following dream, where a person experiences drowning sensations. Remember how the teeth dream referred to 'getting your teeth' into something, so what kind of 'drowning' is going on in the  following dream and what advice might be offered? Remember, you can never truly interpret another person's dream, but it's good to practise. The dreamer is a young man who, at the time of the dream, is going through a separation with his girlfriend, while his parents are also splitting up.

 I am over at the sports ground and my friends want me to come over to them on the running track. Instead I go to a street vendor (who happens to be beside the pool) and I buy some candy floss from him! Then I go for a swim but I just can't stay afloat. I sink down and start to drown. When I come up I shout but nobody hears. This happens several times and each time I surface I scream for help. I see my friends but they won't help. I eventually get out and go over and sit on the race track. I'm in complete distress but nobody seems to notice. Quickly I calm down and everything is OK.

Question: What do you think the dream is about?

the inner place

This dream probably refers to the fact that the dreamer is actually drowning in his emotions in real life. He continually surfaces but, as in real life, gets no support from his male friends. The only place where he doesn't feel he is drowning is literally 'on the race track'. The dreamer was a promising athlete but he more or less abandoned it after meeting his girlfriend. Perhaps the dream is telling him to get back 'on the race track' to prevent him from drowning in his emotions. And the candy floss? Perhaps the dreamer had to learn that life wasn't so sweet after all.

Animal Dreams

Animal dreams are quite common and usually refer to our instincts. Our instincts are very important because they keep us safe and protect us. It is important to note that animals in dreams can often appear to protect us from something or someone.

The dream in question is about a dog, and the dreamer has recently begun to go out with a new guy from her school. Everything is going well for her except that she feels her friends are a little more distant than usual.

> I am on my way to school and unusually it's in the middle of the night. All the street lights are on, and as I walk I am aware of a dog following me. I don't mind at first because I like dogs in general. Yet as we get closer to the school, he catches up and begins to bark at me. I'm scared and run into the school, but now he's even closer. Eventually I reach my class and, thankfully, my friends are there. But just when I think he's gone, he's right beside me growling. Nobody else seems to notice. I wake up.

the

inner

place

Dreams:

Symbols of the Unconscious

Question: What do you think this dream is about?

This is a dream that could easily be misinterpreted by the dreamer. Often characters in dreams that appear threatening are really only there to help us. We need to look at the dog symbolically. What characterises dogs? Firstly, we use them to guard our homes, but they are also renowned for sniffing things out. In this dream, the dog is actually warning her about the school situation. The night-time itself is more threatening. When she gets to her friends, the dog is growling. Has the dog 'sniffed' something? The dreamer in question eventually realises that one of her 'close friends' is actually jealous of her relationship with her new boyfriend and has been spreading malicious rumours about her, and hence her friends' recent distance. The dream was telling her there was something to 'sniff' out amongst her friends.

Note: Cats also appear in dreams. What do they symbolise? One thing is that they are restful, peaceful creatures, usually because they have dealt with any rodents or pests gnawing at our property. A cat in a dream could point to worries that are 'gnawing' away at you. They need to be dealt with so you can snooze and happily laze about like your average cat.

Dreams of Falling

These are also very common and, though frightening, nobody who hits the bottom ever dies. Sometimes the dreamer can wake up just as they fall and it can be quite a disturbing feeling. Falling dreams can refer to different aspects of life. Perhaps they are telling us we need to watch our step, or that somehow we are vulnerable even though we don't realise it. The following dream is from a boy in school. At the time, he was preoccupied with a girl in school whom he was mad about. He seemed to be making promising progress.

> I'm in a theme park (one that comes to our town every summer) and suddenly I see S., but when I go up to her for some reason I can't talk. I feel like a real idiot and I smile and point instead of talking. I can't understand why I can't talk for that single most

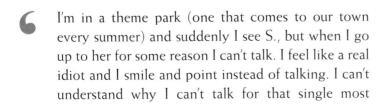

Dreams:
Symbols of the Unconscious

155

important time in my whole life when I want to. My mouth begins to fill with gas, and just as I am about to explode she grabs me by the hand and takes me on a rollercoaster. I remember looking at her and not believing I'm actually with her. I want to blurt out "I love you" but then we take a bend. She goes with the car but I go straight out over the rails. I'm falling down and it gets worse because I'm falling. I wake up in a bit of a panic but thrilled that I dreamt about her as I now have an excuse to talk to her in school. When I told her the dream, she just giggled and laughed! I was dying – she's so incredibly cute. This is it. She's the one. **,**

Question: What do you think this dream is about?

There are many ways of looking at this dream, but it would appear that he's on something of a 'rollercoaster' with this new girl. The dream appears to be warning him about this situation. He can't believe he's in her company on the rollercoaster, but he's not looking ahead. He falls off the rollercoaster, which may be symbolic of what might happen to him with this girl. He is 'falling' in love with her, but may be in line for a more serious and painful fall. He should note when he told her the story of the dream whether she was laughing 'with him' or 'at him'. Big difference.

Body Dreams

According to some, our dreams can tell us things about our physical bodies. The following is an account of a dream that came to a person very soon after they had a transplant operation.

the inner place

' In the dream I am on stage performing and there are five girls watching me from the floor. They have their arms folded and a very aggressive look on their faces. After my performance, they grab my arm in a

very aggressive way and drag me to a room. I know I have upset them but don't know why. I beg them to tell me what I've done and I'll make it up to them. In the room, Gerry Ryan is waiting to act as a mediator.

He asks me what I've done and is there any way I can make it up to them. They set me a task. In the next scene I am running up a hill with Gerry Ryan by my side. He's holding a fluffy microphone and asking me questions as we run. We get back to the room and the girls have calmed a little but are still quite adamant that I have done something wrong. But one of the dream figures is saying that I should be given a chance.

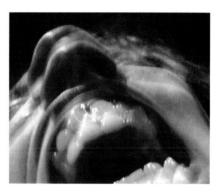

It was a traumatic dream for me and I woke up in a sweat. I was only able to interpret the dream after I gave it a title. I gave the dream the title 'Rejection'. Yet I had this dream four days after my kidney transplant. I was told that within the first five days there was a good chance that my own body would reject the kidney because it was foreign to my body.

When I looked at the dream in this way I realised that in the dream 'I' was the kidney and the other girls were my other organs in my body rejecting the kidney. But they were really advising me because the task that they gave me was to do exercise, and that was exactly what the doctors had said. So I exercised but I also wrote to my new kidney. I told it that I wanted it to stay. I reckoned though it must feel sad and lonely missing its other owner.

NIGHTMARES

I'm lying in my bed except it seems like I'm also in the kitchen of my grandmother's old house. I wake and know there's someone in the room. I know there's someone at the foot of the bed but it's dark and I'm not sure. Then some force starts to pull the

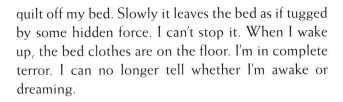

quilt off my bed. Slowly it leaves the bed as if tugged by some hidden force. I can't stop it. When I wake up, the bed clothes are on the floor. I'm in complete terror. I can no longer tell whether I'm awake or dreaming.

Nightmares are common to most dreamers at some stage and they vary in their intensity. Sometimes they can be once-off, or they can be recurring over weeks, months or even years. Yet even though they are disturbing in nature, nightmares are usually an attempt by the unconscious to relate something that needs immediate attention. The nightmare is disturbing so that it can't easily be ignored. While the nightmare might be unsettling, its message may be extremely beneficial to the dreamer. Take the following example of a recurring nightmare.

I'm back in my old primary school and it's always playtime in the yard. Each time I want to stay with my friends but I end up being separated from them and end up in the toilets. They're really dirty and there's used make-up tubes and lipsticks everywhere. It's really disgusting and I can't get out. The bell goes for class but I know I'm going to be late because I can't get out. I look for a way out and it seems like there's a way out through the mirror onto the yard. But it's cracked and broken and I know I'll get cut. I'm petrified that I'll get into trouble if I'm late. I wake up in an awful state and am really upset.

(Female, 18)

the

inner

place

The dreamer in question eventually got to the root of the nightmare with the help of a friend. It could mean various things, but in this case the unconscious wanted to bring healing into the girl's life. She started at the end, where the dream suggested that the 'way out' would be through the mirror but she might get cut or hurt. She admitted that her self-image was really poor and she wore lots of make-up, even though her friends said she was naturally very good-looking. She admitted that for most of her

Dreams:

Symbols of the Unconscious

life she was convinced she was ugly. This was a painful admission. but there was more to the dream. She realised that she was always playing with girls from her fifth class in the nightmare. Though painful, she admitted to her friend that once in fifth class her classmates had gathered round her in a circle and taunted her by repeatedly telling her that she was ugly. A cruel game born out of childish jealousy had imprinted a lasting legacy. The girl might never have confronted that awful memory, but her nightmare presented it to her only so that she could be healed.

Many dreams can be disturbing in their nature, like falling off a cliff, drowning or being attacked by an animal. Yet it would appear that the unconscious knows that often disturbing dreams really get noticed by the dreamer. All dreams strive for healing and wholeness, even the nightmarish ones.

NIGHT TERRORS AND SLEEP PARALYSIS

> You will not feel the terror of the night,
> Nor the arrow that flies by day,
> Or the pestilence that stalks in darkness,
> Or the destruction that wastes at noonday.

(Psalm 91)

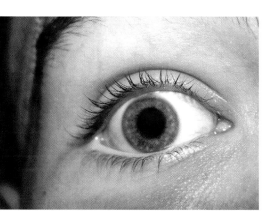

As noted earlier in this chapter, the body has to paralyse itself temporarily in order that it doesn't act out its own dreams. Yet what happens if the person wakes up and the body is still paralysed? Not nice. Those who experience sleep paralysis are frequently very tired, and it often happens to shift-workers. When the person wakes, they are often besieged by feelings that something evil is close by, and

the

inner

place

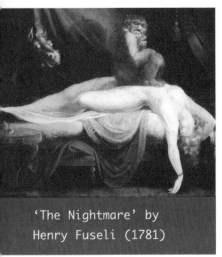

'The Nightmare' by
Henry Fuseli (1781)

because they are in that in-between place of sleep and dreams, they may even have hallucinogenic experiences. Sleep paralysis is extremely frightening and, if misunderstood, it can lead to many and varied interpretations.

The experience of waking up and being unable to move, coupled with the feeling of an unknown presence, often manifests itself in popular culture as the alien abduction phenomenon. Many people, especially in the US, report to have been visited by extraterrestrial agents during the night, or, more simply, little green men. However, these reported experiences are often accompanied by telling elements of sleep paralysis, such as the inability to move, the feeling of dread and a crushing weight on the chest. Sleep paralysis is a very disturbing sensation, but it shouldn't be confused with other phenomena. So the next time you think you have been visited by entities from Pluto during the night, it's best not to tell too many people. Chances are, you weren't.

Sometimes supernatural explanations are given for sleep nightmarish phenomena. Another disturbing experience is that of night terrors. It is important to note that neither sleep paralysis nor night terrors occur during REM time, so they are distinct from nightmares. Night terrors occur at a very deep stage of sleep, when the person suddenly wakes with a persistent feeling of fear and terror. This is often accompanied by a feeling of a dark presence in the room. Because of the nature of this experience, often supernatural explanations are given, such as ghostly phenomena. People often feel that they see a dark figure in the room or at the foot of the bed.

the

inner

place

DISCUSS

Do you think night terrors or sleep paralysis are best explained with supernatural explanations or as sleep phenomena? Give reasons for your answer.

Dreams:
Symbols of the Unconscious

NIGHT PRAYER

It has long been a Catholic tradition to pray throughout the day. Many Catholics follow the *Divine Office*, which prescribes prayers for morning, evening and night-time. Night prayer takes the form of a psalm, scripture readings and a concluding prayer. Here are some extracts from the prayers of the Church. You can read them or take them down to have for yourself.

PSALMS

'What can bring us happiness?' many say.
Let the light of your face shine on us, O Lord.

You have put into my heart a greater joy
Than they have from an abundance of corn and new wine.

I will lie down in peace and sleep comes at once
For you alone, Lord, make me dwell in safety.
(From Psalm 4)

Turn your ear, O Lord, and give answer
For I am poor and needy.
Preserve my life, for I am faithful:
Save the servant who trusts in you.

You are my God, have mercy on me, Lord,
For I cry to you all the day long.
Give joy to your servant, O Lord,
For to you I lift up my soul.
(From Psalm 85)

My soul is waiting for the Lord,
I count on his word.
My soul is longing for the Lord
More than watchman for daybreak.
Let the watchman count on daybreak
And Israel on the Lord.
(From Psalm 129)

the
inner
place

I will bless the Lord who gives me counsel,
Who even at night directs my heart.
I keep the Lord ever in my sight:
Since he is at my right hand I shall stand firm.
And so my heart rejoices, my soul is glad;
Even my body shall rest in safety.
For you will not leave my soul among the dead,
Nor let your beloved know decay.

You will show me the path of life,
The fullness of joy in your presence,
At your right hand happiness forever.
(From Psalm 15)

SCRIPTURE READINGS

They will see the Lord face to face, and his name will be written on their foreheads. It will never be night again and they will need no lamplight or sunlight, because the Lord God will be shining on them. They will reign for ever and ever.

(Revelations 22:4-5)

Hear, O Israel: the Lord our God is one Lord; and you shall love the Lord your God with all your heart, and with all our soul, and with all your might. And these words which I command you this day shall be upon your heart; and you shall teach them diligently to your children, and shall talk of them when you sit in your house, and when you walk by the way, and when you lie down, and when you rise.

(Deuteronomy 6:4-7)

Dreams:
Symbols of the Unconscious

May the God who gives us peace make you completely his, and keep your whole being, spirit, soul and body free from all fault, at the coming of our Lord Jesus Christ.

(1 Thessalonians 5:23)

CONCLUDING PRAYERS

Visit this house, we pray you, Lord:
Drive far away from it the snares of the enemy.
May your holy angels stay here and guard us in peace,
And let your blessing be always upon us.
Through Christ our Lord.

Lord, give our bodies restful sleep;
And let the work we have done today
Be sown for an eternal harvest.
Through Christ our Lord.

In your mercy, Lord,
Dispel the darkness of this night.
Let your household so sleep in peace,
That at the dawn of a new day,
They may, with joy, waken in your name.
Through Christ our Lord.

Lord our God,
Restore us again by the repose of sleep
After the fatigue of our daily work:
So that, continually renewed by your help,
We may serve you in body and soul.
Through Christ our Lord.

the
inner
place

SECTION B

CHRISTIANITY

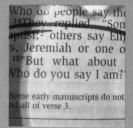

Who do people say the
"They replied, "Som
ptist, others say Eli
s, Jeremiah or one o
s"But what about
Who do you say I am?"

Some early manuscripts do not
nd all of verse 3.

Chapter Eight

RETURN TO ORIGINS

RETURN TO ORIGINS

Many of us belong to groups or organisations that inspire us or give meaning to our lives. Yet sometimes a system loses its way or becomes uninspiring. Sports clubs and teams lose their spirit. The football team that is preparing itself for the All-Ireland will have all sorts of inspiring messages hollered at it; 'C'mon boys! Remember the men of '56. Remember the fighting spirit. Those were real men who ran till their legs were nothing but bloodied stumps! C'mon boys!' All that kind of stuff. Sometimes it would appear that inspiration lies in the past, not in the future.

In popular culture, the iconic figures usually belong to the past and, instead of being branded old-fashioned, they are constantly the coolest thing around. For example, the actor James Dean was killed as far back as 1955, when his Porsche 550 Spyder careered off the road. Dean belongs to the same generation as your grandparents, yet remains the coolest of fashion icons.

James Dean

The key to understanding the return to origins is the sense that there has been something that has been lost sight of. A couple may remember how brilliant it was the first few times they met, but now it's stale and the other person seems boring. Something has been lost. When things become lifeless and uninspiring, people return to the first moments to see if something can be recaptured.

DISCUSS

Can you think of other figures from the past that continue to inspire trends, fashions or people today?

RETRO-STYLING: CONTEMPORARY RETURN TO ORIGINS

Retro-styling is a common term applied to cars, accessories and fashion, and refers to modern styles that have their inspiration and origins in past designs. Today, many girls wear retro-designed clothes and accessories, and it was actually teenage girls that sparked retro-styling into many areas of life, including furniture and kitchen accessories. The return to retro was signalled by Sixties-style fashion – the bell-bottom jeans, dragged and frayed, scruffy cuffs and dropped waist. That's retro. In fact, much of modern fashion for women can be traced back to James Dean, who was the first truly 'modern' fashion figure. With the arrival of Dean, Terylene trousers were out, and denim, leather and white vests were in. Dean was the first one to embody a typically fashionable stance; hunched shoulders, slightly bent knees and a brooding demeanour. Along with squinty eyes, he frowned far more than he smiled. Typical male cat-walk stuff.

Recent cars that are heavily retro-styled are the VW Beetle and Mini. Both these cars disappeared for decades, only to be restyled for modern times. Sometimes retro-styling is used to link a product to an older narrative or story. When some people buy a car, they just buy a car, but others prefer to buy into a myth or a heroic image. The Ford Mustang was made famous by the film *Bullitt*, starring Steve McQueen. The film featured one of the greatest car-chase scenes ever and, needless to say, the star of the chase was the Ford Mustang, or 'Stang'.

the

inner

place

In 2005, Ford, due to depressed sales worldwide, decided to relaunch the Ford Mustang. This was a sensitive task, as the car was more than just a car – it was part of a dream, a fantasy. Yet the 2005 Mustang worked due to its incorporation of the previous Sixties design and styling, i.e. retro-styling. In other words, the new car looked like a Ford

Ford Mustang 2005

Mustang. The new car incorporates the long menacing bonnet with the short-clipped boot, deep C-cuts on either side, three-element tail lights and the chrome running horse in the grille. If you buy a Ford Mustang, you get from A to B, but you also get to dream along the way.

DISCUSS

1 Can you think of other examples of retro-styling? Are they still fashionable?

2 Why do you think designers are inspired by the past?

CONTEMPORARY IMAGES OF JESUS AND THE NEED TO RETURN TO ORIGINS

As we've seen, there is a trend in contemporary culture to return to the origins of a style or to its inspiration. Today, contemporary culture has thrown up images of Jesus which, though passing off as authentic images that return to the origins, are actually distortions of the original prophet from Nazareth and, more importantly, of his message. We will now examine some contemporary images of Jesus from popular culture, i.e. literature, film and music, for the following reasons:

inner

place

- To assess whether they are accurate representations of Jesus of Nazareth.

- To reflect on whether these images have created a distorted image of Jesus.

- To determine if we need to return to the original Jesus and the gospels to see what he was really like.

1 LITERATURE

The Da Vinci Code

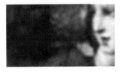

The novel *The Da Vinci Code*, written by Dan Brown, took the world by storm when it was published, and in the process sold millions of copies. It is a story about Jesus but, seemingly, with explosive revelations, all based on the myth of the Holy Grail. The Holy Grail, according to legend, is the cup that Jesus used at the Last Supper. According to the legends, it contains the secret of happiness. It is a fact that Jesus used a cup at the Last Supper, but as to whether it still exists is a matter for debate.

In the book, Robert Langdon is a Harvard Professor who stumbles upon some codes that lead him to the works of Leonardo da Vinci. He is accompanied by a French cryptologist, Sophie Neveu.

According to the book, Leonardo was a member of an ancient secret society called the Prior of Sion, whose role it was to protect the secret of the Holy Grail. Leonardo placed clues in his pictures as to the true identity of the Grail.

In this following extract, both Sophie and Langdon are shown da Vinci's *The Last Supper* by Leigh Teabing at the Chateau Villette.

> Langdon smiled. 'As it turns out, the Holy Grail does indeed make an appearance in The Last Supper. Leonardo included her prominently.'
>
> 'Hold on,' Sophie said. 'You told me the Holy Grail was a woman. The Last Supper is a painting of thirteen men.'
>
> 'Is it?' Teabing arched his eyebrows. 'Take a closer look.'
>
> Uncertain, Sophie made her way closer to the painting, scanning the thirteen figures – Jesus Christ in the middle, six disciples on His left, and six on His right.

the
inner
place

'They're all men,' she confirmed.

'Oh?' Teabing said. 'How about the one seated in the place of honour, at the right hand of the Lord?'

Sophie examined the figure to Jesus' immediate right, focusing in. As she studied the person's face and body, a wave of astonishment rose within her. The individual had flowing red hair, delicate folded hands and the hint of a bosom. It was, without doubt...female.

'That's a woman!' Sophie exclaimed.

Teabing was laughing. 'Surprise, surprise. Believe me, it's no mistake. Leonardo was skilled at painting the differences between the sexes.'

Sophie could not take her eyes from the woman beside Christ. 'The Last Supper is supposed to be thirteen men. Who is this woman?' Although Sophie had seen the classic image many times, she had not once noticed the glaring discrepancy.

'Everyone misses it,' Teabing said. 'Our preconceived notions of this scene are so powerful that the mind blocks out the incongruity and overrides our eyes.'

'It's known as scotoma,' Langdon added. 'The brain does it sometimes with powerful symbols.'

'Another reason you might have missed the woman,' Teabing said, 'is that many of the photographs in art books were taken before 1954, when the details were still hidden beneath layers of grime and several restorative repaintings done by clumsy hands in the eighteenth century. Now, at last, the fresco has been cleaned down to da Vinci's original layer of paint.' He motioned to the photograph. 'Et voila!'

Sophie moved closer to the image. This woman to Jesus' right was young and pious looking, with a demure face, beautiful red hair, and hands folded quietly. *This is the woman who single-handedly could crumble the Church?*

'Who is she?' Sophie asked.

the
inner
place

'That, my dear,' Teabing replied, 'is Mary Magdalene.'

Sophie turned. 'The prostitute?'

Teabing drew a short breath, as if the word had injured him personally.

'Magdalene was no such thing. That unfortunate misconception is the legacy of a smear campaign launched by the early Church. The Church needed to defame Mary Magdalene in order to cover up her dangerous secret – her role as the Holy Grail.'

'Her role?'

'As I mentioned,' Teabing clarified, 'the early Church needed to convince the world that the mortal prophet Jesus was a divine being. Therefore, any gospels that described earthly aspects of Jesus' life had to be omitted from the Bible. Unfortunately for the early editors, one particularly troubling theme kept recurring in the gospels. Mary Magdalene.' He paused. 'More specifically, her marriage to Jesus Christ.'

The book claims further incredible revelations, when Teabing later explains:

'The legend of the Holy Grail is a legend about royal blood. When the Grail legend speaks of "the chalice that held the blood of Christ"…it speaks, in fact, of Mary Magdalene – the female womb that carried Jesus' royal bloodline.'

A Response

So, was Jesus really married to Mary Magdalene? Did they really conceive a child? We'll consider a few points here.

- Jesus did have a special relationship with Mary Magdalene and, as Brown suggests, she wasn't a prostitute. According to the gospels, she stood at the foot of the cross and anointed Jesus' body after he died. Yet there is no evidence to suggest that they were married.

- Today we are shocked by the suggestion that Jesus may have been married. But at the time, it would not have been scandalous for Jesus to have had a wife. If Jesus was married, the gospels would simply have reported it as fact. We know Jesus wasn't married because there is no mention of it in the gospels.

- We know that Mary Magdalene wasn't married either because of the fact that she is called after the place where she is from, Magdala. If she was married, her name would have made reference to her husband or son.

- The idea that Jesus had a child called Sarah with Mary Magdalene has no foundation in any ancient source. It is simply a fictional detail made up by a contemporary author. It did manage to get everybody's attention, but it's only fiction.

'St Mary Magdalene' by El Greco (1576-78)

If the claims made in Brown's novel have no basis in truth, yet are accepted by many as 'gospel', there is a clear need to return to the origins of what we know about Jesus – the actual gospels themselves.

DISCUSS

1 Why do you think Dan Brown's novel was so popular?
2 Why do you think the figure of Jesus continues to fascinate a modern audience?
3 Based on the evidence, do you think any of Brown's claims are valid? Give reasons for your answer.

the

inner

place

2 MUSIC

'Losing My Religion' by REM

In relation to Jesus, the return to origins is based on the need to discover who Jesus really was and what he was like. We feel that we should return because the images that are presented to us seem at odds with our sense of who he was and what he stood for.

In the video for the song 'Losing My Religion', a particular image is presented of Jesus.

Two questions are worth keeping in mind as we examine and analyse the video: first, why is this particular image of Jesus presented, and second, is this Jesus of the gospels?

In the opening scene of the video, Jesus is presented as an old man resting against an angel, while both are resting on the limb of a tree. The old grey-haired Jesus is dressed in orange clothes and has a pair of wings. 'Jesus' then falls out of the tree and tumbles onto the ground. 'Jesus' now appears like a fallen angel, and Michael Stipe sings along with the vocals 'like a hurt, lost and blinded fool'.

A plump figure dressed in robes then points at 'Jesus', just as Pilate pointed to him during his trial. 'Jesus' has a wound in his side, and a man next to him begins to probe the wound by sticking his hand into Jesus' side. 'Jesus' is presented as weak and humiliated by such a violation of his tortured body.

'Jesus' is in obvious discomfort but he endures the spectacle. According to Tom Beaudoin in his book *Virtual Faith*: 'The Jesus of "Losing My Religion" looks exhausted, worn out and sorry… This Jesus is just a haggard old man, acting as if he is not quite sure why he is on earth in the first place.' In the closing scenes, Jesus is lashed against crossed beams, and a crowd throws stones at him. Finally, a group work ropes around his body, but we are unsure whether they are trying to release him or making sure he doesn't get off his cross.

DISCUSS

'The Jesus of "Losing My Religion" looks exhausted, worn out and sorry… This Jesus is just a haggard old man.' Why do you think REM depicted Jesus in this way? Are they trying to mock the figure of Jesus, or are they presenting an image of Jesus that they think people will actually identify with? Do you think Jesus was actually like this? If so, why?

the
inner
place

3 MUSIC

'Heart-Shaped Box' by Nirvana

In 'Heart-Shaped Box' by Nirvana, Jesus is presented yet again as an old man. In the opening scene, a bearded old man lies in his hospital bed, but the atmosphere is such that it could be his deathbed. Three band members sit at the bedside, bored out of their minds. In the next shot, the 'Jesus' figure is in a field of poppies, wearing nothing but a loin-cloth and a Santa Claus hat. He is thin and bony, a figure so pathetic that he is deserving of our sympathy.

The backdrop is reminiscent of *The Wizard of Oz*, suggesting that Jesus is no more than a fairytale figure, a Santa Claus character made up for children. He hangs from his cross like the scarecrow in *The Wizard of Oz*, ineffective and almost comical. Crows alight the cross and pick at the figure hanging upon it. No one seems to care. Tom Beaudoin remarks: 'It is as if he is so domesticated that he no longer instils any emotion, including fear.'

Kurt Cobain seemed to have been preoccupied with images of Jesus during his short life. He had a tapestry of *The Last Supper* sewed onto the back of his ripped-up jean jacket, and he even seems to have adopted his own Jesus look. His biographer notes:

> His blonde hair had grown to a length three inches below his shoulder. With his five-day beard growth, he bears a striking resemblance to some portrayals of Jesus Christ. Even Kurt's expression in one of the photos – a pained and faraway look, as if he is marking his moment in time – is similar to the image of Christ in Leonardo da Vinci's *The Last Supper*.

Kurt Cobain

DISCUSS

1 'He is thin and bony, a figure so pathetic that he is deserving of our sympathy.' Do you think this is an accurate image of what Jesus was really like? Why do you think Nirvana depicted Jesus like this?
2 Why do you think Kurt Cobain adopted what seemed to be his own image of Jesus?

the

inner

place

ASSIGNMENT
Can you think of other examples of songs or videos that depict Jesus in a particular way? Show them in class and analyse them using the following points:

What kind of an image of Jesus is depicted in the song or video?

Is it an accurate image of Jesus?

Why is Jesus depicted in this particular way?

4 FILM

The Passion of the Christ

The film *The Passion of the Christ* was controversial for many reasons, principally because it was so graphically violent and was thought to be laying the blame for Christ's death on the Jews. Here we need to examine the violence of the film because we need to question whether it was really this bad or was this just gratuitous violence from Hollywood. Ultimately, it is necessary to return to the original texts of the gospels to establish the truth of Jesus' death.

One of the most controversial scenes in the film was the flagellation or scourging. This was a common form of punishment in the ancient world for criminals. Yet this punishment was so extreme that it was also a form of execution. This is clear from the scene where Pilate says: 'See to it that the punishment is severe, Abenader, but do not let them kill the man.'

the
inner
place

In the film, the guards first bruise Jesus with rods, then break open his skin with a whip. The scourging itself consists of a sequence of shots depicting the guards hitting Jesus with a whip that has pieces of metal tied to the top of it. The incessant whipping removes the flesh from his back, revealing arteries, ribs and bloodied tissue. His entire body is covered with bruises and cuts, and it would appear that most of the flesh has been removed from his back.

DISCUSS

Why do you think this film was a remarkable success when first released? Do you think people wanted to see Jesus tortured or do you think it might have strengthened people's faith in him? Do you think the film is faithful to what really happened to Jesus?

JESUS: SEPARATING FACT FROM FICTION

One of the struggles we all face is that of being misrepresented. It's like the story of the new girl who comes to school and who is just that bit prettier than everybody else. She goes out on a Saturday night, has a dance with some lad, and by Monday morning she, reportedly, has 'shifted' four different lads. One girl huddles six others around in a tight circle and, swearing them to secrecy, tells all. There's only one verdict: the new girl is the biggest 'slapper' ever to grace the corridors of the school. As for the girl who started it, character assassination is all in a day's work. But maybe if the new girl is lucky, one of the six will have the courage to question the validity of the story and maybe go up to the girl and find out for herself. She will go to the primary source and try to separate fact from fiction. The other five will happily go around judging the new girl on rumour, innuendo and misrepresentations. It's easier to judge people like this instead of going to the bother of finding out what people are really like.

DISCUSS

Do you agree that we are all misrepresented at some stage? Why do people do that to us and who in our group is most likely to have their character taken away?

the

inner

place

OTHER CONTEMPORARY IMAGES

If you look at any of the gossip magazines, you will see that those who are most likely to be misrepresented in life are the rich and famous. Jesus wasn't rich but he certainly is famous, and with that privilege comes truckloads of rumour, innuendo and misrepresentation. As noted recently, Dan Brown huddled a couple of million together in a corner and told them that Jesus really had a thing going with Mary Magdalene and that they had a baby. Not true, but it obviously makes for a good story. The REM and Nirvana videos also offered an interpretation of Jesus that seems far removed from the Jesus of the gospels.

Examine some of the following images of Jesus that seem to have emerged in recent times. How accurate do you think they are?

1   The 'Hippie' Jesus

In terms of fashion, there is actually the 'Jesus look'. It's a broody, long-haired, scraggy look, with droopy shoulders and lazy gait.

It's very much like the hippies of the flower-power generation. They were into peace and love and were pretty much harmless, fun-loving people. We don't know whether Jesus did have long hair or not, but he did preach a message of love and forgiveness, and he encouraged peace where there was conflict. He was also a bit of a wanderer.

But making Jesus out to be something like a harmless 'peace man' hippie is an extremely selective view of the real man. It's a bit like introducing Roy Keane to somebody at one of his charitable events; they might assume that he is simply a lovely, caring and genuine picture – togged out, he is quite different. Similarly, liking Jesus to a hippie is to ignore what he was really like.

2   Jesus the 'Boy-Band Member'

Another image of Jesus could very well place him in a politically correct, clean-cut boy-band. This Jesus, like the boy-band member, is extremely nice, attractive and clean-living. This Jesus is seen as someone who is compassionate and sensitive and very much in touch with his emotions. Like the boy-band member, Jesus would hug lots of people and cry from time to time, again

the inner place

while hugging people. This Jesus would do an awful lot of charity work and make some attempt to save the planet from bad things.

This Jesus is really nice and has loads of fans. People love him and even scream at him. He has lovely long shiny hair. Yes, Jesus was compassionate and he certainly preached a message that encouraged us all to help others. But while boy-band members are really amiable guys, they don't exactly inspire us and they are notoriously forgettable. Had Jesus been a boy-bandish type person, he would have been quickly forgotten. People did scream at Jesus, but it was to have him crucified.

DISCUSS In your opinion, where did the above images of Jesus originate from? How accurate do you think they are?

3   'Simon of Seriousness'

Tommy Tiernan

The comedian Tommy Tiernan refers to an image of Jesus as 'Simon of Seriousness'. This Jesus is a pious bore or a 'holy Joe'. 'Simon of Seriousness' would be a bore. Yet the evidence from the gospels suggests, very strongly, that Jesus wasn't boring, but far from it. For a start, boring people don't get executed under the suspicion of causing a revolution or popular uprising. When was the last time you met a bore who got in trouble because people thought they were a rebel? It doesn't happen. Jesus was also a gifted storyteller, and hundreds followed and listened to his stories. Nobody would listen to 'Serious Simon'. He would talk about gigabytes, or about himself.

the inner place

While Jesus doesn't come across as mad funny to the modern reader, he definitely appreciated the effect of humour on his audience. He spoke about the blind leading the blind and planks in people's eyes. If such images are taken seriously or literally, they come across as completely stupid. When Jesus used such images, or told his parables, it's probably best to imagine at times the faintest grin flashing across his face as, slightly amused, he watched the confused heads of his audience get even more confused.

DISCUSS

1. What are the characteristics of a boring person?
2. Do you think it's accurate to label Jesus as a bore? Give reasons for your answer.

THE NEED TO RETURN TO PRIMARY SOURCES

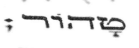
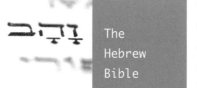

The Hebrew Bible

We have examined many images of Jesus from contemporary culture, but they are images that seem to distort the real Jesus of the gospels. We noted how everybody gets misrepresented from time to time and that some are only too happy to go with the distorted picture rather than with the real one.

Later in this book, we will return to the primary sources to try to discover what Jesus was really like. Even though Jesus lived a long time ago, we are lucky to have many documents dating back to that time, to which we can refer. The four gospels remain the best source of information about Jesus of Nazareth, and in the next few chapters we will be examining the evidence from the gospels to build up a more accurate picture of what he was really like.

the inner place

RETURN TO THE ORIGINS IN CHRISTIANITY

Just as contemporary culture has lost its way when it comes to representing Jesus through film, literature and music, Christianity too has felt the need to return to the gospels to rediscover the authentic message of Jesus. This has happened periodically throughout the ages. Here we will examine three examples.

1 St Francis of Assisi

Religious traditions are no exception to the need to return to origins. Within Christianity, prophetic figures have erupted who were convinced that the Church needed to return to the Gospel message. One such figure was Francis of Assisi (1181–1226). St Francis, the founder of the Franciscan order, was the son of a wealthy cloth merchant, and during his younger days he enjoyed this privileged status.

Assisi

After being held prisoner for a year during a local war, Francis returned home to question his old values. He began to look outside himself to the plight of others less privileged and he spent much of his time working with lepers. Once while praying in front of a cross, he felt challenged to go and rebuild some dilapidated churches. After he sold some of the family's fine cloth to raise money for his project, he was renounced by his father. He decided to dedicate himself to a hermit's life and to care for social outcasts.

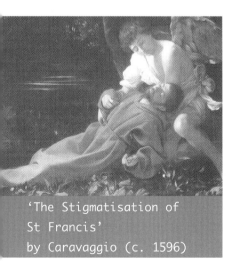
'The Stigmatisation of St Francis' by Caravaggio (c. 1596)

In 1208, Francis' life took yet another turn when he heard Jesus' mission to his apostles to leave all and go follow him (Matthew 10:7–19). He gathered together some followers and founded a new movement based on the Gospel message. They spread throughout Italy, living lives of prayer and work and calling others to conversion based on their own example. Soon their message spread beyond Italy, for Francis was convinced that the

the inner place

friars were called to bring their lived witness of the Gospel to the whole world.

2   The Second Vatican Council

In 1962, Pope John XXIII opened the Second Vatican Council. It is the most modern example of a return to the origins of Christianity. The Pope was aware of the need for the Church to address the modern world, and so he began the process of renewal based on the teachings of Jesus Christ. Three thousand bishops from around the world met in St Peter's Basilica in Rome. They met to listen to the promptings of the Spirit in order to hear anew the voice of Christ. In total, the Council produced sixteen documents, which in turn led to a new focus in the teachings of the Church. Among these are:

St Peter's Basilica, Vatican City

- The Church was to be understood as the whole People of God, and not just the hierarchy, clergy and religious.

- The need for believers to become involved in issues of social justice. Belonging to the Church is not limited to the word and sacraments. The Church's mission includes acting against injustice.

- A renewal of the celebration of the sacraments to allow for greater participation.

- The need for dialogue with other Christians and followers of other religions.

- God uses other Christian churches and non-Christian religions in offering salvation to humanity.

the inner place

3   Liberation Theology

In 1968, the Catholic bishops of Latin America gathered in Medellin, Columbia. They admitted that for too long the Church had sided with oppressive governments in Latin America, to the

detriment of the poor. They decided to opt for the poor instead of the wealthy and powerful. This was the beginning of liberation theology. The bishops returned to the original gospels and teachings of Jesus in order to establish that Jesus was essentially someone who wanted to liberate the poor from their oppression.

Gustavo Gutierrez was one of the first liberation theologians to write about Jesus as a liberator. He believed that theology shouldn't be just an academic pursuit but, instead, it should be rooted in human experience, especially in issues of social justice. He understood Jesus as primarily a liberator of the poor and oppressed. Jesus ate with sinners and tax collectors and didn't shun them. Jesus didn't give them money because, for the most part, it wasn't money they needed. They were poor in terms of their standing in society. What they lacked was esteem and respect. According to Gutierrez, Jesus established a new world whereby all who are poor could be liberated by our option for the poor and the excluded.

DISCUSS

1 Why do you think Christianity has had to return to its origins?
2 In what ways was St Francis like Jesus?
3 Give an example of the new focus of the Catholic Church after Vatican II.
4 According to liberation theology, what was the nature of the relationship between Jesus and the poor?

the inner place

Chapter Nine

THE HISTORICAL JESUS

What would a brief biography of Jesus' life look like?

Jesus of Nazareth was born around 6 or 7 BCE, a few years before the death of King Herod, who died in 4 BCE. He was brought up by a family of Jewish peasants in Lower Galilee. We know little of the intervening years, but around 27 or 28 CE he was attracted to the movement of John the Baptist. Jesus was baptised by John somewhere in the Jordan valley, but soon after he embarked on his own ministry, when he was around thirty-three or thirty-four years old. This ministry lasted for just over two years and was based mostly in his home area of Galilee and in Jerusalem during the great feasts.

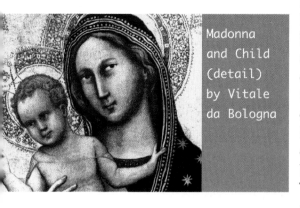

Madonna and Child (detail) by Vitale da Bologna

In 30 CE, while Jesus was in Jerusalem, he sensed that the simmering tension between himself and the religious authorities was reaching a climax. He celebrated a farewell meal with his inner group of disciples on Thursday evening, 6 April, by modern reckoning. He was then arrested in Gethsemane on the same night and was brought before some of the Jewish authorities. They handed him over to the Roman authorities, to Pontius Pilate, on the morning of Friday, 7 April. Pilate condemned Jesus to crucifixion. He was first scourged and mocked by Roman soldiers and was then crucified outside Jerusalem on the same day. He was dead by the evening of Friday, 7 April. He was about thirty-six years old.

(Adapted from *A Marginal Jew: Rethinking the Historical Jesus* by John Meier.)

We know about Jesus from several different sources. One of the most obvious sources is the gospels themselves. They provide the most detailed information about Jesus because they were written by people who collected the information about Jesus' life and death.

After Jesus died, those who followed him began to formulate the stories and passed them on by word of mouth. This is known as the oral tradition. As yet, very little had actually been written down about Jesus. The early followers believed that the end of the world was close and so they felt there was no need to record the details of Jesus' life.

'St Paul' by Bernardo Daddi (1333)

Eventually the different Christian communities began to write down some aspects of his life. There were many different stories going around about Jesus so there was a need for consistency. The written word was one way of combating memory loss. St Paul was the first to write about Jesus and he wrote his first letter to the church in Thessalonica in 49 CE.

Around forty years after Jesus died, something was beginning to happen that would threaten the legacy of Jesus of Nazareth. Those first-hand witnesses who had met Jesus and witnessed the events of his life began to die, and with them the vital stories of his life. Very quickly it was necessary to write down in a systematic manner the details of Jesus' life. These written testimonies are called the gospels. The first gospel was written around 70 CE by Mark, to be followed by Matthew, Luke and John. Matthew, Mark and Luke are known as the synoptic gospels because they share some of the sources that were used when collecting the stories about Jesus' life.

the

inner

place

There are many reasons why we can treat the gospels as credible documents. First, they were written very close to the events of the life of Jesus of Nazareth, as most were written in the first century. A fragment of John's gospel has been dated to 125 CE.

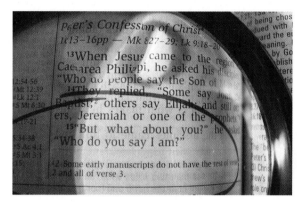

Secondly, the different gospels contain eyewitness reports that corroborate one another, even though they were written at different times for different communities. The gospels also faithfully recount all the aspects of Jesus' life and ministry. They don't edit out the embarrassing details. That Jesus died as a common criminal is a scandal. The parables often threw up awkward and difficult messages about discipleship, but all were included. It is important to establish the gospels as accurate portrayals of Jesus' life because even today, as we saw with *The Da Vinci Code*, many still try to discredit the origins of the Christian heritage.

the

inner

place

What is interesting is that there are other sources of evidence about Jesus that are far more independent. The gospels were written by people who believed in Jesus and wanted to spread his message. But there were various references to Jesus from independent historians whose writings are an authoritative source of evidence that Jesus was indeed a historical character.

Pliny the Younger (61–113 CE) was a governor of one of the Roman provinces and he wrote to the emperor, Trajan, asking for advice on what to do with the Christians in his province. The Romans were concerned with any group or sect that they felt may have been a threat to their rule. The Roman historian Tacitus (56–117 CE) was very hostile towards 'Christus' and the Christians. He wrote: 'Christus, the founder of the name, had undergone the death penalty in the reign of Tiberius, by sentence of…Pontius Pilate.' Finally, Flavius Josephus, a Jewish historian, described disturbances in Palestine during the reign of Pontius Pilate. He attributed these disturbances to Jesus and his followers, even though he said of Jesus that he was '…a wise man, doer of wonderful works, a teacher of men who receive the truth with pleasure'.

DISCUSS

1 Why did it eventually become necessary to write down the details of Jesus' life?

2 How do we know that Jesus was really a historical character?

Jesus was constantly getting into trouble in Palestine. Was it a very troubled region?

Palestine was a very troubled region for several different reasons, but chief among them was the Roman occupation. For hundreds of years before Jesus, Palestine was constantly invaded by different forces: the Babylonians, Persians, Syrians, Greeks and finally the Romans. So when Jesus

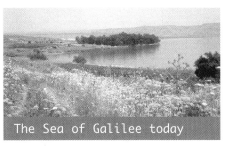

The Sea of Galilee today

was born in Palestine, the political rulers were the Romans. Obviously people didn't like that because it meant they were paying their taxes to a foreign emperor and to Rome. That was also why they didn't like tax collectors.

The Romans decided that they would rule Palestine through co-operation with the powerful Jews at the time. Yet they were still very wary of any group or person who might in some way be a threat to their rule, hence the heavy-handed tactics against Jesus and the early Christians. This meant that the region was extremely tense and volatile.

the

inner

place

Because the Romans decided to rule through co-operation, it meant that they allowed the Jews to hold onto their religious structures, namely the Temple in Jerusalem. The Temple was the centre of Jewish life and contained the Holy of Holies, where it was believed God dwelt (it was also where the original Ark of the Covenant was housed). The Temple was run by a council of seventy members, known as the Sanhedrin. They were a ruling council and court of law for Jews who broke Jewish laws, especially inside the Temple grounds.

When Jesus made his fateful journey to Jerusalem some time around 30 CE, he faced two structures of power: the political structure headed by Pontius Pilate, and the religious structure headed by the high priest, Caiaphas.

DISCUSS

1 What were the two structures of power in Jerusalem during the time of Jesus?
2 What contemporary political region does Palestine remind you of?

If Jesus was just an itinerant preacher, why was he perceived as a threat?

Considering that the Romans eventually killed Jesus, it is hard to understand how he ever posed a threat. His message was against violence of any kind. Instead, he preached a message of compassion and forgiveness. Yet those around Jesus applied a certain title to him, one that would have had both religious and political implications. That title was 'Messiah'.

During the many years that the Jews were invaded by foreign powers, the belief slowly emerged that God would send someone special to free them from oppression. This person would be the 'Messiah' or 'anointed one'. Some ancient texts prophesied that the anointed one would be a suffering messiah, but popular opinion had it that he would be

the
inner
place

a political liberator. The last thing the Romans wanted was a political liberator, someone who would be a definite threat to their rule.

The title 'Messiah' was applied to Jesus by many around him, but he was never comfortable with the title because of its political associations. Jesus had no notion of leading any army against the Romans, yet by being associated with the title he was perceived as a threat. Eventually, during his trial, Jesus admitted he was the Messiah, but few could understand the type of liberation he would really bring.

After his death and resurrection, the early Christians realised that Jesus was actually the Messiah. Most Jews rejected this idea because he wasn't politically motivated. However, the early followers understood Jesus as the Messiah or 'anointed one'. They used the Greek translation of 'anointed one', *Christos* or Christ. So, Jesus the Messiah became Jesus Christ.

DISCUSS

1 Why was Jesus perceived as a threat to the Romans?

2 Why was Jesus eventually called Jesus Christ?

Jesus seemed to get into trouble with different groups. Who were they?

Besides the Romans, there were four different groups in Palestine at the time of Jesus.

The Sadducees were by far the most influential and powerful group because they were wealthy and they were also the priests in charge of the Temple. Ordinary Jews went to the Temple to make sacrifices to God, but only a priest could actually make the sacrifice in the inner court. The Sadducees made up half of the Sanhedrin, and the high priest was always elected from their ranks. They were favourable to the Roman occupation because the Romans allowed them to maintain their wealth and influence. Some Jews resented them for this.

the inner place

The Pharisees were laymen who were the teachers of the Law or the Torah. Yet they were very strict about the observance of the Law and were concerned about Jewish identity. They believed that only through strict observance of the Law could the Jewish people maintain their distinct identity amidst all the different cultures thriving around the Mediterranean at that time. According to many gospel accounts, Jesus regularly came into conflict with the Pharisees over their strict interpretation of the Law.

The Roman tribute-money, which the Pharisees and Herodians produced (Mark 12:13–17), was the silver denarius, bearing the image and superscription of Tiberius Caesar

The Pharisees were against Roman occupation but they didn't really do anything about it. The Zealots, however, believed that the only way to deal with the Romans was through violence and revolt. They posed a real and militant threat to Roman rule. They were particularly hostile to paying taxes to the Romans and they believed it to be a complete injustice.

The final group operative in Palestine at the time of Jesus were the Essenes. These were extremely devout Jews who believed that the only way to lead a proper life was by retreating to the desert. They led lives of strict isolation, prayer and devotion. Whilst opposed to Roman rule, they would never have considered violence or a military campaign.

ASSIGNMENT Try to identify groups in contemporary culture who remind you of the four groups in Palestine at the time of Jesus. For example, the Zealots are much like any terrorist group or group of rebels you might hear about in the News.

the inner place

What did Jesus mean by the kingdom of God?

Long before Jesus, there was an expectation that God would intervene in the history of the Jewish people and establish God's rule or kingdom on earth. Many Jews believed that this kingdom would establish a new political rule for them. When Jesus preached about the kingdom of God, it was a radically different vision than that of the Jews. It was not about power or revolutions. According to Jesus, the kingdom of God was already taking place in him.

In the Sermon on the Mount (Matthew 5:1–12), Jesus teaches how, in the kingdom, peace is an alternative to violence and 'happy are the peacemakers'. The kingdom of God is based on forgiveness, as is evident in the 'Our Father'. The kingdom was not created for an elite group around Jesus, but was to include the outcasts and sinners. Jesus constantly ate with sinners, tax collectors and prostitutes, the social outcasts at the time, and so table-fellowship was central to Jesus' ministry. The kingdom belonged to the outcasts and the lowly in society, those without power or privilege.

Judaea

The kingdom, therefore, would not be created around wealth and prosperity. Instead, the kingdom was based on the sharing out of goods amongst those who were less well off. In the parable of the rich young man, Jesus explained how it would be 'easier for a camel to go through the eye of a needle than for someone who is rich to enter the kingdom of God' (Matthew 19:24). Even though the kingdom of God was central to Jesus' teaching, he rarely taught about the kingdom directly, but instead he revealed the kingdom through his miracles and parables.

In his book *The Shadow of the Galilean*, Gerd Theissen writes a narrative account of following in the footsteps of Jesus back in first-century Palestine. In the book, Theissen never actually meets Jesus but he always arrives in a place just after Jesus has left. In other words, Jesus never actually appears. Instead, we meet his shadow. In the following extract, the group are going along the shore of the Sea of Galilee to Bethsaida when they are confronted by some beggar children.

GERD THEISSEN
The Shadow of the Galilean

> Suddenly the beggar children whom we had met at the toll gate emerged. They held out their hands and barred our way.

the

inner

place

'What are you doing?' I asked.

'We're playing at toll collectors.'

'What frontier is this?'

'This is the beginning of the Kingdom of God.'

I wanted to explode with anger, but I restrained myself. Why shouldn't I play their game? So I did.

'What must I do to enter into your kingdom?'

The children laughed. The oldest one said:

'Unless you become like children again, you will not enter the kingdom of God' (Mark 10:15).

'Who rules in your kingdom?'

'We rule in this kingdom. The children. The kingdom of God is ours.'

'And what duty must I pay?'

'Give us something to eat.'

'Is that all?'

'There is no kingdom you can enter so easily. All you must do is give away what you possess. Then you belong to it.'

I didn't know if it was a game or in real earnest. I said: 'All right. Here is the duty for your kingdom.'

And I gave them a couple of loaves of bread and some fruit. Their faces shone. They gave way. We were allowed to pass. We had crossed this frontier as well.

ASSIGNMENT

the

inner

place

In your opinion, does the above fictional account of entering the kingdom of God provide a good example of who exactly can enter into God's kingdom? For whom is the kingdom of God really intended?

Chapter Ten

PARABLES AND STORIES ABOUT THE KINGDOM OF GOD

PARABLES

Parables are stories told by Jesus using people and events from everyday life to convey a message about the kingdom of God. Some might regard the parables as stories more relevant for people way back in Palestine a couple of thousand years ago. But maybe the stories have lost their impact because we've heard them so often. Any story told over and over and listened to over and over loses its power. Yet those who heard them first would have had a completely different reaction. So what kind of effect did parables have on people? In order to answer this question, we need to look at a present-day story, yet one with a similar quality to a parable.

The Dog in the Plane

This story, 'The Dog in the Plane', is not a parable from the gospels, but it will serve to illustrate something of the nature of parables. It begins with an old lady in a New York airport trying to buy a ticket for her pet dog. The airline staff refuse her request but are at pains to reassure her that her dog will be perfectly OK down in the cargo hold – absolutely nothing to

worry about. If this was a modern-day parable, it might be about the need for honesty in all we do. The story continues:

Arriving in Jerusalem, her destination, she's left waiting at the cargo counter for so long that she suspects something is seriously wrong. The staff continue to reassure her that all is well; it simply takes longer to offload cargo, as the priority is always to reunite passengers with their luggage first. She waits. Behind the scenes, panic reigns. A single glance inside the pet-carrier assures everyone that the woman's dog, a miniature schnauzer, is stone cold dead. Two cargo-handlers receive a blank cheque, a list of nearby pet stores, and instructions to return ASAP with another dog, one as close as possible in appearance to the corpse. The woman at the cargo desk receives more assurances that her dog will be along in a few moments.

Eventually the baggage-handlers race in with a miniature schnauzer, tuck the live animal in the cage, and send it along on the little rubber track to the front counter. The animal's owner takes one look in the cage and swiftly gets hysterical!

'That's not my dog! What have you done with my dog?' Attempts by the staff to convince her that this is her dog fail miserably. 'That can't be my dog! My dog died! I brought it here to bury in my own yard! What have you done with my dog?'

the

inner

place

DISCUSS

1 Why do you think this story has an impact?
2 Can you think of other stories with a similar impact?

Parables and Stories
about the Kingdom of God

If you've already heard the above story, the point will be lost on you. If you haven't, the ending comes as a surprise. In other words, it's not what you expected. The theologian John Dominic Crossan identifies this very quality in story as central to the effectiveness of parables. They display a reversal of expectations. What happens is not what we expect.

The Petrol Station

Now we need to add another element to what parables are about. Again, we'll use a modern story to illustrate another quality of parables. It is a story about fear. This story emerges from time to time, so you may have heard it already. Also, as you read the story, consider if it has a modern-day message.

A friend of mine told me the following story about his sister. One night she was coming home from work and decided to stop in for groceries at a petrol station. As she got out of her car, she noticed a young guy, maybe eighteen, dishevelled and unkempt, who, for all appearances, looked like a drug addict. She was wary of his glance, but was somewhat heartened by the sight of a man in a suit at the counter. She did her business and returned to her car. It was a dark and misty night, but just as she got in she noticed the same young man in a battered car staring at her. She couldn't be sure, but was he about to get out of his car and approach her. His stare was intense and frightening.

She started up her car and left at speed. As a corner loomed up ahead, she noticed the lights of a car approach from behind. Whoever it was, he was driving aggressively and accelerated his car to within feet of hers. The whine of his engine screeched

the

inner

place

through her ears. She was only miles from home, so she accelerated more, but as she did so, the car behind accelerated and then began to flash its lights! What kind of a lunatic was he? Did he really think she would pull over?

She prayed, begged and wished for the lights of her house to be around the next corner. Her husband would be at home. If only this lunatic would go away!

She rounded the corner, and there ahead were the lights from her house shining out onto the road. She accelerated more, but so did he. As the house approached, she took the drive too fast. She drove in on the lawn and skidded along the wet grass. She clambered from the car and there he was: the young guy from the station running at her car! She screamed and beat her fists into the air. He shot past her into the undergrowth.

Through her blurred eyes, she saw her husband at the door running down to her. He grabbed her tight, and then, from the undergrowth, emerged her pursuer. He walked up to her, and before she could warn her husband, the man pointed back to the shrubs and said, 'Sorry, but I couldn't catch him. The guy in the suit from the petrol station. He got into the back of your car while you were paying inside. I tried to warn you but you sped off. Just as well I could keep up. I kept flashing so he would know I was behind you. Better call someone, the guy must be a lunatic.'

the
inner
place

DISCUSS

Why does this story have an impact on its readers? How does it manage to grab your attention? Can you think of other stories that have a similar effect? Tell them in class.

Parables and Stories about the Kingdom of God

The Emotional Reaction

The above story, whilst not a gospel parable, has the kind of qualities and the same effect that parables had on their audience. Like the story of the dog in the aeroplane, there is a reversal of expectations. Yet there is also another quality to this story in so far as it taps into our emotions; in this instance, fear. So far we have established the following:

●   In parables, there is a reversal of expectation.

●   The audience becomes emotionally involved.

There is a further quality in parables that is present in the above story. You may already have identified that the story plays on our bias or prejudice. We presume that the drug-addict-type character is the real threat. That's our bias. The shock at the end of that story is that it is the drug addict (even though we've no evidence he was one) who was trying to help the woman. The man in the business suit, whom we assumed to be helpful or non-threatening, actually turns out to be the baddie. The story confronts and challenges our bias, and this is also exactly what parables did when Jesus told them. So we can now add another two qualities to parables:

●   Parables often play on some bias or prejudice.

●   The story demands that we rethink some bias or some narrow world-view.

ASSIGNMENT   Apply the above qualities to the story of the Petrol Station.

What is the reversal of expectation?

How is the audience emotionally involved?

What is the bias in the story?

How are we forced to rethink our bias?

Parables and Stories
about the Kingdom of God

The Parable of the Good Samaritan

The story about the woman returning home from work could be interpreted as a modern retelling of the parable of the Good Samaritan. A lawyer asked Jesus: 'Who is my neighbour?' Jesus then told the parable.

A man was going down from Jerusalem to Jericho, and fell into the hands of robbers, who stripped him, beat him and left him half dead. Now by chance a priest was going down that

Jericho

road; and when he saw him, he passed by on the other side. So likewise, a Levite, when he came to the place and saw him, passed by on the other side. But a Samaritan while travelling came near him; and when he saw him, he was moved with pity. He went to him and bandaged his wounds, having poured oil and wine on them. Then he put him on his own animal, brought him to an inn, and took care of him. The next day he took out two denarii, gave them to the innkeeper, and said, 'Take care of him; and when I come back, I will repay you whatever more you spend.' 'Which of these three, do you think, was a neighbour to the man who fell into the hands of the robbers?' He said, 'The one who showed him mercy.' Jesus said to him, 'Go and do likewise.'

the inner place

It's important to note that at the time when Jesus told the parable of the Good Samaritan, his audience, the Jews, despised Samaritans over something that happened years before that. When the original audience heard that parable, they would have been shocked that a priest would have ignored the stricken traveller. They would have been shocked too that a Levite would have ignored the man, because they were the tribe to which the running of the Temple was entrusted. Yet they would have been completely infuriated and dismayed to hear that a Samaritan

(spit!) would have helped the man... 'Nonsense!'... 'Rubbish!'... 'Go back to Nazareth!'... 'What's he on?'... 'The only thing good to come out of Samaria was the road to Galilee!' The story wouldn't have gone down well, but that didn't seem to interest Jesus. He was more interested in disturbing, challenging and confronting people's narrow minds and prejudices. This was typical of him.

DISCUSS

1 What are the similarities between the drug-addict-wielding-a-syringe type character in the story 'The Petrol Station' and the Good Samaritan?

2 What do you think was the message Jesus was trying to get across in the parable of the Good Samaritan?

3 Do you think the parables would have been powerful stories for the original audience? Give reasons for your answer.

SO WHAT WAS THE PURPOSE OF THE PARABLE STORIES?

1 UNFORGETTABLE STORIES

If parables were really good stories at the time they were told, then, like any good story, they should be events in themselves. If the stories were just intended to deliver a message, they would lack the impact they seemed to have. Parables were an event in so far as they affected the listener in some way. Take for example little horror stories told late at night. It's not really possible to sleep soundly after them.

the inner place

Parables and Stories about the Kingdom of God

Like the girl who is about to drive home from her boyfriend's and (anxious that she stay a little longer) he asks her will she be taking the 'Canal Road' home. 'Yeah, why?' she asks. 'Oh it's just, I don't want to scare you, but a young girl drowned there years ago in an accident. Some people have said that as they pass the spot they feel like there's someone sitting in the back seat. They don't want to look in the rear-view mirror but they can't help it. They glance up nervously and, maybe it's just a jumper up on the back window, but they see something, and next thing they're in the canal. I don't know how many have gone in there, all with the same story. Safe journey babe.' 'Well maybe,' she thinks, 'I'll stay a little longer.' Parables had that same ability to stay alive in a person's mind. It's like they had little hooks on them and, once they got inside the brain, it was hard to get them out. Like little horror stories.

2 SHATTERING WORLDS

The Jews expected a political kingdom that would free them from the Romans. Jesus used parables to show that the kingdom was actually drawing near right now and, as it did, the old world was disappearing and a new one was being created. And this is exactly what happens to those who hear parables. Their cozy world of who they would help and who is in their inside circle of neighbours or friends is blown apart. Jesus provoked outrage and a very definite hostility from his audience. He was subverting, disturbing and shattering their little narrow, comfy worlds. This, he was saying, was what the kingdom of God would be like. The kingdom did not come with God's outstretched arms trying to give everyone a big hug and going 'there, there'. No. Instead, the kingdom came with a giant wrecking-ball, shattering all our securities and boundaries. Then, amidst the wreckage, when we are open to see things in a radical new way, we can experience the presence of the kingdom. Think of the person you most hate in school, the girl or boy that you loathe. Think of going up to them and genuinely trying to do

the

inner

place

Parables and Stories
about the Kingdom of God

something good for them. Right there...at that moment...that's the kingdom of God. Now: 'Go, and do the same yourself.'

3   A MORAL MESSAGE AND THE 'BYSTANDER PROBLEM'

A good parable should be able to deliver its message in such a way as to leave the person rethinking their world-view and their moral vision. The power of the Good Samaritan is that the story is two thousand years old, but it still gets people to think. The parable delivers a very definite moral message. Not only do you help your friends, but you help your enemies, like the Samaritan helped his sworn enemy, the Jew. The point of the story as Jesus makes clear is: 'Go, and do the same yourself.'

As we are about to see, though the story of the Good Samaritan is thousands of years old, it has as much to say about contemporary society as about first-century Palestine. The question is: if you saw someone in trouble, someone you didn't know, a complete stranger, would you 'do the same yourself'?

In 2005, a newspaper carried the following report: On a bus in London, a young man stood up to defend his girlfriend when a man started pelting her with chips. A struggle began and the young man was stabbed to death by his attacker. The bus was full of people, yet the frightening aspect of the story is that no one intervened in the situation. No one tried to help. One woman wrote of the incident:

> What do you do in that situation? I definitely hesitated – I was thinking there's no way I'll be the first person to do something here, there are so many other people about. And then, suddenly, I had a very quick realisation that no one else was going to do anything. I find it astonishing that no one else approached an injured man in that situation. I suppose some people might not have thought it was life-threatening. And I suppose some people might have been squeamish. But nevertheless, there was blood, and a guy injured, and you were there. You don't just leave him, and leave someone else to deal

the

inner

place

with it… At one point this other guy came over. I'm not sure, but I think he got on the bus to have a look. He was leaning over, looking, and he was wearing a jacket. So I said: "Can you give me your jacket so I can put it over him?" He just said "No". That was it.

One explanation as to why people do not help is what psychologists have termed the 'bystander problem'. The University of New York staged emergencies in different situations to see what the response of people would be. The results were surprising, and one of the main factors in determining who would help was the number of people who witnessed the event.

In one experiment, for example, Latane and Darley had a student alone in a room stage an epileptic fit. When there was just one person next door listening, that person rushed to the person's aid 85% of the time. But when subjects thought there were others also overhearing the seizure, they came to the student's aid only 31% of the time. In another experiment, people who saw smoke seeping out from under a doorway would report it 75% of the time when they were on their own, but the incident would be reported only 38% of the time when they were in a group; in other words, responsibility for acting is diffused. Individuals will presume that someone else will make the call, or they presume that because no one else is acting, the apparent problem – the seizure-like sounds from the other room, the smoke from the door – isn't really a problem.

(*Irish Independent*, 15/8/05)

the

inner

place

DISCUSS

1 Why do you think people don't offer help to others when they obviously need it?

2 What do you think you would do given some of the situations above?

3 In the light of the above newspaper article, why do you think the parables might still have a relevant message for modern readers?

Parables and Stories
about the Kingdom of God

Chapter Eleven

THE PARABLE-MAKER: DISTURBING THE PEACE

THE STORY OF THE RICH YOUNG MAN

Jesus told stories that we call parables, but the gospels are also full of stories about Jesus. One such story is about how one day he met a rich young man.

> **DISCUSS**
>
> 1 Hands up who wants to be rich. Why do you want to be rich?
> 2 Why do you think so many people want to be rich?
> 3 In your opinion, does being rich make people happy?
> 4 In Ireland, do you think we look up to rich young people? Should we?

The Story

One day, a young man went up to Jesus and said: 'Master, I have absolutely loads of money. What do I have to do to get into heaven?' And Jesus said, 'Make loads more and keep it all for yourself! Make more money. Money is great, and make sure to give none to the poor! When you get to heaven, you'll be first in...' Well no, actually that's not what happened at all. Here's the real story.

> As he was setting out on a journey, a man ran up and knelt before him, and asked him, 'Good Teacher, what must I do to inherit eternal life?' Jesus said to him, 'Why do you call me good? No one is good but God alone. You know the commandments: "You shall not murder; You shall not commit adultery; You shall not steal; You shall not bear false witness; You shall not defraud; Honour your father and mother." ' He

said to him, 'Teacher, I have kept all these since my youth.' Jesus, looking at him, loved him and said, 'You lack one thing; go, sell what you own, and give the money to the poor, and you will have treasure in heaven; then come, follow me.' When he heard this, he was shocked and went away grieving, for he had many possessions.

(Mark 10:17–22)

The young man was shocked by what Jesus said and would obviously have preferred to have heard the first version. Now the rich young man was a sad young man. It would seem that life is just not fair. But is there any evidence to suggest that Jesus is actually right, that wealth may not lead to happiness? Could it be true that offloading some riches for the benefit of others might actually make us happier people?

WEALTH AND HAPPINESS

One universal pursuit is happiness, but what makes us happy? The parable of the rich young man suggests that wealth doesn't make us happy. If Jesus is right, then it's little wonder the young man is shocked; surely more money would make us all happier.

What do you think would make you happy?

the

inner

place

ASSIGNMENT

Listed below is a range of potential sources of happiness. Which situation would you pick to be in and which do you think would make you happier? In each option, you must make a choice.

The Parable-Maker: Disturbing the Peace

1 Buying/Gratitude

A You've always wanted a faster car, and eventually you get the money to go out and buy it. It's secondhand and small, but that's the only way you'll ever afford the insurance. Imagine your first set of keys in your hand. You rev it up and off you go.

OR

B You play sport but you get a bad injury and the doctors tell you that it's so bad you may never be able to play sport again. One doctor who is a specialist immediately puts you on a brand-new medication. There's a fifty per cent chance it will work. It does. The doctor comes out to the waiting room and tells you you're in the clear. You are incredibly grateful to her and remain grateful for your health.

2 Male/Female

(Obviously you can't choose here, but which do you think are the happier?)

A Men

OR

B Women

3 Forgiveness/Revenge

A You've just left college and one night coming home from the shop you see an old landlord who refused to give you back your deposit. It wasn't your fault that the other idiots you lived with trashed the place. You decide to get even. After he walks away from his car, you go over and pour a pound of sugar into his petrol tank. Cars don't run on sugary petrol. You've just got even.

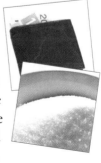

the

inner

place

OR

B You are in the same situation as above, but this time when you see your old landlord, you notice that his wallet is hanging out of his trouser pocket. It's certain to fall out on the street. So you run over to him and let him know. He thanks you and off you go home with the sugar for your cup of coffee.

4 Friendship/Being Alone

A You are at home watching TV when you unexpectedly get a phone call to go out and meet some of your friends. It's cold and a bit wet outside and the fire is lighting. Shoes off, feet up on the couch. But you get up and head off into town to meet your pals.

OR

B You are at home watching TV when you unexpectedly get a phone call to go out and meet some of your friends. It's cold and a bit wet outside and the fire is lighting. Shoes off, feet up on the couch. You decide it's too much bother and so you stay in.

5 Charity/Lottery

A You buy a ticket for some charity and the prize is a chance to go to a developing country to help build homes for homeless people in a shanty town. After the experience, you become heavily involved in the charity and it becomes a feature of your life.

OR

B You win the lottery and it's life-changing money; new house, new car, etc. You have loads of cash. A new music system would be good and a completely new wardrobe. In fact, you could buy most things you want.

The Parable-Maker:
Disturbing the Peace

The Answers

1   In the first scenario, you get to go out and buy something; in this instance, a faster car. There has been much research in recent years into whether buying does really make us happier, and the answer is that it doesn't. Firstly, it is documented that those who have materialistic goals are simply not happy. If a person bases their happiness on materialistic items, it's simply impossible to be ever satisfied. Products are continually upgraded; cars become faster; luxury goods become more luxurious. The buyer can never arrive. Secondly, if a person is geared towards wanting, it's proven that 'wanting' is never satisfied. In studies, people were given what they wanted, but three years later they still wanted things. In the second choice, the person was full of gratitude. Gratitude does lead to happiness and it's recommended to assess your life regularly and identify the aspects of your life that you are thankful for. There's always something.

2   In the second scenario, it's not so clear-cut. Men tend to simplify things. Generally, women are happier than men in so far as they have a much better ability to be emotional. Women express their emotions, whereas men tend to control them. The bad news for women is that they are also sadder because they can deal with and express that emotion better. For instance, women cry more. So who is happier? You can fight and argue about that one in class.

3   The third scenario pits revenge against forgiveness. People who can forgive are happier because they have the ability to leave and let go of bad experiences in their past. People who think about revenge stay stuck in the past and dwell on negative experiences. People who forgive can let go of bad memories and experiences, and are happier for it.

4   In the fourth scenario, both may make a person happy, but many studies show that meeting friends and being part of a community leads to greater happiness than being alone. Of course, it's not so black and white, because introverts will be happier alone, whereas extroverts will be happier with other people, but generally speaking having friends

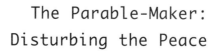

The Parable-Maker:
Disturbing the Peace

and being with them makes us happy. Remember, a form of punishment in the prison system is an isolation cell.

5   Did you pick winning the lottery? The research on lottery winners is very interesting because they all revert to their original levels of happiness after six months, which may have something to do with developing materialistic values. If you picked the trip to do charitable work, then you're on your way to being happy. Firstly, being altruistic or thinking of others makes us happy, and also experiences such as travel and meeting people make us happier than buying. The trip away was a challenge that was overcome, and being with others universally makes us happy.

JESUS AND HAPPINESS

**'I have said these things to you
so that my joy may be in you,
and that your joy may be complete.'**
(John 15:11)

It seems that the advice that Jesus gave the young man was sound, though shocking – you're better off not being attached to your money and it won't make you happy. The messages about altruism and forgiveness in some of the parable stories also seem to point to a happier life. Jesus wasn't out to challenge or confuse people just for the sake of it. He had a better vision for what would constitute a happier life and he wanted to share that with anyone willing to listen.

What Jesus says about happiness seems to be borne out by studies on how the human brain affects our happiness. The area for 'want' in the brain is different from the area for 'like'. To put

the

inner

place

208   The Parable-Maker:
Disturbing the Peace

this another way: what we always want won't be what we like or what will make us happy. In the brain, there's no link between 'want' and 'like', or between 'want' and 'happiness'. People seem to think that if they get what they 'want', it will make them 'happy'. Not so. Jesus seems to be right about a lot of things when it comes to happiness.

So how would he have fared on the above exercise?

1   At the Last Supper, Jesus repeatedly gave thanks to the Father. Indeed, the word 'Eucharist' actually means 'thanksgiving'. Catholics are repeatedly encouraged to give thanks to God for the blessings they have received. Jesus encourages an attitude of gratitude.

2   There is plenty of evidence that Jesus could express a range of human emotions.

3   Jesus always encouraged his disciples to forgive their enemies. The mathematically minded apostle Peter wondered how often. The answer Jesus gave was seventy-seven times, but he was probably being smart.

4   Jesus spent lots of time with people, and significantly his advice was for his followers to gather together: 'Where two or three are gathered in my name, I am there among them' (Matthew 18:20).

5   No lottery in Palestine in 30 CE, but Jesus constantly encouraged his disciples to think of the needs of others.

ASIDE   Nowhere are Jesus' teachings on happiness more clear than in the Sermon on the Mount. There Jesus outlines the very values of the kingdom of God that will lead to happiness:
'Happy are the poor in Spirit, for theirs is the kingdom of heaven.
Happy are those who mourn, for they will be comforted.
Happy the meek, for they will inherit the earth.
Happy are those who hunger and thirst for righteousness, for they will be filled.
Happy are the merciful, for they will receive mercy.
Happy are the pure in heart, for they will see God.

the

inner

place

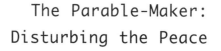

Happy are the peacemakers, for they will be called children of God.
Happy are those who are persecuted for righteousness' sake, for theirs is the kingdom of heaven.'

(Matthew 5:3–10)

Jesus seems to have something important to say when it comes to giving us insights into what will actually make us happy. Jesus said: 'Ask and you will receive, so your joy may be complete' (John 16:24).

Break into groups and make a list of the attitudes, actions and values that would actually make people happy, based on what you have read so far in this chapter. Identify at least three qualities in a person that would make them happy.

THE PARABLE-MAKER: DISTURBING THE PEACE

'Parables alert us to what it might mean to live in the world in a radical new way. These narratives are about relationships. They are concerned with what people do, about new ways of being together because of their relatedness to what he calls the reign of God. They tease the mind and imagination into new, extravagant, radical ways of grappling with reality.'

(Eamonn Bredin, *Disturbing the Peace*)

The parables always upset and disturbed people because they forced them to examine their relationships in a radically new and challenging manner.

The Parable-Maker:
Disturbing the Peace

- Nobody liked the idea, but the Samaritans should be accepted and welcomed.
- Most would have driven the prodigal son out of the farm and down the lane with a kick. The father welcomed, forgave and accepted him for who he was.
- Most looked up to the rich young man, but Jesus exposed his true condition to be that of a sad young man.

That Jesus was compassionate and merciful is beyond doubt, but there was another side to his personality that goes largely unnoticed: Jesus disturbed and shattered the peace. With precision and ease, he disassembled people's cozy little worlds.

- 'He's my friend but you're not, so you can't come to my party.' Jesus knocks that one on the head in the parable of the Good Samaritan.

- 'I'll get that cow back if it's the last thing I do.' Perhaps a natural instinct, but in the long run it's better to forgive her and try to get along (The Prodigal Son).

- 'Look at me everyone, I'm loaded. Look at my cool car and my cool clothes. Everyone should be like me.' Not really. The whole rich thing will not lead to happiness.

The Jesus that emerges from the parables is quite different from traditional images that we might have about what Jesus was really like. Yet his purpose was to offer us a radically new and improved way of living our lives. He offered us happier lives. It's now time to take a look at what Jesus would really have been like.

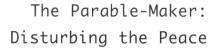

WHAT WAS JESUS REALLY LIKE?

JESUS THE PROPHET

When the people saw the sign that he had done,
they began to say, 'This is indeed the prophet who is
to come into the world.'
(John 6:14)

In chapter 8, we noted how Jesus is often misrepresented as a weak, harmless, inoffensive and irrelevant type of person. Jesus was full of compassion and love for the sinner and the outcast. Yet Jesus was not afraid to challenge the comfortable world-views of his day. His love had an edge to it, and that edge was especially sharpened for his critics. There are many different titles given to Jesus, but in his own time he was best understood as a prophet.

> **ASIDE** A prophet is someone sent by God in God's name for a particular mission. Prophets speak openly and fiercely. But Jesus was not just another prophet in a long line of prophets stretching back into the Old Testament. Instead, he was God's final messenger, bringing a final message of salvation to the world. Prophet is also the term that Jesus seemed most at ease with. Typically, the prophet announced that the people had to change their behaviour in some radical way. Typically too, the prophet was fierce and outspoken, preaching of judgement and right behaviour. This was the category that many who

witnessed the real Jesus put him into. Those who actually listened to him and heard him preach and witnessed his actions were very clear about what sort of a character he was.

As a prophet, Jesus continuously challenged the system and threatened people's security. He had no regard for popularity and, instead, repeatedly said the unpopular thing. He hung around with the outcasts and the sinners and mocked the self-righteous. The religious leaders despised sinners, and so, for Jesus, as prophet of God, to deliberately welcome sinners was an absolute scandal. Jesus disturbed the leaders' selfish and elitist existence and his words made them squirm in their seats. He insulted them, proclaiming: 'I came not to call the righteous, but sinners', and they despised him for it. In turn, they blackened his name, calling him a 'glutton and drunkard, friend of tax collectors and sinners'.

In one particular story, Jesus heals a paralysed man, an outcast and sinner, and infuriates the Pharisees.

One day, while he was teaching, Pharisees and teachers of the law were sitting near by; and the power of the Lord was with him to heal. Just then some men came, carrying a paralysed man on a bed. They were trying to bring him in and lay him before Jesus; but finding no way to bring him in because of the crowd, they went up to the roof and let him down with his bed through the tiles into the middle of the crowd in front of Jesus. When he saw their faith, he said, 'Friend, your sins are forgiven you.' Then the scribes and the Pharisees began to question, 'Who is this who is speaking blasphemies? Who can forgive sins but God alone?' When Jesus heard their questions, he answered them, 'Why do you raise such questions in your hearts? Which is easier, to say, "Your sins are forgiven you", or to say "Stand up and walk"? But so that you may know that the Son of Man has authority on earth to forgive sins' – he said to the one who was paralysed – 'I say to you, stand up and take your bed and go home.' Immediately he stood up

the
inner
place

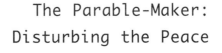

before them, took what he had been lying on, and went to his home, glorifying God. Amazement seized all of them, and they glorified God and were filled with awe, saying, 'We have seen strange things today.'

(Luke 5:17–26)

The Pharisees would have condemned the sinner and seen his illness as just punishment for his wrongdoings. They would have refused God's compassion and forgiveness. For this, they provoked the wrath of the Father's son: 'Woe to you Pharisees! For you love to have the seat of honour in the synagogues and to be greeted with respect in the marketplaces. Woe to you! For you are like unmarked graves, and people walk over them without realising it' (Luke 11:43–44).

As prophet, Jesus challenged, disturbed, unsettled and provoked all that he saw wrong and unjust in his society. Jesus was not weak but was courageous and outspoken. He was not harmless but challenged the authorities to their rotten core, and was even branded a blasphemer. Jesus was a champion of the little people but for this he was condemned as outrageous and a troublemaker. His outspokenness would have a price and he would pay for it with his life.

ASIDE

Nostradamus: Prophet of Future?
Often when we mention the word prophet, people think of someone who can see into the future. When Jesus was called prophet, it wasn't a reference to his ability to predict things that were about to happen. Nostradamus is accredited with having had the ability to see into the future. The sixteenth-century French seer is accredited with having foreseen the French Revolution, the coming of Adolf Hitler and the death of King Henry II. According to some accounts, he predicted that civilisation as we know it would end in 1999. It didn't.

the

inner

place

The Parable-Maker:
Disturbing the Peace

1. What kind of a person is a prophet?
2. Why did the religious leaders despise Jesus?
3. As a prophet, whom did Jesus challenge to change their ways?

Do you know of anyone who challenges unjust structures in society? Do such people provide an important function in society?

JESUS – MAN OF PRINCIPLE

In the film *Scent of a Woman*, Al Pacino plays a retired general who embarks on a trip to New York with Charlie, played by Chris O'Donnell. The general finds out that Charlie is in big trouble in school because he witnessed an attack on the principal's car but he won't rat on the students involved. At the end of the film, Charlie and another boy are brought before the school disciplinary committee for interrogation and disciplinary action. Charlie refuses to rat on the students involved, but in doing so he will probably lose out on a scholarship.

Things look bleak for Charlie until the unexpected arrival of the blind general, who makes an impassioned plea for Charlie's career. The plea is born out of a genuine compassion and love for the boy in the face of what seems to be an injustice against him. The general launches a fierce and thunderous tirade against the unjust structures of the school, which are victimising Charlie. He is ferocious in his attack, and angry and furious with the stern and self-righteous principal.

When Jesus met his contemporaries, they often made comparisons between him and other figures. It's natural to

the inner place

compare Jesus to characters we know, and there is something in the character of the general played by Al Pacino that reminds us of what Jesus would really have been like. Like the general, Jesus had compassion for the vulnerable and lowly, yet his compassion was fierce and uncompromising.

FILM

Look at the closing scenes as mentioned above in the film *Scent of a Woman*. Does the figure of the general as played by Al Pacino strike you as similar to the image of Jesus disturbing the peace and challenging the system? Give reasons for your answer.

JESUS AND THE SEARCH FOR MEANING

In the first section of this book, we noted how people engage with the search for meaning in many different ways. It is tempting to believe that wealth and success will satisfy us, but the evidence suggests that they won't – that extra wealth, ultimately, won't make us happier.

Quite often, modern research tends to agree with many of the teachings found in the gospels. It would appear that following these teachings might just make us happier. An attitude of thanksgiving automatically gives a person a positive outlook on life. Forgiveness allows us to let go of the past, whilst many studies show that charity work and thinking of others have immediate benefits for the giver.

There are many wrong turns on the road that leads us along the search for meaning, and at times it can be helpful to have a source of advice and direction. The message that Jesus gives in the gospels can lead to a more meaningful and happier life. He challenges us to look at our lives and our search for meaning, but he always offers an alternative, one that modern research is now willing to embrace. For anyone who is willing to listen, the message of the gospels is worthy of serious consideration.

the

inner

place

The Parable-Maker:
Disturbing the Peace

Chapter Twelve

TEENAGERS AND THE KINGDOM

DO WE KNOW ANYTHING ABOUT JESUS THE TEENAGER?

Unfortunately, we know little about Jesus' teenage years, or the 'hidden years', as they are sometimes referred to. The gospels say very little about the years between his birth and the start of his public ministry. We do know that he was a carpenter's son and that much of his time was spent working as a 'tekton' or 'woodworker'. He would have worked in his own workshop, making bits of furniture. He also spent some time on 'building sites', putting in wooden beams in homes, etc. His job at that time involved quite a bit of technical skill and a lot of muscle. The image of Jesus as some sort of weakling, as portrayed in many films, does not match with the historical data. He would have to have been well built and strong. If he was working on building sites today, he would have been known as a 'chippie', i.e. carpenter.

Jesus was fully human, so we have to imagine that he went through the same difficulties as any other teenager. He lived a human life like everybody else, even though he was unique in his relationship with God.

When did people know there was something special about Jesus?

The following story about the England football star Wayne Rooney tells of how he came to be recognised as having 'special' talents.

> Wayne played for the Liverpool Schools U-11s side,
> for whom he had scored more than seventy goals in

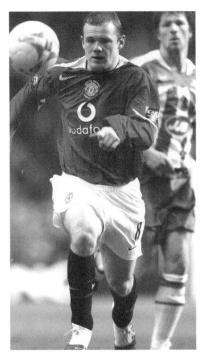

the season. In one game, Rooney ran down the middle of the pitch with the ball. The coach – as coaches do – encouraged him to play the ball out wide and get in the box for its return. His father, who may have sensed his son's capabilities, encouraged him to dribble past the defenders, before beating the goalkeeper to score himself.

As the advice bellowed from the touchline, Rooney – maybe only to shut them up – stopped and hit the ball from forty yards. It flew past the young 'keeper into the net. The suggestions stopped short on the sideline. The small crowd looked for some explanation. Rooney turned to where his coach and his father were standing and shrugged.

(Sunday Independent, 24/10/04)

The only story that would seem to tie in with Jesus' early adolescent years comes from Luke's gospel, and it reveals how Jesus, from an early age, was showing signs of being special. According to Luke 2:41–50, every year his parents went to Jerusalem for the Passover festival. On one occasion, on their way home, they noticed that Jesus was missing. Where was he? Jesus, it seems, had decided to stay behind in the city. They weren't impressed. So they went back to look for him, and after three days they found him in the Temple. Not good. But Jesus was happy and seemingly unaware of any commotion. In fact, he was deep in discussions with the teachers of the Temple. He was twelve years of age.

inner

place

After three days they found him in the Temple, sitting among the teachers, listening to them and asking questions. And all who heard him were amazed at his understanding and his answers. When his parents saw him they were astonished; and his mother said to him, 'Child, why have you treated us like this? Look, your father and I have been searching for you in great anxiety.' He said to them, 'Why were you searching for me? Did you not know that I must be in my Father's house?' But they did not understand what he said to them. Then he went down with them and came to Nazareth, and was obedient to them. His mother treasured all these things in her heart. And Jesus increased in wisdom and in years, and in divine and human favour.

(Luke 2:46–52)

Though only twelve, this would seem like classic teenage stuff. He runs away from home for three days or so, and then answers his mother back when she has a word or two with him. Finally, his parents end up admitting that they just do not understand him. Like Wayne Rooney, Jesus probably just shrugged his shoulders.

Was Jesus grounded after this? If he was grounded, it was the longest one ever recorded in history. Nothing is known of Jesus between that incident and approximately twenty years later.

TEENAGERS AND THE KINGDOM OF GOD

Though this may come as a surprise, there are many similarities between Jesus and teenagers. Here are a few.

- Jesus' parents didn't understand him.
- He was constantly saying the wrong thing and getting into trouble.
- He had immense energy for compassion and justice.
- He often seemed to be very shy and headed off to the wilderness.
- He loved hanging around with his friends.
- He absolutely loved going out. Check the gospels. He was never one to stay in.
- Loads of people disapproved of those with whom he hung around.
- He attracted loads of bad headlines, e.g. 'glutton and drunkard'.
- Despite what everyone said, his Mammy thought he was brilliant.

There are a few certainties about teenagers. Yes, they do seem to get into a lot of trouble (later in this chapter we'll find out why). They have an incredible knack of attracting all the bad headlines. True, some teenagers deserve the negative publicity they get, but unfortunately it often hides far more revealing, positive and inspirational stories. In short, teenagers can be great creators of the kingdom of God. Read the following story that never made the headlines and decide for yourself.

A STORY OF TEENAGERS IN ACTION

Then the righteous will answer him, 'Lord, when was it that we saw you hungry and gave you food, or thirsty and gave you something to drink? And when was it that we saw you a stranger and welcomed you, or naked and gave you clothing? And when was it that we saw you sick or in prison and visited you?' And the king will answer them, 'Truly I tell you, just as you did it to one of the least of these who are members of my family, you did it to me.'
(Matthew 25:37–40)

I remember the evening my Dad first showed me the pictures of the children from the orphanages. He had been to Romania to try to help those who had been forgotten during a harsh and uncaring communist era. I had heard the story but this was the first time I saw the images that bore witness to what happens when children are forgotten and abandoned.

That was two years ago and now I know that the images I saw that evening don't tell the true and horrific story. The pictures do show twenty-year-olds in shrunken and malnourished bodies. They show child after child tied to beds, shackled like animals to prevent self-injury. It's easy to imagine their tiny frames rocking backwards and forwards, condemned as they are to lives of sometimes severe physical and mental handicap. But what I know now is that the pictures don't reveal the ever-present stench of stale urine and decrepit sanitary facilities. You can't hear the screams and groans of the abandoned in the silent images. You can't feel the deathlike pallor that seems to cling to every inch of every ward.

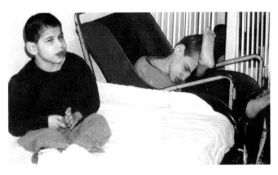

That night those same pictures were strewn over my bedroom floor. Up until then my life had been comfortable and carefree. But I was growing up quickly and learning that the world outside my bedroom window had dark secrets that were now slowly beginning to invade my every waking thought. It's hard to explain but after hearing my Dad's shocking story I could think of nothing else. Child after child stared vacantly from the pictures on the floor and as I fought back tears my mind was awash with countless feelings and frustrations. On

inner

place

the walls of my room were pictures of my sisters, happy, smiling and free. Something seemed very wrong with the world.

The next morning in school I was restless and couldn't concentrate. At break I showed the pictures to my friends and recounted the story of the orphanages. It's still hard to explain their reaction and mine. It's hard to explain what was going on inside all of us. We were huddled and silent. Then I just said that we have to do something about this. These were my friends, I knew they'd understand. We had no words in the face of such horror. Instead, our actions would speak for us. That morning, perched on chairs and desks, we were stunned but determined. We were looking into the faces of the unwanted. Something had to be done.

We invited two members of Focus on Romania to talk to us in school. They recognised how we felt and they put a challenge to us. Would we be able to fund a holiday for thirty young adults in institutional care in Romania? Could we raise 10,000 euro? We were delighted to help.

The next few months witnessed a flurry of fashion shows, mini-marathons, raffles, auctions, coffee mornings and a film night. We raised 14,000 euro. But it wasn't just about the money. They also asked us would we go on the trip ourselves. So fifteen girls from Mount Sackville offered to fly to Romania. That way we would ensure that these children and young adults would have the most memorable holiday that we could provide. As we packed our bags, we tried to include everything they might need. We brought shoes, clothes, medicines, even nail polish. Anything that would brighten up their days.

inner place

When we arrived, the young adults were in their room, some rocking on their beds, others screaming. One guy was just sitting on his wheelchair, oblivious to what was going on, and then the other, more lively ones would be just simply 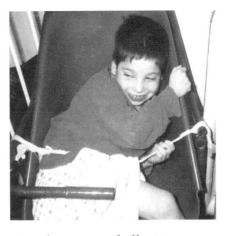 crying out for a hug or a simple gesture of affection. At the beginning the whole thing seemed overwhelming. No matter how much you've heard or seen on TV or video, nothing can prepare you for what you see and smell when you physically go there yourself. Some of the girls found it more difficult than others at the start but it wasn't long before we got stuck in. We had the children out of their beds and down to the beach. It was just ten minutes away yet they'd never been to its sandy shores. Our day was packed with swimming, building castles, dancing, singing and playing games. The language barrier was never really a problem because they were just crying out for some love and attention. I now know that simple acts of kindness are a universal language.

inner

place

We tried to make each day different, with long walks, sing-songs on the basketball courts, shoot-outs, trips to the slides, and one night we organised our own disco with a small CD player and glow-in-the-dark ping-pong balls and lights. They were always so grateful for everything. Everything we did excited them and it made us all realise how little they had and how lucky we were coming from such an affluent society.

On the Wednesday I was lucky enough to have the opportunity to go to another orphanage, Negru Voda. I had heard much about it but I must admit I was also apprehensive. When we finally arrived at the institution it looked like one of the dreariest and daunting places I had ever been in. We paid a visit to the main canteen. This was the part I was very apprehensive about – all of us were. We had seen

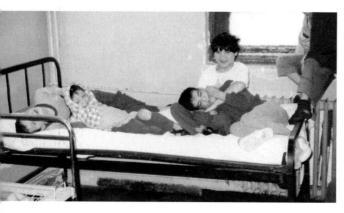

photos and videos of Negru Voda, but again nothing prepares you for the smell or atmosphere about the place. The young adults living were out on the grass while we were there, so all the rooms were vacant. It was a hot day and the smell was worse than usual. We passed by the wire fence, which kept all the children confined to a grass patch where some would sit in a corner and rock and others would sit sedated in wheelchairs. We walked inside and the dreariness of the place was felt by everyone. We walked the long corridor, passing each room with several beds, some without sheets and blankets. We continued on down the corridor until we reached the so-called 'soft room', and as we opened the door a boy was lying there on a mat under a blanket. He was lying in his own urine, with flies surrounding his

inner

place

head. That was one of the images which will have a lasting effect on all of us.

Some of the things we saw will haunt our memories forever. Yet in some ways we too were blessed to be amongst the abandoned and the unwanted. One sunny day I remember walking into one of the rooms and one of my friends was there with a younger girl. She was putting cream on her chapped and dry hands. She was immersed in this activity. Then, finished, she looked up at the young girl. But she looked into eyes so full of gratitude, love and appreciation. There, in that silent moment in a Romanian orphanage, two lives were changed.

(Aoibhin Garrihy, 17)

And the king will answer them,
'Truly I tell you, just as you did it to one of the least of these who are members of my family, you did it to me.'

DISCUSS This story about teenagers responding in dramatic fashion to the needs of others is one of many that could be told here. Why do you think teenagers in particular respond so well to those who have been abandoned by society?

inner

place

DISTURBING THE PEACE

In chapter 8 of this section, we looked at different images of Jesus, from the 'Hippie Jesus' to 'Simon of Seriousness'. Jesus, however, is to be understood as a prophet and a disturber of the peace. He challenged what he perceived to be the unjust systems of the day.

When a Romanian Government delegation visited Ireland, a group representing Focus on Romania was invited to meet the delegation. A reception hosted by the Romanian ambassador was held in a Dublin hotel. Present was the Romanian prime minister and what seemed like a harmless group of school girls, the youngest members of Focus on Romania. The prime minister reckoned he saw a good photo opportunity in front of the assembled Romanian media. He'd look well beside the school girls. Things didn't work out as planned.

The girls agreed to the photo shoot, but they weren't there just to look good. Along with the other members, they closed around the prime minister in a tight circle. There was no escape. The girls demanded that he immediately close the dreaded Negru Voda orphanage. When would he do it? Could he give them a commitment? The circle tightened and the seasoned politician was under serious pressure. Trapped, he agreed to close the orphanage.

(Adapted from *Dancing on the Waves: Romania's Orphans and the Grand Canal* by John Mulligan.)

DISCUSS

Do you think teenagers are good at challenging unjust systems? Why? Have you any examples of teenagers standing up for what they believe to be right? Tell the story to the class.

inner

place

ADOLESCENT IDENTITY

One thing that teenagers have a difficulty with is their identity. One day you're a child, the next you're an adult. Except it's not like that. There's the in-between time when you're neither a child nor an adult. We call it adolescence. 'Who am I? What am I supposed to do? What's my role in life? I'm too young to go out, too young to drive the car, but "old enough to know better". I'm "old enough to pay for that yourself now" but "not yet old enough to work".' Sorting out one's identity is difficult. Jesus faced the same problems, and throughout his life he came to realise his special relationship with God and his special mission.

When it comes to identity, there is little doubt that teenagers tend to be more misunderstood than any other segment of society. It is also fair to say that teenagers seem to get into more trouble than any other group. Often headlines dominate newspapers regarding the inappropriate or offensive activities of teenagers. Yet being a teenager isn't easy on many different fronts, especially when it comes to identity.

One of the reasons for this difficulty is that teenagers are caught in the transition from childhood to adulthood. It is the time of betwixt and between. The lack of a clear and defined identity is unsettling. It would also appear that society is unsure as to how to treat teenagers. Should they be treated as children or adults? In the second book of this series, we will examine how primitive societies used rites of passage to mark the transition of the child into adulthood. In our society, this process takes almost ten years, but in primitive cultures the process of change took no more than a few months. After the rites of passage were completed, the person acted like, and was treated like, an adult. They assumed an adult role and adult responsibilities in that society. In modern culture,

inner

place

it can take up to ten years before a person is formally treated like an adult.

Coupled with the unsettling place that teenagers occupy in society, it has emerged in recent years that part of the difficulty with teenage identity comes from the workings and biology of the developing teenage brain.

DISCUSS

1 Why do you think there is a problem for teenagers around their status in society; in other words, around whether they are children or adults?
2 If you had a teenage son or daughter, what type of behaviour would you have to see evidence of before you would treat them as an adult?
3 Why do you think parents and adults have difficulty in knowing when to treat you in a more adult way, as opposed to a childish way?

THE TEENAGE BRAIN

The human brain does not come fully developed at birth, and during the adolescent years some very interesting things are happening inside the teenage brain. Teenagers are often accused of having a short fuse, and many parents are left bewildered as to why their sons or daughters slam and bang doors at the slightest provocation. According to research, part of the problem occurs in the frontal lobes, that part of your brain just behind your forehead. People who suffer damage to the frontal lobe area often have difficulty in controlling their temper. The frontal lobes should act to control our urges and ensure that we behave appropriately.

This area of the brain goes through a growth spurt until about eleven or twelve, but then may actually go into reverse. Without a fully functioning frontal lobe area, teenagers are biologically more prone to mood swings and flashes of temper. One of the explanations for this reverse in frontal lobe activity is that the brain has to concentrate on other areas of development so as to

prepare the child for becoming an adult capable of survival and reproduction.

In other research, teenagers were shown a range of facial expressions and were required to identify each expression. Surprisingly, teenagers scored less than younger children. For example, teenagers were less able to identify a threatening from a non-threatening facial expression. This may not seem significant but, according to some researchers, this has serious implications for the teenage ability to assess threats in general. Teenagers, it would appear, end up in more fights than adults. Is this because teenagers are less capable of assessing when a situation is becoming heated or potentially threatening?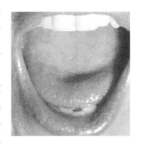

Again, it is the frontal lobe area that seems to be the problem. Studies show that adult brains exhibit stronger activity in this area than do the brains of teenagers, and so are better equipped to assess danger. Adults often deem some teenage activity incredibly stupid and dangerous. Adults seem baffled by the risks that teenagers take and parents constantly worry about what their teenagers are getting up to. Now it would appear they have good reason to worry because teenagers simply haven't developed key areas of their brains. The frontal lobe does the thinking and assessing for us, so if it's in a stage of development it's not adequately deciding on what type of activities are too risky.

So parents shouldn't expect rational explanations from their teenage son or daughter. When asked as to why they did something incredibly stupid, teenagers often reply that they really have no idea: 'Just did it.' According to brain research, they're not lying.

(Robert Winston, *The Human Mind*)

DISCUSS

Would you agree that teenagers take more risks than adults? Is it possible that teenagers also take risks to fit into a group, to be accepted? Could risk-taking also be linked to alcohol abuse?

JESUS GAVE SOME HELPFUL ADVICE

In Matthew 6:5, Jesus gives the following advice: 'Whenever you pray, go into your room and shut the door and pray to your Father who is in secret; and your Father who sees in secret will reward you.' Now, researchers believe that prayer and meditation

may be of particular relevance to teenagers. Researchers at the University of Pennsylvania decided to perform brain scans on eight monks who entered into a meditative state through prayer. They hoped to find out what happens in the brain during prayer and meditation. The monks were seated in a brain-scan room, which was specially darkened. In order to achieve the best results, incense candles were burned. The monks were wired up so as the researchers could monitor the blood flow throughout their brain.

The first thing they noticed was a reduction of blood flow to the posterior parietal lobe. This gives a person a sense of their place in space and time. Secondly, they noticed a heightened activity in the frontal lobes. What was remarkable was the fact that in other tests they established that the concentration of blood flow in this area continued even after the monks had finished meditating. The researchers, led by Professor Andrew Newberg, believe that of all groups, teenagers would benefit most from prayer and meditation. Along with its obvious spiritual benefits, prayer

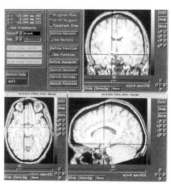

inner

place

strengthens the exact areas of the brain that would serve teenagers best.

DISCUSS

1 Do you know of anyone who practises prayer or meditation on a regular basis? Do they believe that it is beneficial for them?

2 Do you think teenagers would benefit from a regular time of silence and prayerful meditation? Would it be good to get a break from a busy, hectic and demanding world for a while every now and then?

WHO, THEN, ARE YOU?

Every human being has to come to an understanding of their own identity so as to establish their role and function in society. Jesus realised that his unique relationship with God had very clear implications for his role and function in his own lifetime. Because it was a unique relationship, it dictated that he had to abandon his job as carpenter and commence a ministry throughout Galilee. It was a ministry that would bring him into conflict with the highest authorities in the land and eventually lead to his death.

Yet Jesus had a personality that enabled him to confront the corrupt religious and political structures of the day, while at the same time showing extraordinary compassion and love to the ostracised and lowly.

In recent times, psychologists have identified certain personality types. According to this theory, each person has particular personality traits. One trait is not better than any other, but it would seem that we all have a particular personality that facilitates us to operate within society and social groups in a particular way. Here we will briefly outline one personality test.

inner

place

THE ENNEAGRAM

The Enneagram is a popular theory of the different types of personality people have. Its origins are unclear. Some claim it originated from the Sufi practice of the master leading the disciple. Eventually, through different writings, it made its way to the West, where it has been used to map spiritual progress and differentiate personality types. According to the Enneagram, all of us have different personalities. Understanding the different personality types means that we can better understand the reasons why people behave the way they do. We can understand how we are all motivated in different ways and how we have different needs and energies. According to the Enneagram (from the Greek for 'nine points'), there are nine personality types and each is identified by its number. There are positive and negative aspects to each personality. The Enneagram is an important tool for personal development because it helps us to understand the needs and energies of ourselves, our friends and those with whom we work.

As you read through the nine personality types, you may recognise yourself or someone you know. You can research these in more detail with the help of your teacher.

Type One: These are the perfectionists in our midst and you'll find that their rooms and desks are very neat and tidy. They are very conscientious and honest, yet sometimes too critical of themselves and others.

Spiritual Growth: 'You shall love your neighbour as yourself.' (Mark 12:31)

In general, we are far too hard on ourselves. We never let up. Jesus teaches us that we are fundamentally good rather than flawed. We cannot love others unless we love ourselves.

inner

place

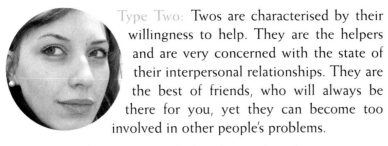

Type Two: Twos are characterised by their willingness to help. They are the helpers and are very concerned with the state of their interpersonal relationships. They are the best of friends, who will always be there for you, yet they can become too involved in other people's problems.

Spiritual Growth: 'At daybreak he departed and went into a deserted place. And the crowds were looking for him.' (Luke 4:42)

We need to give proper time to our own needs and so not allow our compulsive generosity to rule our lives. Saying 'No' to others should not make us feel guilty. They have no right to the last drop.

Type Three: Threes are very much success-orientated and are usually high achievers. They are more interested in their careers than in their relationships and are concerned very much with appearances, as they like to impress. They are usually optimistic and sociable but can become workaholics.

Spiritual Growth: 'An argument arose among them as to which one of them was the greatest. But Jesus, aware of their inner thoughts, took a little child and put it by his side, and said to them, "Whoever welcomes this child in my name welcomes me, and whoever welcomes me welcomes the one who sent me; for the least among all of you is the greatest".' (Luke 9:46–48)

Position, prestige and privilege cut no ice with Jesus. Our emphasis on the significant roles we play does not impress him.

Type Four: Fours are artistic and creative. They are in touch with their emotions and are comfortable with sadness and pain, and even seem to welcome it. They believe they are special and they enjoy one another's company. Much of the creativity in a culture

inner

place

comes from this type, but they can become depressive and wallow in emotive states without seeking help.

Spiritual Growth: 'Then Pilate took Jesus and had him flogged. And the soldiers wove a crown of thorns and put it on his head, and they dressed him in a purple robe.' (John 19:1)

Jesus experienced abandonment and rejection in dramatic fashion towards the end of his life. Yet, in spite of being humiliated, he relied on God's help and placed himself in God's care.

Type Five: These are the observers in a group and they prefer ideas to emotions or relationships. They need to be left alone to deal with problems by retracting into themselves. They often become academics and are amongst the best thinkers in the world. They can, however, be accused of being overly distant from everyday life.

Spiritual Growth: 'Give and it will be given to you.' (John 6:38)

Our unwillingness to risk sharing what we have with a generous heart frequently prevents us from receiving more ourselves. If we hoard what we have and are stingy with our gifts, we are unlikely to be open enough to receive the unexpected.

Type Six: Loyalty and friendship are important to sixes, but they are constantly fearful that something will go wrong, and so they mind their relationships very carefully. They find it difficult to make decisions because of their intense loyalty to whatever or whoever they pick. They make for very good friends.

Spiritual Growth: 'Then he said to Thomas, "Put your finger here and see my hands. Reach out your hand and put it in my side. Do not doubt but believe".' (John 20:27)

We like certainties and find it difficult to cope with doubt, ambiguity or loose ends. We are afraid of committing ourselves

inner

place

without supporting evidence. But God is patient with us and gently leads us to inner conviction and faith.

Type Seven: These people are fun-loving, energetic and outgoing types. They are great company. They suit teenage years because they are energised by socialising, yet often avoid painful situations or emotional problems. They are optimistic and are usually uplifting friends, yet some may view them as shallow.

Spiritual Growth: 'And everyone who hears these words of mine and does not act on them will be like the foolish man who built his house on sand. The rain fell, and the floods came, and the winds blew and beat against that house, and it fell – and great was its fall!' (Matthew 7:26–27)

Staying on the surface of life is ultimately doomed to failure. Real growth and long-term happiness demand rock-solid foundations of depth. Concentrating on the superficial is no way to build for the future.

Type Eight: These are very powerful characters who are motivated by powerful situations. They are outspoken and will react to perceived injustices against themselves and others. They will fight for what is right and will stand up to unjust structures. They can, however, appear as aggressive and intimidating at times.

Spiritual Growth: 'The Spirit of the Lord is upon me,
because he has anointed me to bring good news to the poor.
He has sent me to proclaim release to the captives
and recovery of sight to the blind,
to let the oppressed go free,
to proclaim the year of the Lord's favour.' (Luke 4:18–19)

We have been given power so that we can help those who are powerless. Our strength should be used to help the weak and the marginalised. Our words can speak for those who have no voice and our deeds can support those who need protection.

inner

place

Type Nine: These are the mediators and peacemakers in society. They avoid emotional conflict and try to resolve things peacefully, yet they often lack self-confidence. They are easygoing to the point of being accused of being lazy, but they have the extraordinary ability to do an amazing amount of work in a short space of time. They cram before exams.

Spiritual Growth: 'The hour is coming, indeed it has come, when you will be scattered, each one to his home, and you will leave me alone. Yet I am not alone because the Father is with me.' (John 16:32)

Our lack of a real sense of selves brings with it a deep loneliness. We feel empty inside, as if there is nobody at home. But Jesus reminds us that God's Spirit dwells within each of us. Once we realise that we, too, are important, and that we are never alone, we will not be afraid to make the inner journey to encounter the God in our hearts.

(The suggestions for spiritual growth are taken from *Enneagram 2: A Spirituality of Brokenness* by Eilis Bergin PBVM and Eddie Fitzgerald SDB.)

DISCUSS Why do you think it is important to realise that all of us have different personalities? How do you think this would help you to get on with other people? In what way does it help you to understand yourself?

inner

place

Chapter Thirteen

DEATH AND RESURRECTION

In May 1898, a shroud was put on public display in Turin, Italy. It bore a faint imprint of a man who had obviously been crucified. This piece of cloth became known as the shroud of Turin. The shroud is still in Turin and is revered by many as the cloth that covered the corpse of Jesus of Nazareth. It is one of the most fascinating and examined relics in modern history. Later we will learn more about the shroud and the macabre experiments that were carried out to ascertain its authenticity. But for the moment we need to examine how the historical Jesus of Nazareth came to meet his end. How did he die and what happened in a graveyard in Jerusalem on 9 April in 30 CE that gave birth to the largest and most widespread world religion? It is to those very questions that we will now turn.

THE PROPHET GOES TO JERUSALEM

Probably the single most documented historical fact about Jesus of Nazareth is that he was executed in Jerusalem during the reign of the procurator Pontius Pilate. Pilate represented Rome in Palestine and enforced its laws. Most importantly, he ensured that nobody posed a threat to Roman rule. Yet given Jesus' teachings about forgiveness and compassion, it is hard to understand how he would have been seen as a threat to anyone. The man who thought that you should turn the other cheek if struck, hardly seems the violent type. However, it must be remembered that Jerusalem was a volatile and very tense place, and it didn't take much for the Romans to remove someone, even if their level of threat wasn't

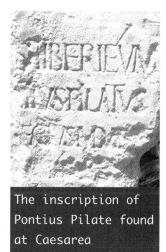

The inscription of Pontius Pilate found at Caesarea

significant. Pilate was known to be particularly ruthless, and one source at the time says that he used 'briberies, insults, outrages, wanton injuries, constantly repeated executions without trial, ceaseless and supremely grievous cruelty' (*Embassy to Gaius*, 302).

WHY WAS JESUS ARRESTED?

The Romans
It is easy now to say that Jesus posed no threat to the Romans, as he had no political ambitions, yet if he came to their attention and they did some homework on him, he might appear in a less saintly light. First, Jesus had a group of followers and, significantly for the Romans at least, one of the disciples was Simon the Zealot. The Zealots were those who believed in violent opposition to Rome. Another two disciples, the brothers James and John, were nicknamed 'Sons of Thunder'. So they were hardly choirboys. That's not to mention Judas 'Iscariot' or 'dagger man'. From Jesus' point of view, he included everyone in his group – sinners, Zealots and tax collectors. The kingdom was for all. Yet the Romans would have taken a different view. We know that Jesus wasn't a Zealot or violent character, so, out of the thousands in Jerusalem at Passover time, how did he manage to come to their attention?

The Jewish Authorities and the Temple
Earlier we reviewed some videos by REM and Nirvana that depicted Jesus as weak, enfeebled and pathetic. The following account of Jesus' activities in Jerusalem depicts him as anything but weak or pathetic. Throughout his ministry, Jesus attacked the Pharisees and their rigid interpretation of the Law. But that was up in Galilee, the middle of nowhere. Now he was in the capital where the Roman armed forces were based, along with the site of Jewish religious power, the Temple. If Jesus wanted to bring his message and ministry to the very heart of Judaism, then he would have to go to the Temple.

Many images of Jesus would have us believe he was harmless and nice. This Jesus would have walked into the Temple and said: 'Hi! I'm Jesus! I want to tell you all about happy things!' Big smile.

the
inner
place

'Have a nice day!' Nobody would have noticed. Just another in a long line of idiots from Galilee. Yet as for the real Jesus, when he went into the Temple, all hell broke loose.

This scene needs to be really imagined for all its dramatic impact. Imagine if your friend had a problem or grievance with your school principal. You follow them up to the office and wait outside. You expect to hear low voices, murmur, murmur, murmur. Imagine instead that you hear the principal's computer screen hitting the wall and the desk being overturned. This is not good, because your friend has just made a strike at the heart of authority and power in your school. There is only one end to that story: expulsion. That student has to be got rid of. Overturning the principal's desk impresses nobody.

Yet, this is exactly the way Jesus treated the Temple, the centre of Jewish power and authority. He had been wrecking people's worlds and attacking religious authority all the way through his ministry, through parables, miracles and gibes at the Pharisees, but this was the ultimate affront.

'Jesus Accused by the Pharisees' by Duccio Di Buoninsegna (1308–11)

'Then they came to Jerusalem. And he entered the Temple and began to drive out those who were selling and those who were buying in the Temple, and he overturned the tables of the money changers and the seats of those who sold doves; and he would not allow anyone to carry anything through the Temple' (Mark 11:15–16).

the inner place

DISCUSS

Do you think Jesus really was the rebellious type as feared by the Romans or, if not, what was it about him that got him into so much trouble?

WHY WAS JESUS PUT TO DEATH?

Jesus before the Sanhedrin

Jesus was arrested and brought before the Sanhedrin, the Jewish court of law, for his first trial. Jesus had broken religious laws by wrecking the Temple, but his real crime was his attack on Jewish authority. The Sanhedrin didn't just want him punished, they

wanted him removed from the situation. The Sanhedrin enjoyed a privileged existence under the Romans and didn't want anything or anybody to disrupt that relationship. They were fearful that Jesus might make a stir amongst the Jewish population, and part of their cosy relationship with the Romans was to keep the population peaceful. As Caiaphas, the high priest, stated: 'You know nothing at all! You do not understand that it is better for you to have one man die for the people than to have the whole nation destroyed' (John 11:49-50).

Yet the final insult to the Jewish authorities came when Caiaphas asked Jesus if he was the Messiah, the Son of God (Mark 14:61). The Jews were very strict in their belief that there was only one God. When Jesus replied: 'I am', there could only be one response. Jesus was now equating himself with God, and so he was immediately condemned of blasphemy. He must die. But there was a problem. The Sanhedrin could not kill anyone, only Pilate could do that job, so they had to convince Pilate that Jesus was a threat not only to them but to Roman authority. Jesus had already admitted that he was the Messiah, which was understood as a political title, so this provided enough ammunition to go to the Romans.

Jesus before Pilate

Pilate had no real interest in any religious crime that Jesus may have committed, but he would have been concerned if Jesus was a trouble-maker and disturbing the peace. Pilate's job was to keep Jerusalem peaceful, so anyone causing a stir was potentially a problem. As noted above, Passover time was particularly volatile because it celebrated the liberation of the Jews, and Jesus had a

the
inner
place

Death and Resurrection

dubious set of followers, Zealots among them. Pilate interrogated Jesus about the type of king he was, and was ultimately unconvinced that Jesus posed any type of threat. He had come into Jerusalem on a donkey. Hardly the leader of a revolution! Yet Pilate wanted to keep the Sanhedrin happy, so he had Jesus scourged and humiliated.

The Sanhedrin, however, were determined to have Jesus killed, and Pilate was forced to put Jesus and Barabbas before the crowd to choose between the two. One of them would die. The crowds, swayed by the Sanhedrin, picked Barabbas. Jesus was condemned to death. The crime was treason. Jesus had posed a threat to the State.

ASIDE

The Scala Sancta

In a church opposite the Basilica of St John Lateran in Rome may be found a set of stairs that pilgrims ascend on their knees. The stairs was brought to Rome in the fourth century and was taken from the headquarters of Pontius Pilate in Jerusalem. It is believed that Jesus went up these very steps when he faced trial before Pilate. Drops of blood that are visible on some glass-covered steps are allegedly from Christ's wounds.

QUESTIONS

1 Why did the Sanhedrin want Jesus put to death?
2 Why did the Sanhedrin get the Romans involved?

DISCUSS

Why might Pilate have been unconvinced that Jesus was really a threat to Roman authority?

the

inner

place

WAS THE MANNER OF JESUS' DEATH AS HORRIFIC AS PORTRAYED IN SOME FILMS?

The Execution

The film *The Passion of the Christ* depicts a very violent end to Jesus' life, yet evidence would seem to suggest that the manner of Jesus' torture and death was particularly horrific. The scourging gets little mention in the gospels, but evidence suggests it was a very gruesome procedure. Two men would have whipped Jesus with the scourges, which were tipped with shards of metal or bone. The scourges were designed to lacerate the flesh, and the entire body, back and front, would have been whipped and covered with bruises, cuts and blood. His flesh, veins and arteries would have been exposed by the incessant blows, and a severe scourging could even damage internal organs. Jesus' face may have been unrecognisable after the event and he would scarcely have been able to stand.

It was only about five hundred yards from the Antonia Fortress to Golgotha, where Jesus was crucified. It would have taken four Roman soldiers to crucify Jesus. His arms were first held taut over the crossbeam, which rested on the ground, and two nails were hammered into his wrists. Then the limp body was hoisted up onto the upright and affixed on a prepared notch. His feet were nailed to the wood, two nails through each tibia.

As Jesus hung on the cross, the real torture (not depicted in films) was his efforts to breathe. Due to exhaustion and shock, Jesus would naturally have slumped and hung simply from his wrists. Yet in this slumped position, with the arms extended

above the head, breathing was extremely difficult. He would then have had to place all his weight onto the nails in his feet, and in so straightening himself he could breathe once more. However, the excruciating pain on his feet, plus exhaustion, meant that he would have slumped again, only then to try to straighten his body to breathe once more. This was the horrific and torturous rhythm of movement that the condemned man had to endure. Eventually his arms would have become cramped, along with the chest wall. Breathing was now dependent on the walls of the diaphragm, which eventually would have cramped and failed. Unable to take a breath, Jesus suffocated to death. According to tradition, Jesus was later lanced in his side with a spear to ensure that he was dead.

ASIDE

What is the Veil of Veronica?
There exists a custom in the Vatican whereby three relics are bought out for public viewing in what is known as *ostensio* or 'public viewing'. They are the Veil of Veronica, a fragment of the true cross and the tip of the lance that pierced Christ's side. The Veil of Veronica is the veil with which St Veronica wiped Christ's face as he made his way to Calvary. It is believed that the features of his face are imprinted on the cloth.

St Veronica brought the cloth to Rome after she discovered it had healing powers, and she gave it to Pope Clement, who put it in the care of the Church. It was placed in the Vatican basilica, where it was worshipped by pilgrims, who believed it bore the true likeness of Christ.

DISCUSS

Christians believe that the human Jesus crucified on the cross was really the Son of God. How do you react to the brutal and merciless execution of God's own Son?

the
inner
place

HOW DO WE KNOW THAT THE RESURRECTION TOOK PLACE?

Our primary source of evidence about the Resurrection comes from the writings of St Paul and from the gospels. Within the gospels there are two resurrection narratives: the empty tomb and the appearances.

The Empty Tomb

The first tradition is the empty tomb. The gospels tell us that Mary Magdalene and some other women went to the tomb to anoint the body three days after Jesus died. The tomb was empty, even though a large stone had been put in front of it in case the body was stolen. In Mark, an angel informs the women: 'He is risen!' In John, the women tell Peter and another disciple who came to the tomb. Peter 'saw and believed'. Yet in Mark, when the others were told that the tomb was empty, they did not believe. Clearly they were not anticipating such an event.

Jesus' tomb

One particular problem some have with the empty tomb tradition is that they believe the disciples simply stole Jesus' body. Yet this is unlikely. A large stone was placed across the front to prevent such a stunt, and guards were placed to guard it. The more convincing reason, however, is the disciples' motivation. Jesus, their associate, had just been executed for treason. This was a serious crime, and disciples could be found guilty by association. So why would they steal the body of a criminal and a failure in order to implicate themselves in his treasonous activities? It would have made no sense.

Death and Resurrection

The Appearances

The evangelists were convinced that appearances of the risen Jesus took place. These accounts are important because the empty tomb on its own could easily point to the theory that the body was stolen. Significantly, the appearances were physical encounters. In John 21, Jesus eats breakfast on the lakeshore with the disciples. Earlier in the same gospel, in John 20, Jesus enters the room through closed doors and Thomas puts his hand in Jesus' side to help him believe it is really Jesus. Yet questions have been raised about the account of Jesus' appearances in the gospels.

'The Meal in Emmaus' by Rembrandt van Rijn (c.1628)

Were the appearances of Jesus simply that of a ghost? If Jesus was a ghost, then yes, he would have been able to walk through walls. But the Jesus of the appearance narratives was very physical, as noted above. According to accepted tradition, ghosts can't eat anything, nor can you touch them. Just as well.

Perhaps Jesus never really died and they simply resuscitated him? Some believe that the disciples used a concoction of herbs to put Jesus to sleep, only to resuscitate him later. Yet the evidence against this is that it is a historical fact that Pilate crucified Jesus. Those who crucified him were paid to do it, and they usually did their job very well. Usually, a criminal was only crucified, but Pilate had Jesus scourged first because he felt it might keep the Jewish leadership happy. Therefore, when Jesus eventually was put on the cross, he was in a very weakened state. Survival was unlikely and, as it was the Sabbath the next day, the guards had to ensure that he was dead, and so they lanced him in the side.

There is also a second reason to suggest that Jesus wasn't resuscitated, and it centres around Jesus' actual physical appearance. Again, in John's gospel, his appearance in the room through a closed door suggests he wasn't exactly the same earthly Jesus. In John and in Luke, the disciples crucially don't recognise him. In Luke 24, the disciples are on the way to Emmaus but they fail to recognise Jesus until he is at table with them and breaks the bread. If he had merely been resuscitated, they would have

the
inner
place

recognised him instantly. Instead, Jesus had risen from the dead and was not merely the earthly Jesus restored to life.

Perhaps the disciples just made up the whole thing? Firstly, as noted above, it would have been foolish to invent the story that a treasonous criminal was still around and meeting up with his associates. Secondly, the primary witnesses to the appearances and empty tomb were women. At the time, women could not give evidence in a court of law, as their testimony wasn't deemed credible. If the disciples were going to make up the story, they wouldn't have picked women as the primary witnesses.

DISCUSS

In your opinion, does the evidence suggest that the Resurrection really took place, or did Jesus' followers just make up the story?

ASIDE

Jesus' shoe size
According to an ancient tradition, when St Peter was fleeing Rome after his imprisonment, he met Jesus on the old Appian Way. Peter said to him, 'Lord, where are you going?' 'Domine, quo vadis?' Seemingly, Jesus left his footprints on a cobblestone. A cast of his 'footprints' is in the church called 'Quo Vadis'. According to the cast, he wore a ten and three-quarter sandal.

Appian Way

The Shroud of Turin – Evidence of Jesus' Death and Resurrection?
At the time of Jesus' crucifixion, it was common for the bodies of executed criminals to be thrown into a ditch once they were confirmed dead. Only a person of standing would have been able to go to Pilate and ask for Jesus' body. All of the gospels agree that Joseph of Arimathea took Jesus' body from the cross, and John mentions how he was helped by Nicodemus. Joseph interred the body in a tomb belonging to his own family.

the inner place

According to John's gospel, they embalmed the body in accordance with Jewish custom. Yet they probably didn't have sufficient time, given the proximity of the Sabbath, and the synoptic gospels agree that Jesus' body was simply placed in a shroud.

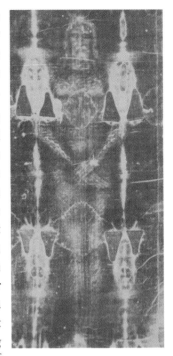

In May 1898, a shroud was put on public display in Turin, Italy. It measured fourteen feet by three and a half. On the cloth was a faint imprint of a man who had obviously been crucified. According to many, this was simply a medieval forgery, yet a good one. There were bloodied marks on the wrists and feet – obvious signs of crucifixion. Yet there was something very odd about the marks on the shroud. Unlike in an ordinary crucifixion, in this case the man had also been scourged. Later tests revealed that the man had been bent over a post and whipped by two men with scourges that had three thongs, and at the end of each thong were five strands, each weighted with two pieces of lead. The man on the shroud had been hit 120 times by two men. The marks cover him from the top of his head to the soles of his feet. Along with the scourge marks, there was a bloodied mark on his side. His head was also covered with wounds. Crucially, the man on the shroud bore the marks of Christ's crucifixion.

For the first time, in May 1898, the shroud was photographed by a man named Paul Vignon. Later towards midnight in his apartment, the photographer removed the first of two plates from the developing fluid. What he saw almost made him drop the plates. Instead of the blurred, indistinct image on the shroud, he was now looking at a very distinct face. If this was a forgery, then it was extraordinarily clever, for its real impact was only as a photographic negative. What painter would have thought of forging a photographic negative? Also, the shroud first came to light in the fourteenth century, many hundreds of years before the invention of photography.

In May 1931, the shroud was displayed again, and this time a French anatomist, Pierre Barbet, examined photographs of the shroud in minute detail. The first problem was that a nail that had penetrated the wrist had emerged on the back of the hand. Surely

the inner place

it should emerge through the other side of the wrist. A forger's mistake? So Barbet nailed a corpse's wrist, and when the nail hit the bone, it emerged on the back of the hand, the exact same spot as on the photograph. The shroud also showed two different blood stains for the wrists, but a man hanging on a cross would have shifted position in order to relieve the weight from the feet, as we noted earlier. Barbet also noted the blood and water marks on the side. As part of his investigation, he thrust a knife into a corpse above the heart – the result was blood and water, or pericardial fluid.

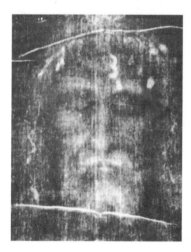

In June 1969, Cardinal Pellegrino decided to determine by scientific means whether the shroud was a forgery or not. A scientific commission was set up and for two days examined the shroud. They removed minute samples. Among the samples were pieces of pollen. Significantly, some of these were traced back to the Jordan valley in Israel, others to France, Turkey and Italy. It constitutes powerful evidence that the shroud indeed originated in the Holy Land. In 1976, other startling discoveries were made, this time by two American scientists who were experts in 'image-enhancement'. This was a process that was developed for space probes, to change two-dimensional images of Martian landscapes into three-dimensional images. When they subjected the shroud to this technique, a clearly defined three-dimensional image appeared of the head. Crucially, it would have been impossible for a painter to produce an image with such detail for the computer to produce this statue-like image. They also discovered that two coins had been placed over the eyes, two 'leptons' – the exact same coins as mentioned in the parable of the widow's mite.

In 1988, carbon-14 dating tests were carried out on the shroud, which dated it at between 1260 and 1390 CE. It seemed that the shroud was a medieval forgery after all. But in a further twist to the tale, recent research discovered that the piece of the shroud that was used for the dating was actually a piece that had been sown in after the shroud was damaged by fire. The piece dated

the

inner

place

Death and Resurrection

was not an original piece of cloth. To date, the mystery of the Shroud of Turin remains just that, a mystery.

What are Stigmata?

The Capuchin friar Padre Pio was born in 1887 in Italy, and at seventeen he joined the monastery. For eleven years everything was fine, but in September of 1915 he began to feel pains in his hands, feet and side. Three years later, the monk collapsed at the altar of the church in Foggia. When the others found him, he was unconscious, but there was also something quite incredible about his body. He was bleeding from his hands, feet and side. No doctor could heal the wounds and he would bear them until the end of his days.

Padre Pio

In Christianity, the word 'stigmata' refers to marks that appear on a person's body that correspond to the wounds Christ received during the Passion. The marks therefore appear on the hands/wrists, feet, side and head. Often these marks form wounds that bleed. In some cases, the blood found in the wounds can actually be of a different type than the person's own blood. Sometimes the wounds have exuded a perfume. Most times the marks are visible, but in the case of Catherine of Sienna they were invisible. One of the first documented cases of stigmata is that of Francis of Assisi in 1224. It was reported that the skin that grew out of his wounds formed into calluses that bore the shape of nails.

As yet, there has been no conclusive explanation for this phenomenon. Those who have stigmata are always very devout, and often the wounds become more painful. Some argue that stigmata are psychosomatic wounds brought on by the power of the person's own unconscious and extreme levels of worship. Alternatively, stigmata could genuinely be the manifestation of a divine gift that can be classified with the extraordinary phenomena associated with mysticism. Officially, church authorities have responded with caution when authenticating cases of stigmatisation. The Catholic Church has on rare occasions accepted the occurrence of stigmata as authentic but has never defined the origin or nature of the phenomenon.

the
inner
place

Chapter Fourteen

THE EARLY CHRISTIAN MOVEMENT

In this chapter, we will learn about the early Christian community, which was founded on its faith in the resurrection of Jesus from the dead. Unfortunately, these early followers were to endure a prolonged and systematic reign of persecutions under successive emperors. Christianity only became legalised in the fourth century, when the emperor Constantine was converted to Christianity. Faith in the risen Christ lasted for three centuries under threat of torture and death. Using today's calendar, if Christ had been crucified in 1723, his followers would have endured persecutions right up until today. For three hundred years, the early Christians endured torture, humiliation and even death for their faith.

ASIDE

A Tomb is Found

According to a very ancient tradition, the apostle Peter was executed by the emperor Nero in Rome during the first century. He is regarded as the first bishop of Rome and, accordingly, the first pope. It was believed that he was buried in a cemetery near to Nero's circus. A special shrine was erected over the grave in the second century. Then in the fourth century, the emperor Constantine erected a basilica on the site. During the Renaissance, this basilica was replaced with the present St Peter's Basilica.

St Peter's Basilica

Recent excavations in the Vatican and under St Peter's uncovered an ancient cemetery. It was decided that a team of archaeologists should carry out further excavations – under the ancient cemetery. The team had to work very carefully, as they were directly underneath the altar of the basilica, along with its massive canopy. Under the cemetery, the archaeologists found a white marble sarcophagus. They bored a small hole in the wall of the tomb and inside they found a skeleton. Forensic tests dated the skeleton to the first century. It belonged to a man who was in his sixties when he died. His death was caused by crucifixion. St Peter, according to Christian tradition, was crucified upside down. The marks on the skeleton revealed that this man had been crucified – but upside down. Though it can never be conclusively proven, it would appear that the altar in St Peter's Basilica is located directly above the remains of St Peter, first bishop of Rome and first pope.

RESPONSE TO THE RESURRECTION

Most of our information about the early Christian Church comes, not from the gospels but from another book in the New Testament, the Acts of the Apostles. It was written by Luke, who also wrote Luke's gospel. The Acts of the Apostles details the experiences of the followers of Jesus after his death and resurrection.

It is important to note that these same followers never anticipated that Jesus would rise from the dead. They had no previous concept of what that might even mean. Yet after the Resurrection, they were faced with the challenge of trying to understand what it meant. If Jesus rose from the dead, then what did that say about him?

Initially after Jesus' death, the disciples were afraid for their lives. Jesus was executed for treason and, by implication, they too could get into serious trouble. In fact, immediately after Jesus'

the

inner

place

Coptic painting

arrest, Peter denied him three times. Yet, according to the Acts of the Apostles, their attitude changed when the day of Pentecost came around. On Pentecost, the followers gathered in one room and 'all of them were filled with the Holy Spirit' (Acts 2:4). This event is regarded as the birth of the Christian Church because it was then, spirit filled, that the followers began their mission to spread the good news. But what exactly would they say?

In Acts, we are told that from the beginning Peter emerged as a leader of the Church, and it is Peter who first announces that Jesus is the Messiah, God's specially anointed one. Before the Resurrection, the disciples may have still believed that the Messiah was the one who would liberate them from the Romans. But the Resurrection was to affect their understanding of who Jesus was in a radical manner. He was not just another prophet or miracle-worker. He was the Messiah or, in Greek, 'Christos'. Jesus was the Christ. As Peter proclaims:

'Therefore let the entire house of Israel know with certainty that God has made him both Lord and Messiah.'

(Acts 2:36)

the inner place

DISCUSS

1   Why did the followers of Jesus initially deny any involvement with him?
2   What event is regarded as the birth of the Christian Church?
3   What gave the followers the courage to preach about Jesus?

NEW IMAGES FOR JESUS

It is clear from Peter's profession of faith that the first thing that the early Christians had to do was find new images to explain who Jesus was. The first image that they used was that of Christ. Jesus was the promised messiah, yet his was not a political revolution. Instead, Jesus the Messiah or Jesus Christ brought about a spiritual revolution. Jesus sacrificed his own life so that all would be saved.

The disciples had great difficulty trying to understand Jesus' death on the cross. Why would the Messiah have to die in such an appalling and embarrassing manner? The early Christians had to search for images to try to convey what happened at Golgotha, what happened on the first Good Friday. They went back into their Jewish history. There they found a story and an image that could easily be reinterpreted for Christians, as they tried to grapple with the meaning of Jesus' death.

ASIDE

The Catacombs

In the sixteenth century, a series of underground tunnels was found in Italy, especially in Rome. These subterranean chambers were the burial places of the early Christians. They were known as the catacombs. Under persecution,

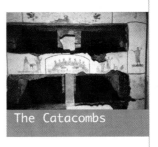

The Catacombs

it was advantageous for Christians to meet out of sight so that they wouldn't be caught or reported to the authorities, who banned such gatherings. The catacombs were channelled underground for several miles and, on either side, chambers were dug out to receive the dead. Martyrs and popes were also buried underground when sometimes the Eucharist was celebrated near an important grave. In the nineteenth century, the scientific study of art in the catacombs began revealing many significant frescos and images that gave invaluable insights into the beliefs and practices of the early Christians.

the inner place

THE LAMB OF GOD

In the book of Exodus we are told the story of the liberation of the Hebrews (Jews) from their Egyptian overlords. Yahweh (God) sent Moses to free the Hebrews from slavery, and to help him Yahweh sent plagues on Egypt. The Pharaoh was stubborn. Eventually Yahweh sent the final and terrible plague – the death of the first-born male in each household. Yet the homes of the Hebrews would be saved. That night the angel of death would pass over their homes and their lives would be spared. This would be known as the Passover. The next morning the people had won their liberation and they were free. Yet to what did they attribute their freedom?

On the night of Passover, they were given special instructions. They had to prepare some unleavened bread (bread with no yeast). They also had to sacrifice a lamb and put its blood on the doorpost. This would mark their house and the angel of death would pass over. In the years to come, the Hebrews would always claim that they were saved by the blood of the lamb, the sacrificial lamb.

the inner place

Now when the early Christians were searching for a way to understand the cross, they looked to the Passover lamb. The lamb had been sacrificed to save the Hebrews of old from slavery and death. Now the Christians believed that Jesus had been sacrificed to save them also. Jesus was the new lamb, the new Passover, and it was his blood that was shed so that many might be saved.

THE PERSECUTIONS AND THE SPREAD OF CHRISTIANITY

As soon as the early Christians began to preach about Jesus, they once again came to the attention of the Sanhedrin. Peter and the other apostles were warned about preaching about Jesus and were even arrested and flogged (Acts 5:40). One of the early Christians, Stephen, eventually paid the ultimate price. He was brought before the Sanhedrin where he argued his case, but he was accused of blasphemy and was eventually stoned to death by members of the Sanhedrin (Acts 7). This was witnessed and approved of by a Jew named Saul, who eventually became Paul. More of him later. After the death of Stephen, intense persecutions of the Christians began in Jerusalem.

In order to escape the persecutions, many Christians fled Jerusalem, but as they did they brought the good news of Jesus with them. Peter and John travelled to Samaria to spread the message. In Caesarea, however, something extremely significant happened that would change the face of Christianity for ever. Up until this point, it was only Jews who were followers of Jesus, but in Caesarea Peter baptised non-Jews or Gentiles. While this caused controversy back in Jerusalem, from then on it was not necessary to be a Jew first before one could be a Christian. Christianity would quickly spread throughout Palestine and eventually to the rest of the Mediterranean.

Nero

The worst persecutions, however, were in Rome. They began around 64 CE when the emperor Nero burned part of the city. In order to diffuse blame, he turned his attention to a small group known as the Christians. They had a bad reputation anyway. They were accused of cannibalism and atheism because they refused to worship the Roman gods. The persecution lasted for another three hundred years. Under Valerian, a most savage phase of persecutions began. Christians were imprisoned, exiled, tortured and forced into slavery. Many prominent Christians suffered,

including Cyprian, bishop of Carthage, and Pope Sixtus II. Many others were burned at the stake. The final phase of persecutions began with the emperor Diocletian, who attempted to eliminate Christianity completely. The persecutions ended with the conversion of the emperor Constantine who, in 313 CE, produced the Edict of Milan, which granted religious freedom to Christians.

QUESTIONS

1 Why were the early Christians persecuted?
2 When did the worst persecutions begin?

DISCUSS

Given the length of time that the persecutions lasted, why do you think the early Christians persevered with their faith?

ST PAUL AND THE EARLY CHRISTIAN COMMUNITIES

Earlier we mentioned that when Stephen was being stoned, the whole affair was witnessed by Saul. Saul was a Jew who persecuted Christians, but according to the Acts of the Apostles he had a conversion experience while on his way to Damascus. Jesus appeared to him and said: 'Saul, Saul, why do you persecute me?' (Acts 9:4) He was blinded by the experience but later recovered his sight and was baptised. Saul, who became Paul, began to spread the message of Christ and became one of the greatest ever Christian missionaries.

Paul undertook three journeys around the Mediterranean, and everywhere he stopped and visited he started a new Christian community. Later he wrote letters to these same communities, supporting and encouraging them. So, for example, when Paul visited Corinth in Greece during his second journey, he later wrote a letter to the community there. These same letters are read today at Mass, usually for the second reading. The letter that Paul wrote to the community at Corinth is known today as St Paul's Letter to the Corinthians.

We get many of our insights into the life of these early Christian communities from Paul's letters. Here we will examine St Paul's Letter to the Philippians to discover the lifestyle, belief and behaviour of an early Christian community.

THE COMMUNITY AT PHILIPPI

Philippi was a city located in north-eastern Greece, about ten miles from the Hegean Sea. It was the first Christian community that Paul founded in Europe, and many think it was his favourite.

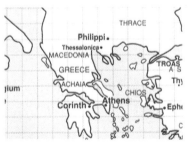

What was distinctive about many Christian communities was that they shared all their goods in common. We also learn about this from the Acts of the Apostles, where we are told: 'All who believed were together and had all things in common' (Acts 2:44). In Philippi, they developed a culture of sharing, and once when Paul was in prison they sent money to him. This remarkable lifestyle was based on

the

inner

place

Philippi today

their belief in the abundance of God. They believed that 'God will fully satisfy every need of yours (Philippians 4:19).

Another aspect of life in the Christian community at Philippi was their attitude of love towards one another. This attitude included sharing, support and forgiveness, and it was modelled on Jesus' love for them. A central element of this letter is the hymn in chapter 2. Here we read how Christ 'humbled himself and became obedient to the point of death, even death on a cross' (Philippians 2:8). Jesus humbled himself and accepted death because of his love for us. St Paul tells the community that they must model their love for one another on Christ's love for them: 'Let the same mind be in you that was in Jesus Christ' (Philippians 2:5).

Despite their attitudes of love for one another, the community at Philippi also experienced tensions with those outside the community. They were facing considerable antagonism from fellow citizens because of their lifestyle, which was a challenge to the prevailing culture at the time. St Paul tells them not to be 'intimidated by your opponents' (Philippians 1:28). In 3:2 he tells them to 'beware of the dogs'. Here he is referring to the Jewish Christians who were still insisting that a person had to be circumcised and become a Jew before they could become a Christian. Yet Paul encouraged them to get on as best they could with their fellow citizens and to try to be a 'shining example' for them. They should accept all that is good in their community, while rejecting all that is false. Some seem to have been able to stand up for themselves. Paul encouraged them to be strong in the face of adversity, telling them that 'it is God who gives you the victory' (Philippians 1:28).

the inner place

DISCUSS
1 What kind of lifestyle did the early Christians have?
2 What kind of relationship did they have with non-Christians?

SECTION C

MORALITY

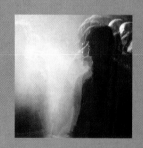

Chapter Fifteen

BECOMING MORAL

WHY BE MORAL?

Morality is concerned with how different human situations and experiences are considered right or wrong. A characteristic of being human is freedom and choice. Based on our intellect, we can make decisions and decide what is the right thing to do. Simply because we might know the right thing to do doesn't necessarily mean that we do it. Freedom means we can do either the right thing or the wrong thing.

Morality is a natural human phenomenon, as people in every culture and society decide what constitutes right or wrong behaviour for their group. As humans, we have a sense of when something is a moral situation. We have a sense of when something is wrong. Morality is not just some cold intellectual faculty, but is a complex process that involves our reason and emotions. We might not always do the right thing, but our morality can often give us a sense of what the right thing to do should be.

In the following extract, the journalist India Knight reflects on how teenagers can sometimes treat one another. It is about teenagers being mean in the extreme. She reflects on the first time she witnessed a teenage group attacking another teenager.

> For me it was four years ago, on a London bus, just after school had ended. The top deck was invaded by 10- or 12-14 year olds, who were beating up another girl and dragging her up and down by her hair. The other people on the bus were, obviously, horrified, but none of them (myself included) moved to help: you could see each one having the

"What if they stab me/kick me in the head?" thought.

Eventually the bus conductor opened the doors and let the girls, who were wearing school uniforms, out. One of them had a little Hello Kitty rucksack. They dragged the hysterical, bleeding girl by her hair down a side street and out of sight, where God knows what happened. Everyone left behind looked as if they were about to be sick and reached for their mobiles. Their school would have been alerted at least, though I doubt the police got there in time.

I avoided that bus route for years, and then moved away. Thinking about that bus journey, and about what I completely failed to do – that is intervene in any way whatsoever – still makes me feel guilty, pathetic and angry. Those feelings of anger came back last week when a friend was telling me about her fifteen-year-old son, who is at one of east London's many dire sink schools. He's had problems being bullied before, but when he came home last week and ran upstairs without saying hello, and locked himself in his bedroom, his mother knew something was wrong.

Eventually she got him to explain what had happened: he'd been beaten up by six girls in the year above him. When they'd finished they'd each spat on him. They spat so much that he was covered in their saliva as he walked home, being jeered at and trying with all his might not to cry.

(The Sunday Times, 12/6/05)

,

the

inner

place

QUESTIONS

1   In the above story, what suggests to you that the journalist knew she was faced with a moral situation when she was on the bus?

2   Why did she not intervene, and how did it make her feel afterwards?

Becoming Moral

DISCUSS

1   How do you feel when you read such accounts of bullying by teenagers?
2   Do you feel that it is a moral situation – that it has to do with something being right or wrong? What makes you think this?
3   Do you think teenagers can be excessively mean to one another? Why is that so? Share your stories with the class.

REASONS FOR BEING MORAL

People have different reasons for being moral. There are both human and religious reasons for being moral. In the above story, the journalist felt 'pathetic' and 'guilty' for not intervening in the moral situation. She seemed to know what she should do, but just didn't do it. Yet clearly she would have been happier for doing the right thing. Her morality wasn't based on any religious sense, but instead was based on her own humanity. She knew that to intervene would have been the right thing to do, but she also valued her own safety.

Our own humanity can cause us to assess moral situations and, ultimately, enable us to lead happier lives. But we can also have a moral sense based on the laws of the land. We might have a sense of duty to uphold the law. The State creates a legal system that enforces laws.

People can also be moral for religious reasons. If a person has faith in God and believes that they are a follower, then they will try to obey God's laws on how we should relate to God, ourselves and the world around us. In the Christian tradition, morality is also a way of expressing and responding to God's love for us. We will examine the role of religion in morality in more detail later.

As we've mentioned, there are different reasons for being moral. A genuinely religious person will be a moral person, but a moral person need not necessarily be a religious person. Most of us react to moral situations, but often for very different reasons. Consider the following true story.

the inner place

Policeman in Trouble

Jack D. dropped out of school at fifteen and embarked on a life of petty crime. He wasn't much of a criminal and, after a spell in jail, he decided to go straight. He settled down, got a job with a construction firm, married, had a little son and even had his own place. Things were going well, probably for the first time in his life. All he had to do was stay out of trouble, stay away from his old friends and associates, and he would be fine.

He arrived for work at 8 p.m. and settled down to the night that lay ahead of him. His job involved doing the night-shift on the construction of a new road just on the outskirts of town. He drove a Caterpillar D9, a massive bulldozer. Jack had a temper, and sometimes he liked his job because he took his frustrations out on the earth and dirt and gravel that he had to shove around.

It was getting dark when Jack noticed a police car speed into the construction site. He was alone on the night-shift and his first reaction was to get out and run. Jack had done time for some crimes, but others had been swept under the carpet, so to speak, in his own mind at least. His mind raced as he tried to think of what they may have caught up with him for. But the car sped past him and on down to a lower ridge, where the new road stopped short. The lights kept flashing their warning blues and reds and Jack just wanted to turn his machine around and go the other way. He started up the V12 engine and began to turn away, but his head was doing a spin; maybe he should go down and see what was up. The other week the police came for a homeless man who had been found unconscious and they took him to hospital. Though he didn't particularly want to get involved with the cops, Jack felt in some way responsible, and so he trundled on down to the police car. If he could help, he would.

When he reached the car, the policeman was in an absolute panic. He explained his situation.

the
inner
place

Becoming Moral

A call had come in that a woman was in a medical emergency and, with the nearest hospital nine miles away, the policeman took the call and said he would go to assist. He was sure the road he was on led to the housing estate, but instead it was still under construction. Ahead was a twenty-foot drop.

Jack listened intently while shielding his face in the shadows for fear of being recognised.

The policeman was almost in tears, so Jack decided to help out his old enemies. A twenty-foot drop was nothing to his D9. He told the policeman to back up his car and follow him as he dug a trench through the earth and down to the road the policeman wanted to be on.

The car sped off in a hail of dirt and grit and Jack went back to work feeling good that for once he was on the right side of the law. He quit his shift at 7.30 a.m. and took his van home. When he got in, he found his wife sitting up sobbing in the sitting room. She was holding their son tightly and tears were flowing down her cheeks. Through her sobs she told him about the piece of food that had lodged in their son's throat, about her panic and about the policeman who arrived just in time to save their son's life.

DISCUSS

1 Would you consider Jack to be a morally upright type of person?
2 What sort of a conflict was going on inside his head when he saw the police car?
3 Why do you think Jack eventually helped the policeman?
4 What were the consequences for Jack of doing the right thing?
5 Why do you think Jack reacted the way he did? Was he motivated by the law, his religious convictions or his own humanity?

the

inner

place

ACTIONS AND CONSEQUENCES

When Jack saw the police car, his first thought was of the consequences for himself getting involved with the law: 'If I get involved, maybe I'll get in trouble' (bad history there). But then he thinks again and remembers how a homeless man was recently taken away by the police to hospital. Now he is considering the consequences for others and not just himself. If he does nothing, if he turns away, there might be serious consequences for someone else.

When faced with moral dilemmas, we first think of the consequences of our actions. In an earlier section, we examined the parable of the Good Samaritan, and studies which show that often people will not help another in trouble. We don't want to get involved in case we get in trouble ourselves. Sometimes there seems to be an instinct of self-preservation that overrides all other thoughts. Jack thought about self-preservation first, only later thinking about the needs of others.

GROUP WORK

What would you do in the following situations? In all of these situations, consider the possible consequences for yourself and others if you decide to do nothing.

a You're bringing your pet dog for a walk. He has been in the family for eight years and he was given to you as a birthday present. Going through a park, he suddenly takes off after a young child and really frightens her. He's unusually aggressive. At home they've been saying his personality has changed, perhaps it's old age. You know he might have to be put down if they discover that he is becoming aggressive with people.

Becoming Moral

b There's a particular student in school whom you are wary of, as he has a violent reputation. One day you see him going through another student's locker. He sees you looking at him. He takes something from the locker and then strolls up to you and eyeballs you for a few seconds. Then off he goes.

c On a night out, you see a guy being set upon by three other youths. They begin to kick him on the ground and one guy begins to kick him in the head. You have a mobile phone and it's a fairly crowded area.

d You start to work in a new restaurant belonging to a friend of the family. The restaurant isn't doing that well. You know nobody, but one girl working on the till befriends you. Eventually you notice that when her own friends come in, she only charges them for a glass of milk, even though they have a full tray of food.

e You have befriended a girl at school who is usually a loner. You felt sorry for her. But now she has attached herself to you and follows you everywhere. Your friends are getting a bit annoyed. At lunchtime, just as you and your friends are planning a night out on Saturday, this girl sits down beside you at the table. Do you tell her what's happening or not?

the
inner
place

From your discussions, some points may have emerged. If we simply consider the consequences for ourselves in a situation and don't think about the consequences for others, something bad might happen. Central to morality is the need to develop an awareness of the consequences of our actions for ourselves and others.

Most would agree that speeding on our roads is wrong, but that doesn't necessarily mean that there will be disastrous consequences for everyone who speeds. Yet the moral person is aware that doing the wrong thing can, and often does, have unfortunate consequences for all involved. Examine the following story in the light of actions and their consequences.

Joyriding with a Difference

Michael J. was the type of guy that everybody looked up to, not in any kind of genuine way, but he had this aura of cool about him. His daddy was rich and he was one of the few who had access to a top-of-the-range BMW. He boasted constantly about being with different girls, but they were always strangers, so nobody knew whether the stories were true or not. Anybody who knew him recognised him for the rich, brash idiot that he was. Yet that didn't stop the hangers-on who were in some way mesmerised by his wealth.

When Declan joined the class late from another school, Michael 'befriended' him, but he never really had any idea of what friendship was about. For Michael, friendship was simply a sign of popularity and power. Some guys hung around with him because they were bullied into it. Michael invited Declan out with him and a few lads, but his purpose was simply to poke fun at the new guy, bully him as a sign of his power. This was one plan that would gloriously backfire.

After a while on the town, Michael, Declan and two others in the know approached Michael's dad's car. Michael pretended it wasn't his own and asked Declan if he felt like going joyriding in it. Michael

the inner place

boasted about being able to break into any car, and Declan was obviously uncomfortable and didn't want to get into trouble. He protested, saying it wasn't the right thing to do, it was someone else's car, but Michael kept the pressure on. If he wanted to hang around with the lads, he'd have to join in. Declan wanted to make some friends. He valued friendship and having a few pals, and so he gave into the pressure and clambered into the back.

After 'breaking' into his own car, Michael 'hotwired' it. He tore off, wheels spinning, and the hangers-on goaded him on. They drove at speed around the car-park and were interrupted by what sounded like Declan getting sick in the back of the car. But it wasn't.

Declan had moved schools because he had fallen in with joyriders before. He wasn't getting sick. Instead, remembering his old ways, he was happily ripping the leather seats to pieces with his penknife.

GROUP WORK

Break into groups and think of examples where people's actions can have bad consequences for others. You could take examples from the following possibilities: lying, cheating, all forms of bullying, peer pressure, dishonesty, etc. Identify situations where people can really get hurt because of the actions of others.

the

inner

place

THE ROLE OF VALUES

In the story of the 'joyriders', the farcical situation arose out of a clear absence of values. If people have good values, they usually act responsibly. In that story, some people clearly lacked values. What values do you think were lacking in that situation and by whom? Alternatively, in the story of the policeman in trouble, what values do you think Jack displayed?

A value can be described as a desired quality or characteristic of thought that we consider good, worthwhile and important. There are many obvious examples, such as honesty, loyalty, care of others, and safety of oneself and others. Values play an important role in morality, because we apply them to any situation that requires a moral decision. It is our values that often determine the type of moral decisions we make.

DISCUSS

1 Describe the kind of values that you think are important in a friendship.
2 What kind of values are important in your school and when would you see them in action?

the

inner

place

Wedding Dilemma

Dear Abby: Recently I attended the wedding of a good friend. Because I am a photojournalist by trade, she asked me if I would videotape her wedding, and I gladly agreed. The wedding was beautiful and the reception went smoothly until the bride's father stopped the band to make an announcement. He said

he had 'lost' his wallet, which contained $1,500, with which he had intended to pay the band. He said if anyone found the money, it could be returned simply by leaving it in the men's lavatory, and no questions would be asked. No money was turned in.

The following day, I looked over the footage I had taken at the reception and was astonished to see that while filming the couple's conversation, in the background was the groom removing a wallet from the evening coat of the bride's father.

Now I don't know what to do. The couple is away for two weeks on their honeymoon. Should I tell my friend? Should I tell her father? Or should I just keep it to myself?

(Jan Harold Brunvand, *Too Good to be True*)

1   What conflict of values would you say is going on in the photojournalist's mind?
2   What advice would you give to her?

the

inner

place

Here are some other examples of how our values affect our moral decisions:

- If a person values **honesty**, they will return the money if they are given too much change in a shop.

- In friendship, if a person values **loyalty**, they will not disclose a secret.

- If a person values **trust**, they will not betray their parents' wishes.

- If a person values their own **safety** and that of others, they will not drink and drive.

- If a person values **courage**, they will stand up for the victim of a bully.

Morality is usually a fairly complex matter. One reason is because sometimes we can have a conflict of values. In the story of the 'joyriders', Declan seemed to value that it was 'someone else's car'. But Declan also valued his need for friendship and acceptance into the group. Declan chose one value over another, but in the process he chose a value that was good for him and not for others. We know the consequences.

Often a conflict of values occurs between group values and personal values. In school, an individual might place a value on the safety of students, and so believe that bullying is wrong. The same person might value the importance of friendship. But what happens if that person's friends get involved in bullying and invite them to join in? Another person might value their health and fitness, but their friends want to go out and get seriously drunk at weekends.

the inner place

DISCUSS

Can you think of other examples where there arises a conflict between personal and group values? What should the individual do in those situations?

Here's another example of a conflict of values. A mother may value honesty, but if her children are hungry she may be tempted to steal simply to feed her children because she values their welfare. Read the following true story.

Looting in New Orleans

In 2005, hurricanes lashed the coast of America, and New Orleans was worst hit. All essential services were destroyed. Aid organisations raced to the scene of desperation.

They witnessed a situation where the police were given instructions to shoot anybody seen looting so as the city wouldn't descend into anarchy. One aid-worker described the situation: 'We've seen desperate people walking out of

shops with diapers, food, water and so on,' Dr Nash said. 'I don't deny there are some inappropriate things going on but I don't think we should be arresting people for taking food and water. They're not looting, they're surviving. Nevertheless, police have said they intend to stamp out looting by whatever means necessary.'

(*The Guardian*, 1/9/05)

DISCUSS

1 In the above situation, do you think it is morally wrong to take food and supplies from a supermarket without paying for them? How do you justify your answer?

2 Were the authorities right to 'stamp out looting by whatever means necessary'?

3 Do you think the owners of the supermarkets cease to have any rights to their property in such situations? Give reasons for your answer.

the

inner

place

Read the following account and then discuss the questions.

Deirdre enjoyed a great relationship with her parents and she had built up a good trust with them. When she asked to be allowed go out, there didn't seem to be a problem, but they wanted her home by 2 a.m. at the latest. They gave her money to get home safely in a taxi and they explained that they didn't mind her going out, but she wasn't to drink.

When Deirdre met up with her friends at the club, everyone was in great form. They were joined by some lads whom the girls fancied. Before long, they were buying Deirdre drink, and then before she knew it she was buying rounds for them. She didn't particularly want to drink but she wanted to fit in, and anyway there was a lad there whom she fancied. She kind of thought about what her parents had said and she felt really guilty.

Everything was going great until the time came to go home. All Deirdre's money for the taxi was gone, but one of the lads had a car and offered them all a lift home. Someone asked if he had been drinking and he said he hadn't. Deirdre had seen him down at least five drinks. She knew he was lying through his teeth but he obviously wanted to impress with the car. Deirdre's mind was in a complete muddle. If she took the lift, she'd get home on time and her parents

the

inner

place

would continue to trust her, but by doing so she was risking her own life, and if she didn't warn the others she was risking their lives as well. If she didn't take the lift, she'd have to walk home alone through an area where a girl was attacked only last week.

At the car, she decided to take the lift, but her stomach was in complete knots. There was something wrong with the whole situation. She thought she might get sick in the back of the car. As the doors shut, she pulled her friend Emma from the car and told her the guy was drunk. Nobody else would listen. They walked home together, and by the time Deirdre got back her dad had fallen asleep in the chair.

DISCUSS

1 What values are evident in this situation?
2 Identify the conflict of values.
3 Do you think the main character, Deirdre, has good values? If so, what are they?
4 Do you think Deirdre lacks some values? What are they?
5 Why do you think she didn't just ring her parents and face the consequences?

the

inner

place

THE ROLE OF CONSCIENCE

Throughout this chapter, we have seen different examples of where people had to try to decide what was the right thing to do. Sometimes they get it right, sometimes they don't. The question is: how are we supposed to know what is the right thing to do? The ability to choose the right thing to do in a given situation, and then to do it, is called your conscience.

Conscience operates when we apply our values, beliefs and intellect to a moral situation. We know conscience is at work when we're not sure what to do and we're trying to make the right decision. In such a situation, we have to refer to a deeper and truer part of ourselves, which informs us about what is the right thing to do. The values, beliefs and teachings that we hold to be part of our truest self help us to formulate our moral convictions and act on them.

Sometimes conscience is described as a voice inside your head. But there can be lots of voices inside a person's head, like 'Go on, have another drink! It's good for ye!' or 'Go on and take it. No one's looking. Sure a big store like this won't miss it.' These aren't exactly 'good' voices. So conscience has to be more than a voice. Some people think that conscience is a feeling you might have, but again people can have lots of feelings, such as 'I feel like getting her back for what she said about me' or 'I'm stressed and I feel like getting wasted out of my skull'. Neither of these are particularly good feelings.

the inner place

DISCUSS Can you think of any other examples of where a person might have a voice in their head or a feeling, but it wouldn't be considered to be morally right?

Read the following account of how a young girl, Aisha, is rescued from an earthquake in Kashmir by a woman named Kausar.

Six-year-old Aisha loves the orange blouse and jeans given to her by the kind woman who rescued her from the chaos of the Kashmir earthquake. She snuggles up to her, trying to forget the devastation of her village home and the deaths of her parents fifteen days ago. What Aisha does not know is that the woman, Kausar, is a prostitute, who has bought her from relatives for 50,000 rupees and plans to put her to work in the sex trade as soon as she reaches puberty.

No official appears to have noticed when Aisha disappeared. After her home in a village called Arja was wrecked, she was taken to her grandmother's house in the nearby city of Bagh. Kausar, her new 'carer', who claims the little one is a distant relative, heard about her plight from family members. Her grandmother was too old to look after the girl. 'I went to Bagh on October 12 and I got her very cheap… I will provide a good education for her. I would not like her to be a cheap, third-class prostitute. I do care about the girl. I will take good care of her, and then reap the benefit. I'm providing for her protection and I don't care what Allah thinks.'

(*The Sunday Times*, 23/10/05)

DISCUSS

1 Kausar wanted to 'care for the child' and 'protect' her. These are good values in themselves, but do you think Kausar was being genuine?
2 Do you think Kausar was using her conscience?
3 Was Kausar behaving morally? Give reasons for your answer.
4 As a Muslim, why do you think Kausar rejected 'what Allah thinks'?

the

inner

place

THE NEED TO INFORM CONSCIENCE

In the preceding story, Kausar says, 'I'm providing for her protection and I don't care what Allah thinks.' She seems to be justifying her actions by 'protecting' the child, yet she is dismissing Allah and her religion. Kausar is simply following her own convictions but is refusing to listen to any other sources of morality, in this example her religion. This story shows the dangers of what happens when a person follows their own inner voice without listening to the wider community.

Unlike Kausar above, a morally mature person recognises the need to inform their conscience from sources other than their own self-interest. A person who has a well-informed conscience recognises that often the final say in a moral matter is not their own. The Irish Catholic Bishops put it thus: 'Being aware of how an issue appears to my friends, how other people in my community, past and present, have understood it, helps me to make the best, most informed decision' (Irish Catholic Bishops, *Conscience*, 1998).

> **ASIDE**
>
> **No Need to Inform Conscience**
> A patrol car near a large shopping mall is alerted to a recent purse-snatching. For once, the victim has a clear description, and the description can't fit that many people. 'A white youth, about eighteen, six feet, hair dyed white, scrawny, almost losing his army pants off his hips, white T-shirt, black vest, lime underwear...'
>
> Sure enough, dodging through the mall parking lot, scattering the contents of the purse behind him, is the kid from the description. They quickly tuck him into the back seat, where he can't help hearing the conversation between the patrol car and the cop inside with the victim. They'll just drive around to the main entrance, get the kid to stand outside for a positive ID, and go on. As they pull up, the driver warns the kid, 'Nothing funny now, you hear? This'll go a lot easier for you if you co-operate.'

the

inner

place

The lad is apparently overflowing with co-operation on this particular day. As he steps out and the victim comes to look at him, the youth nods quickly. 'Oh yeah, I can ID her. That's the woman I robbed all right.'

(N E Genge, *Urban Legends*)

ASSIGNMENT Consider the following examples of people using their conscience in a moral situation. In each situation, you have to decide whether the person needs to inform their conscience or not.

1   A mother notices that her child is seriously sick. She is a doctor and she realises that she must get the child to hospital immediately. If she waits for an ambulance to arrive, it will be too late. She fears for her child's life. She puts the child in her own car and speeds to the hospital. She travels at dangerously high speeds through built-up areas. There are two routes she can take: one through an industrial area, another past a school. It is school closing time and there are many children on the roads coming home from school. She takes the route past the school because it's quicker. She gets the child to the hospital just in time.

Was the woman right to use the shortest route in order to save her child, or should she have taken the safety of the schoolchildren into consideration?

the

inner

place

2   A man is walking along the streets of a busy city. It's Christmastime. He encounters many homeless people and he feels he should do something. He knows it's wrong that society treats them like this. He remembers he has a shotgun at home, so he gets it and uses it to rob a bank of a substantial amount of money. Later, he walks through the streets distributing the money to the poor and homeless. He is arrested by the police after leaving a trail of 'hot money' throughout the city. Many of the poor and homeless have the best Christmas they ever had and they fondly remember the kind and generous man. That year the bank announced profits of 155 million euro.

Was the man right to take from the rich and give to the poor, or should he have helped the poor in another way?

3   A man wakes up one night to hear an intruder downstairs. He is alone with his children. He gets a stick and creeps downstairs. He sees the intruder's shadow and lashes out. The intruder crumbles to the ground. The man hears him groan and decides to hit him one more time on the head to make sure he won't wake up. He fears for his children's safety. As the intruder lies unconscious, the man phones the police.

Should the man have taken the intruder's rights to safety into consideration before hitting him across the head 'to make sure'?

4   A girl gets a phone-call from her mother who is shopping in town but feels unwell. She wants her to come in and pick her up. When the girl gets into town, she can't find a parking space. The only one available is designated for disabled drivers. She parks there and collects her mother, who has now recovered and is feeling OK. They go for a cup of coffee and then return home.

Was the girl right to use the parking space that was reserved for disabled drivers to collect her mother, or should she have left it for a disabled person?

the
inner
place

5   A woman who is financially secure always gives generously to the poor and needy, especially at Christmas. This year she notices that her daughter is quite sad about her looks and is really lacking any self-confidence. She decides to spend the money on her daughter instead and she pays for some cosmetic surgery. The daughter is thrilled. The woman reckons that sometimes charity begins in the home.

In this case, should charity begin in the home?

THE ROLE OF RELIGION

As is evident from the above examples, it is every person's duty to inform their conscience fully for given situations. In the story of the earthquake in Kashmir, the woman, Kausar, rejects Allah and her religion because she knows that her religion would forbid her actions. Religions set out moral guidelines for their followers, and we can generally say that all of the world religions agree to uphold the dignity of the human person.

In many world religions, we find different versions of what is often called 'The Golden Rule'. In Christianity, it is formulated in Luke's gospel as: 'Do to others as you would have them do to you' (Luke 6:31). In the next chapter, we will examine in more detail the particular vision that Jesus had with regard to morality.

Here is how the Golden Rule is formulated in other religions.

Hinduism: 'Do not do to others what would cause you pain if done to you.'

Judaism: 'What is hateful to you, do not do to others.'

Buddhism: 'Hurt not others in ways that you yourself would find hurtful.'

Islam: 'Not one of you is a believer until you desire for your sister or brother that which you desire for yourself.'

the inner place

In *Reason Informed by Faith*, Richard Gula explains the role of religion as follows:

> Following conscience requires that one searches for truth, discerns what is right and good, and then acts according to what one understands that truth to be. That search for the truth is facilitated by following one's religious teachings, and religion has always acted as a form of moral guidance.

Religions set out moral guidelines because, as humans, we are in need of guidance. Left to our own devices, things can go terribly wrong, as the following experiment carried out by a psychology professor demonstrates.

The psychologist Dr Philip Zimbardo of Stanford University conducted an experiment (in 1971) which started by taking ordinary groups of volunteer college students, and dividing them into two. One half was then 'depersonalised' – names were replaced by numbers, their clothes were concealed with laboratory smocks, and they had to wear hoods with eyeholes. They became the 'prisoners' for the experiment. They were housed in a specially mocked-up prison. The other half was similarly depersonalised, but this time with laboratory coats and numbers. They became the 'guards'.

The guards were given control over their 'prisoners', control which they abused, secretly, they thought, late at night. They imposed strip searches in the small hours, and made up additional punishments for their prisoners, such as to clean the toilet bowls with their hands. During the days, they shouted abuse at them, and tripped them up for laughs as they went past.

DISCUSS

1 How would you explain the behaviour of the guards?
2 Do you think the experiment illustrates that humans are in need of guidance when it comes to acting morally? Give reasons for your answer.

CONSCIENCE IN THE CATHOLIC TRADITION

> Deep within his conscience man discovers a law which he has not laid upon himself but which he must obey. Its voice, ever calling him to love and to do what is good and to avoid evil, sounds in his heart at the right moment... For man has in his heart a law inscribed by God... His conscience is man's most secret core and his sanctuary. There he is alone with God whose voice echoes in his depths.
>
> (*Catechism of the Catholic Church*, par. 1776)

RECOGNISING THE MORAL ACT AND ASSUMING RESPONSIBILITY

According to Catholic teaching, a person's conscience allows them to recognise the moral character of particular situations. Walking to the shop is not a moral situation, but getting too much change is. The moment when a person's reason knows that a judgement must be made here – that is their conscience at work. In other words, do I keep the money or do I return it? At all times, the person is obliged to follow what they know to be the right act, because when a person listens to their conscience they are attuned to God.

Alternatively, a person may reflect upon an action committed some time ago. If they now reason that it was a morally wrong act, then they must now seek forgiveness for that act. A person's conscience cannot make them do the right thing, but it does allow the person to look inwardly and to reflect honestly on what they have done. Earlier we referred to how sometimes there can be a conflict of values. A student might participate in an incident where another student is being treated in a hostile or unjust manner by others. At the time, they know that what is occurring

the inner place

is morally wrong, but because of peer pressure they are unwilling to intervene or withdraw from the activity. Later they might reflect on the situation and turn inwardly and recognise that they should have made a stand against the victimisation or bullying that was taking place. According to that person's conscience, they must now seek forgiveness and seek to do the morally right act.

DISCUSS In your opinion, how could the student seek forgiveness and seek to do the morally right thing in the above example?

THE GOLDEN RULE

There is little doubt but that making moral decisions can be very difficult. For this reason, a person must try hard to find out what is the right thing to do. They must try to discover what is God's will. We will see shortly how a person can inform their conscience within the Catholic tradition, but certain rules do apply to all situations.

Take this example. A girl in school knows her friend is taking drugs, and her friend tells her she is in control of the situation. But the girl can see that it is changing her friend's personality and is really having a bad effect on her. She can't concentrate in class and is becoming really paranoid. She has spoken to her friend loads about it, but she won't listen. She knows she should probably tell the girl's older sister, but then her friend would feel really betrayed.

So, what should she do? This is a difficult situation but, as noted previously, there is one rule, the Golden Rule, that can be applied here. It states: 'In everything do to others as you would have them do to you' (Matthew 7:12).

As we noted earlier in this chapter, people can have many different values, and during moral decision-making they apply these values to the situation. The Golden Rule is a value that people can apply to moral situations in order to help them make a moral decision. According to Catholic teaching, there is another rule that can be applied to moral situations: never do evil so that good may result from it. Earlier in this chapter, we examined a situation where a man robbed a bank in order to give money to the homeless. Helping out the homeless was good, but the armed robbery was an evil act that couldn't be morally justified simply because the end goal was to do good.

DISCUSS

1 What do you think the Golden Rule means?
2 If the girl applied the Golden Rule to the situation, what do you think she would do? What would you do in that situation?
3 Why do you think the Golden Rule might be a good guide in moral decision-making? Give some other examples.

THE FORMATION OF CONSCIENCE

In the formation of conscience the Word of God is the light for our path; we must assimilate it in faith and prayer, and put it into practice. We must also examine our conscience before the Lord's Cross. We are assisted by the gifts of the Holy Spirit, aided by the witness or advice of others and guided by the authoritative teaching of the Church.

(*Catechism of the Catholic Church*, par. 1785)

Catholics have a duty to inform and educate their conscience in regard to morality by referring to the Catholic tradition in the following ways:

the
inner
place

- By learning from the sacred scriptures, which contain detailed moral codes, such as the Ten Commandments in the book of Exodus and the Beatitudes in Matthew's gospel. For Christians, the Bible is the inspired word of God and, therefore, the Bible is a primary source for guidance and theology.

- Through becoming familiar with the teachings of Jesus in the New Testament, which offer guidelines for those who want to be his followers. Within the Catholic tradition, Jesus has a unique authority to offer us moral guidance.

- By consulting with the teachings of the Catholic Church as communicated to followers through the Magisterium. The Magisterium of the Catholic Church refers to the role of the Pope and bishops, who interpret the sacred scriptures and communicate the message of Jesus Christ.

- Through prayer and reflection, Catholics can be guided by the wisdom of the Holy Spirit, the gift of which we were given in our Confirmation.

Conscience is something that needs to be nurtured and formed. This is why it is important that people are part of a religious community and receive instruction throughout their lives. By following religious instruction, a person comes to know what are appropriate actions and responses, and how to apply them to a given situation.

THE TEN COMMANDMENTS

'Teacher, which commandment in the law is the greatest?' He said to him, ' "You shall love the Lord your God with all your heart, and with all your soul, and with all your mind." This is the greatest and first commandment. And a second is like it: "You shall love your neighbour as yourself." On these two commandments hang all the law and the prophets.'

(Matthew 22:36–40)

Becoming Moral

The Ten Commandments are part of the covenant or agreement that God made with the Hebrews after saving them from slavery in Egypt. The commandments are a list of rules of behaviour which the people were expected to keep in order to remain faithful to the covenant with God. Yet they are also more than that, because they should be seen as the human response to God's loving care for God's people, as shown in their liberation from slavery.

As we can see from the scripture piece above, Jesus endorsed the Ten Commandments and their role in Christian life. The commandments continue to act as the Christian moral response to God's love. They should be regarded as a unit, as they address love of God and love of neighbour. The first three commandments address love of God, whilst the other seven address love of one another.

In Catholic teaching, the commandments play an important role in the continuing formation of a person's conscience because they spell out our moral obligations towards God and towards our neighbour.

I am the Lord your God; you shall not have strange gods before me.
You shall not take the name of the Lord your God in vain.
Remember to keep holy the Lord's Day.
Honour your father and your mother.
You shall not kill.
You shall not commit adultery.
You shall not steal.
You shall not bear false witness against your neighbour.
You shall not covet your neighbour's wife.
You shall not covet your neighbour's goods.

the inner place

DISCUSS How do you think the commandments can continue to serve as a good means of acting out our moral obligations towards God and ourselves?

MATURE MORAL DECISION-MAKING

Conscience plays an important role in almost every aspect of moral decision-making. Here we will outline the various stages involved when a person makes a moral decision. We will note the role that conscience plays throughout the process.

Medals for Kate

Tim worked in a builders' supply yard at the weekend. Some of the builders who came in boasted to him of how they were overcharging their customers and how they were making loads of money. The lads were so busy mouthing off that they didn't notice that sometimes the prices Tim charged weren't exactly right. Nor did they notice that the change they got back wasn't always right either. But Tim wasn't too bothered at first, because the money was for his girlfriend Kate, who was trying her best to become a professional musician. Kate had her life seriously messed up by lots of people a while back (some of them the same guys who were now being ripped off by Tim) and she was trying her best to get her life back together. But her tuition cost a lot of money, and now Tim had found a way of helping her out. In fairness, he thought, nobody was getting hurt. Yeah, it was wrong but not that wrong.

But then he went to Mass on Sunday. It was a small rural parish and the young priest wasn't half bad at giving a sermon, and he was often funny. Tim didn't mind going, but this Sunday something came up about stealing, and the priest went on about stealing in the workplace in particular. It was the Ten Commandments. That was it. Tim felt himself go red. Yeah, deep down he knew that what he was doing

the
inner
place

wasn't right, even if he was helping Kate. He wouldn't like it if somebody was ripping him off in order to be in their girlfriend's good books. He'd give the money back and just do some overtime instead. Lent was only a couple of weeks away, and he even went to confession to the priest, but obviously he disguised his voice. Dropped two octaves. Sounded like his da.

Stages Involved

- A Moral Situation: From the very beginning, Tim's conscience lets him know that this is a moral situation. He knows it's wrong, but he doesn't seem to have a very well-informed conscience and reckons it's 'not that wrong'.

- Applying Values: Because it's a moral situation, Tim applies his values to it. He's stealing, but it's in order to do something good. There seems to be a conflict of values. He knows he's stealing, so he does value the right not to have your property taken from you.

- Informing Conscience: Later though, Tim's conscience seems to be informed a little. At Mass he becomes aware of the seventh commandment. He goes red, realising that the sermon applies to him. The priest seems to be giving witness to the truth and giving advice to those who steal in the workplace.

- Rules: After this experience, Tim seems to apply different values to the situation. Though he doesn't say it directly, he seems to realise that you can never really do something evil just so that something good may come of it.

- Looking Inwardly: Tim's conscience is allowing him to look inwardly and reflect honestly on the moral situation.

- Doing the Right Thing: He knows the right thing to do and feels morally obliged to do it. He seeks forgiveness (making sure to remain anonymous) and then does the good thing by giving the money back.

- Responsibilities: Tim is still aware of his responsibilities to his girlfriend and her welfare, but now he does overtime to help her out.

the

inner

place

Chapter Sixteen
RELIGION AND MORALITY

THE ORIGINS OF MORALITY

The following true story illustrates the emergence and origins of a moral code under the most extreme of human conditions.

The Shipwreck

In 1816, an expedition set sail for Senegal with four vessels and 365 people on board. One of the frigates, however, hit a reef in high seas, and since it did not carry enough boats to accommodate everyone, it was decided to build a raft. The raft was twenty metres long and was built to accommodate 150 people, but when they started to embark, the raft began to sink. In the end, only fifty could get on the

raft, and at that they had to throw many provisions overboard as the raft was a metre under water. When it set sail, all aboard were in water up to their waists and so crowded they could not take a single step. In the mayhem of their departure, they left without charts or a compass. There was no rudder or oars and so no means of controlling the raft.

The first night the raft met a storm and, with no means to rest, those on board were lashed by waves and freezing waters. The morning was greeted with lamentable cries and wailing. Two of those on board threw themselves into the sea. The second night was worse, and the raft was bombarded with waves so high it was at risk of being overthrown. Some on board, so convinced of their inevitable death, broke open a cask of wine and resolved to meet their end by abandoning the power of reason. Yet sea water entered the cask and destroyed the wine, and so, having abandoned all reason, they set upon the raft with knives to destroy it and bring everyone on board with them into the sea. The ensuing mutiny resulted in the officers on board being attacked with knives, and many were so deranged that they set upon the officers with their teeth. Many were stabbed, bludgeoned and thrown to the sea. Two casks of wine went overboard and all the fresh water.

The third day began with the cries of the wounded and the deranged. Corpses littered the raft and some on board, driven to starvation and unsatisfied by eating leather belts, boxes and even their own excrement, set upon the corpses, but only after drying the meat first to make it more palatable. That night, a shoal of flying fish was captured, and when this was added to the human flesh it was deemed more palatable. No one on board was without wounds and, as the salty sea water washed over them, they all wailed and beseeched the Lord for salvation.

On the seventh day, two on board were found to have bored a hole into the last remaining cask of wine. When they were discovered, it was deemed necessary to throw them overboard in accordance with new laws that had been speedily enforced. It was then that another decision had to be made. When counted, there were twenty-seven on board. Fifteen were likely to survive for some days at least, but the others were suffering from terrible wounds and were deemed to have but the smallest chance of survival. There was only a limited supply of

the inner place

provisions left, and between them they would consume at least thirty or forty bottles of wine. It was suggested to half their rations, but this would be death by degrees. A debate ensued among the fifteen healthy and, amidst the most terrible despairing, they resolved to carry out the repugnant but necessary executions. Four, whose hearts had been hardened by the constant sight of death, cast the sick into the sea. There were now provisions left for six days.

On the thirteenth day of their ordeal, they were all saved by a passing ship. The strongest had barely forty-eight hours of life left in them. The crew of the passing ship cared for them as best they could and rekindled life back into their swollen, lacerated and battered bodies, and hope back into their broken souls.

(Adapted from Julian Barnes, *A History of the World in 10½ Chapters*)

DISCUSS

1. Why do you think those on board the raft created new laws, which were 'speedily enforced'? Do you think they were right to throw the two men overboard?
2. Why do you think that the fifteen decided to throw those weaker overboard, and do you think they were justified in their actions?
3. Do you think morality originated in societies in order to aid survival, or is there another reason?

the inner place

MORALITY AND THE BRAIN

There is little doubt that the origins of morality have something to do with the survival of the group and the individual. Rules and laws against killing or stealing food have obvious benefits for the group. In the story of the shipwreck, for example, the rules

Religion and Morality

originated around the availability of food. The breaking of rules led to exclusion. In addition, the weak were being thrown overboard. In our society, the person who disobeys the rules is sent to prison. It would appear that morality has developed in part due to our need for greater co-operation within the group. The group is obviously more efficient at defence and productivity if it is harmonious and co-operative.

In brain research, volunteers were asked to take part in situations where they had to learn whether to trust one another or not. Those in the group who learned to trust other members and, hence, to co-operate with them, showed activity in certain regions of their brains. These areas were associated with pleasure and reward, and when activated made them 'feel good'. In other words, the brain is hardwired to reward us by the release of chemicals that make us feel good when we co-operate with others. For example, the experience of shouting at parents and slamming doors may serve some purpose, but rarely, if ever, does it make us feel good. The brain doesn't reward that kind of thing.

Other research has presented particular moral dilemmas to volunteers and then conducted brain scans to try to discover what was going on inside the brain while a decision was being made.

ASSIGNMENT You can try the dilemmas for yourself now in class and explain your actions. The situations described are purely fictitious.

> You are watching a view from a footbridge over a railway. You then see a runaway rail carriage heading towards a forked junction. There is a lever in your hand, which you can move to determine the direction of the railway carriage after it hits the fork. If you move the lever forwards, the lever will direct the train to kill just one person. If you move the lever backwards, it will kill five people. Which way do you move the lever?

the

inner

place

Again you are on a footbridge looking at another railway carriage hurtling down towards five people. The only way you can stop it is by pushing the person who is next to you off the bridge and into its path. What do you do?

While you were sorting out which way to pull levers or whether to throw people into the path of a moving train, certain things were happening in your brain. According to researchers, we operate differently depending on the type of dilemma with which we are faced. In the first dilemma, we use an area of our brain that is associated with the workings of our memory. In the second example, where we are actually involved ourselves, we use an area that is associated with processing emotions. This area is called the superior temporal sulcus (STS). Interestingly, this area is used when we try to discern and figure out the emotional and mental states of other people. It is this area that produces sympathy when we see that people are in trouble or are sad.

Research has also shown that our brains are constructed in such a way so as to read the faces of others. It is probably a very primitive function, as it was necessary for survival to be able to interpret the other person's stance and facial expression. If it was threatening, it was time to scarper or attack. Now our brains, and in particular a region called the amygdala, function so as to interpret others' facial expressions. We immediately try to figure out a person's mood when we meet them.

the

inner

place

Try this exercise in class, as you imagine yourself meeting people in different situations:

a   If a person is really happy, how do you react to them?

b   If a person is obviously upset about something, how do you react to them?

c.   If a person is threatening or abusive, how do you react to them?

According to brain research, we usually mirror others' emotional states so as to understand them. If a person is really happy about something, we usually smile and ask what's the story. If they're down, we try to be more sensitive and sympathetic. If someone is angry or threatening, we usually mirror this back to them. According to Robert Winston, 'The architecture of our brains predisposes us to interpret other people by feeling what they do, by putting ourselves in their shoes' (Robert Winston, *The Mind*).

Forgiving others or being compassionate in our response to them are ways of behaving morally. The interesting thing to note here is that morality appears to be part of our humanity and is perhaps even woven into the structure of our brains.

DISCUSS

1   Would you agree that morality has its origins in the human brain, or do you think morality is something made up by religions?

2   Do you think people can behave morally without being religious? Why is this so?

3   In your opinion, what role does religion have in morality?

the

inner

place

RELIGION AND MORALITY

We have just examined recent theories about how humans come to be moral, but locating the moral zone in our brains, while interesting, may not be of much practical use. We noticed in the last chapter how difficult it can be to make moral decisions in moral dilemmas, and we can often get it wrong. Due to the complexities of morality, we all need guidance, and all the world religions offer guidance in matters of morality. Though we may all have a sense of right and wrong, we are in need of guidance when it comes to moral dilemmas, as the following story illustrates.

In a famous case a young woman, Kitty Genovese, was chased along a street in Queens, New York and stabbed repeatedly by her assailant. She was attacked three times on the street over the course of half an hour. The attack was witnessed by thirty-eight neighbours who watched from their windows.

the inner place

During that time, however, none of the witnesses called the police. The case provoked rounds of self-recrimination. It became symbolic of the cold and dehumanising effects of urban life. Abe Rosenthal, who would later become editor of the *New York Times*, wrote in a book about the case. 'Nobody can say why the thirty-eight did not lift the phone while Miss Genovese was being attacked, since they cannot themselves. It can be assumed, however, that their apathy was indeed one of the big city variety.

It is almost a matter of psychological survival, if one is surrounded and pressed by millions of people, to prevent them from constantly impinging on you, and the only way to do this is to ignore them as often as possible. Indifference to one's neighbour and his troubles is a conditioned reflex in life in New York, as it is in other big cities.'

(*Irish Independent* 12/8/05)

DISCUSS

1 What is your reaction to this story? Does it shock and surprise you? Would you have helped in that situation or would you have been one of the bystanders?

2 What does this story have to say about our natural morality?

3 In what way does this story illustrate that people need some sort of moral guidance?

It would appear that we are in need of some assistance when it comes to our morality. It looks like some of us do not have a very developed sense of what is right and wrong. Given that situation, there is a need for moral guidance and help. Later in this chapter, we will examine how moral development occurs. Now, however, we will look at what guidance and help is particular to Christianity and, especially, the Catholic tradition.

the inner place

THE CATHOLIC TRADITION

THE ROLE OF JESUS IN CHRISTIAN MORALITY

❝ Last summer I had a really good summer job. I made a rake of cash with this builder who was a friend of the family. It was a brilliant summer as me ma started to let me go out for the first time and I had loads of cash, so I really had a ball. I'm not mad into religion but when I was young I used to visit me granny and stay with her. If we were in town we always had to go into the church to light candles for the souls. It stuck with me as a good thing to do. Anyway last summer I went into the church in town. I just got paid and I was really happy. The sun was shining in through the stained glass. So I lit a candle for me gran who's dead now. So there I was and I was looking at the statue of Jesus. Then just in me head came this thought. Now I know I sound stupid but I just knew he wanted me to use me money to help someone. And I knew it was the right thing to do. So I went down to the bank and made out a form for homeless children in Dublin. Yeah, I gave them a good bit and I missed the money but it felt mad too. I felt good after it. But me ma was wondering where the money had gone and she sat me down for a big talk about drugs. There ye go. ❞

the inner place

Last Christmas I was watching TV and there was an ad on about a famine in some third world country. The ad was by a charity and it really affected me. I couldn't understand how we could be so wealthy and others so poor. I said a prayer that night for those people and especially the kids but I couldn't get to sleep. I had this feeling that God wanted me to do something myself and I spent the night racking my brain. I really felt God was challenging me to do something. Next morning it was clear – I'd shave off all my hair for the charity. So I rang them up and told them my idea and they were thrilled. They sent me forms so that people could sponsor me. People thought I was mad and everyone kept feeling my long hair, like saying goodbye to it. The girls in school were tying it back to see what I'd look like as a skinhead. Not great. I got my head shaved in a hotel and there were people from the newspapers and all that. I raised over fifteen hundred euro for the charity. When I went back to school everyone was rubbing my head – like I was a pet – well it felt like that. Some teachers didn't even notice. One night soon after, I was at home and the same ad came on. I felt good watching it. When it was over I just gave my head a rub and then went off outside for a walk.

the

inner

place

DISCUSS What is your reaction to the above stories? Have you ever felt challenged by your religious faith to do something for someone else? Or do you know someone else who has? Tell the story to the rest of the class.

The Natural Law

> The natural law expresses the original moral sense which enables [the human person] to discern by reason the good and the evil, the truth and the lie.

(*Catechism of the Catholic Church*, par. 1954)

According to Catholic theology, it is possible for people to reflect upon human experience and human nature and to discern what is good and evil. This is called natural moral law. In other words, by the use of reason, a person can come to know the natural law which is inside all humans. It is called natural law because we come to know it through our reason, and reason is a faculty natural to all human beings. This means that all cultures and societies of people, whether they have faith or not, can come to know what is right and what is wrong based on their reason.

the

inner

place

Students reading about the natural moral law might form the opinion that surely it is open to many interpretations. If a person was stuck in a particular moral dilemma, they might prefer to have more definite help and guidance. The fact is that often we do make the wrong choice and get things wrong. According to Catholic teaching, the natural moral law does provide for greater clarity in our morality because it acts as a foundation for revealed law.

The Old Law

> The Old Law is a preparation for the Gospel.
>
> (*Catechism of the Catholic Church*, par. 1964)

Revealed law refers to the laws of God that have been revealed to humanity throughout the ages, starting with the Law of Moses and the Decalogue, which was given on Mount Sinai during the Exodus (see chapter 15). Yet the Law of Moses was to act as a preparation for the law of the Gospel as revealed through Jesus Christ.

Mount Sinai

As we noted in the last chapter, Jesus incorporated the Ten Commandments into his own unique moral vision:

> 'Teacher, which commandment in the law is the greatest?' He said to him, ' "You shall love the Lord your God with all your heart, and with all your soul, and with all your mind." This is the greatest and first commandment. And a second is like it: "You shall love your neighbour as yourself." On these two commandments hang all the law and the prophets.'
>
> (Matthew 22:36–40)

the inner place

> Now when they heard this, they were cut to the heart and said to Peter and to the other apostles, 'Brothers, what should we do?' Peter said to them, 'Repent, and be baptised every one of you in the name of Jesus Christ so that your sins may be forgiven; and you will receive the gift of the Holy Spirit.'

(Acts 2:37–38)

As the above stories of young people helping others illustrate, people today are being inspired by the person of Jesus to do what is good and to reach out to those who are in need of help. In each case, both young people felt challenged in some way by their religious faith. Both felt that what they did was the right thing to do. It would appear that the presence of Jesus in their lives made a difference not only to them but to those around them.

The scripture quotation above (Acts 2:37–38) refers to the very first converts to Christianity. First they heard the good news; that Jesus who was crucified had risen from the dead. This same Jesus was Lord and Christ. Yet, accepting Jesus into their lives meant that they had to repent and believe. In other words, Jesus called for a fundamental reorientation of a person's life. In Section B we examined the parables as stories about the kingdom of God. We noticed how Jesus was always trying to challenge people and get them to think in a different way about their lives and their relationships with those around them. The coming of God's kingdom brings with it a call to repentance:

the

inner

place

The time is fulfilled, and the kingdom of God has come near; repent, and believe in the good news.

(Mark 1:15)

A RESPONSE TO LOVE

Christian morality is based on a response to God's love. As the account below illustrates, love can be a powerful and transformative force.

When he was discovered in the boot of a battered Lada, Dzhamal Gamidov looked far too small to be an eleven-year-old boy. He was filthy, naked and weighed 2st 5lb. He had been stripped of muscle by a starvation diet and robbed of the power of speech by three and a half years of beatings. But the horror of his bulging eyes bore eloquent testimony to his suffering.

Twenty months later and Dzhamal has recovered enough to describe what happened to him, and last week he bravely recounted an ordeal in chains as the hostage of a kidnap gang whose cruelty knew no limits. His captors – six men and a woman – stuffed him in a dingy basement. They shackled him to the floor by his wrists and ankles. They flogged him. They threatened to cut off his ear and send it to his mother.

Marina Gamidov, his mother, endured another kind of torture. First she received photographs of Dzhamal wearing only his T-shirt and stretching out his hands towards the camera as if pleading for help. These were followed by a shocking video in which he howled for his mother as he was viciously whipped...

The grainy footage showed him crouching terrified by the light of a single bulb, screaming for his mother as the whip came down hard upon his frail body. 'Don't beat me, don't beat me,' he

the

inner

place

shrieked. 'Please Mummy, take me away. I can't bear it any more, I beg you.'

It was December 2003 before help came. The kidnappers were changing hideouts when they came across a group of special forces looking for a different gang. They abandoned the car with Dzhamal in the boot and have never been caught.

Doctors broke down in tears when they saw how pitifully thin Dzhamal had become. When they gave him a little porridge his stomach swelled up like a balloon. His mother could hardly believe that they were being reunited. 'He was so thin that I was scared to touch him. He crawled on all fours faster than he could walk. But he recognised me at once. He looked at me and whispered, "I want to go with Mummy".'

He bit his aunt and scratched his mother and younger sister Zhenia. His hair had to be shaved to stop him from tearing it out. He was locked in a psychiatric ward, but his mother had other ideas about how to help him recover.

'I knew deep in my heart that I could bring him back to normal,' she said. 'I knew all he needed was love and warmth. So I took him away and started re-educating him day by day.' The effect has astonished experts. When Dzhamal was found, the clothes he wore at eight still fitted him. He has since put on nearly 60lb and is going back to school.

(*The Sunday Times*, 2/10/05)

the
inner
place

Religion and Morality

DISCUSS
1 What effect did years of torture and abuse have on Dzhamal?
2 How do you think his mother's love succeeded where psychiatric treatment had failed?

Christian morality is based on love. We are loved by God, and our response is to return that love to our neighbour. Why? As the above account illustrates, love is transformative, and Christians are transformed by God's love. Those who are transformed by the love of God share that love with one another. At the centre of Jesus' teaching and moral vision was the command to love one another.

'You shall love your neighbour as yourself.'
(Matthew 22:39)

If Christian morality is a response to love, then our morality is woven into our relationship with Jesus Christ. This relationship is strengthened through prayer, both personal and communal.

This relationship is also strengthened through our participation in the sacraments, as the following account illustrates.

the
inner
place

This is a story from a long time ago, well I suppose I was around twelve at the time. I was in Mass and I remember it clearly because there was a woman

sitting in front of us with a distinctive headscarf. It had horses' heads on it and horse shoes. Somehow we always ended up behind her. Anyway I suppose I wasn't really paying attention. In Mass I usually used to just go into my own little world. But that one day was the strangest. I was just sitting there and suddenly everything seemed to just change. As if the sun just broke through on a cloudy day. This really strange feeling came over me that's very difficult to describe. At the time I couldn't but now I can. It was just an experience of a really deep love. It was almost like being crushed but in the best possible way. I was powerless but it did happen. People will probably think it's stupid. I couldn't really care less anyway.

(Female, 17)

DISCUSS

1 Why do you think it was love that healed Dzhamal instead of a psychiatric ward?
2 Can you think of other examples of how love can be transformative?
3 Can you think of examples of how Christian love can transform other people?

ASIDE

The New Law

'The New Law is called a *law of love* because it makes us act out of the love infused by the Holy Spirit, rather than from fear; a *law of grace*, because it confers the strength of grace to act, by means of faith and the sacraments; a *law of freedom*, because it sets us free from the ritual and juridical observances of the Old Law.'

(*Catechism of the Catholic Church*, par. 1972)

the

inner

place

The call to repentance and to accept Jesus' moral vision is about responding to God's love and not about blindly accepting a list of rules and observances. Love is the basis of Christian morality and the New Law that replaces the Old Law of Moses.

Very early in the life of the Christian Church was an event that transformed all those who were to follow Jesus. At Pentecost, there occurred an outpouring of the Holy Spirit into the hearts of all those who had heard the good news about Jesus of Nazareth. This outpouring of the Holy Spirit filled those hearts with the love of God, a love that would fuel the early Church through many centuries of hardship and persecution.

Like Christians today, those in the early Christian communities were strengthened in their ability to live out their calling to follow Jesus' unique moral vision through the grace they received in the sacraments. All those who repented were baptised, and they met regularly in their homes for the breaking of the bread, and there they received the grace of the Eucharist.

THE BEATITUDES

The Beatitudes respond to the natural desire for happiness. This desire is of divine origin: God has placed it in the human heart in order to draw [the human person] to the One who alone can fulfil it.

(Catechism of the Catholic Church, par. 1718)

Blessed are the poor in spirit, for theirs is the kingdom of heaven.
Blessed are those who mourn, for they will be comforted.
Blessed are the meek, for they will inherit the earth.
Blessed are those who hunger and thirst for righteousness, for they will be filled.

the
inner
place

Blessed are the merciful, for they will receive
mercy.
Blessed are the pure in heart, for they will see God.
Blessed are the peacemakers, for they will be called
children of God.
Blessed are those who are persecuted for
righteousness' sake, for theirs is the kingdom of
heaven.
Blessed are you when people revile you and
persecute you and utter all kinds of evil against you
falsely on my account. Rejoice and be glad, for
your reward is great in heaven, for in the same way
they persecuted the prophets before you.

(Matthew 5:3–11)

In chapter 11 we examined the story of the Rich Young
Man (Matthew 19:16–21). When we examined the
implications of this story, we realised that the advice to
detach oneself from materialistic goals actually leads to
happiness. Much of Jesus' other advice and teaching
would also lead to a happier life. The same applies to his
vision of the Christian moral life. If we believe that the
goal of human life is to be happy, then the Beatitudes
offer a compelling framework for human happiness. The
Beatitudes also offer an insight into our relationship with
God and with others.

The 'poor in spirit' are those who may feel rejected but
who also appreciate their dependence on God. While
poverty is not something good in itself, it suggests a right
attitude towards wealth and a detachment from riches. 'Those
who mourn' feel helpless, yet their vulnerability facilitates an
intimacy with God, which in turn strengthens their relationship
with God. The 'meek' are not to be walked all over, but instead it
should be recognised that their powerlessness readies them for
God's power working through them. The Beatitudes act like a
parable in so far as they challenge our view of reality. In God's
kingdom, it is not the powerful and wealthy who are blessed, but
instead those who, in their powerlessness and vulnerability,
recognise their dependence upon God.

the

inner

place

Religion and Morality

Our right relationship with others is expressed in looking at those who 'hunger and thirst for righteousness'. They are attuned to their relationship with their neighbour just like those who are 'merciful'. They have experienced God's mercy and now bestow it on others. The 'pure in heart' are people full of integrity, who are honest in all their dealings with others. The 'peacemakers' strive to create reconciliation, wholeness and peace in situations around them. They challenge bitterness and hostility, and instead promote understanding and forgiveness. Finally, 'those who are persecuted' are the ones who are ridiculed or slandered because of their discipleship. They are blessed because they realise the future reward both of their discipleship and their suffering.

DISCUSS

1 In what way do you think the Beatitudes might point to human happiness?

2 Why do you think the Beatitudes pose a challenge to our way of thinking about our relationship with God and others?

3 Which beatitude, if embraced, would offer most to society? Give reasons for your answer.

SIN AND RECONCILIATION

There is little doubt but that humans do terrible things to one another. In Section A we examined some of the atrocities carried out during the Holocaust, and also during the ethnic cleansing in the former Yugoslavia. Moral failure destroys people's lives and

wrecks human relationships. In the Christian tradition, we refer to moral failure as sin.

> The grainy footage showed him crouching terrified by the light of a single bulb, screaming for his mother as a whip came down hard upon his frail body. 'Please don't beat me,' he shrieked. 'Please Mummy, take me away. I can't bear it any more. I beg you.'

Anybody who reads the above account of the treatment of Dzhamal will respond with a range of emotions. But ask yourself this question: if you were Dzhamal's parent, which of the following options might you take with regard to his attackers.

a   Dedicate your life to hunting them down and then kill them, slowly, one by one.

Or

b   Try your best to forgive them.

Though there may be an immediate sense of satisfaction in choosing the first option, we noted in Section B how people who forgive are actually happier people. Take the following examples.

> L was going out with J for six months. He wasn't that mature but he was very funny. She really liked him, but so did S, her seemingly good friend. Then one night J and S met up at a night club. 'Oh we just had too much to drink,' they protested. Fine, but the damage was done and L had no option other than to break it off with J. But it didn't end there. She couldn't stop thinking about what S did to her, so she waged a campaign of revenge. First up was a girlie fight outside of 'Lilac's'. Then the really vicious campaign began. She admits to starting rumours about S. S admits to starting rumours about L. L ignored S in school. S ignored L in school. They

dreaded meeting each other on the corridor. It was a pretty miserable time, but every point scored was worth it.

L was going out with J for six months. He wasn't that mature but he was very funny. She really liked him, but so did S, her seemingly good friend. Then one night J and S met up at a night club. 'Oh we just had too much to drink,' they protested. Fine, but the damage was done, and L had no option other than to break it off with J. But it didn't end there. J was gone but L and S had been friends and they had to try to sort out the mess now. For L, it was one of the hardest things in the world – to face a friend who had betrayed you. But when they eventually got to talk about it – or cry about it – L could see for herself how much pain S was in. Yeah, she forgave her. It wasn't easy, but the reward was that she didn't lose her friend. Not only that. In a strange way, she knows that S would do almost anything for her now.

DISCUSS

1 Why do you think it's so difficult to forgive? Why do we sometimes prefer to hold onto bitterness and feelings of revenge?

2 Looking at the stories above, why do you think we might be better off if we could forgive and move on?

the inner place

ASIDE

When Arsenal and Manchester United took the field to challenge for the FA Cup in 2005, extra police were drafted in to monitor both on-field and off-the-field clashes. Fans reacted with almost hysteria to the most innocent foul and, in fairness, there was a definite edge to most tackles. So why the animosity between the clubs? The answer according to one theory places the blame on an incident seventeen years previously during an FA Cup tie between the clubs in 1988. Brian McClair slapped a late penalty over the bar for United and they lost 2-1. As McClair ran towards the tunnel, Nigel Winterburn slagged him off. Then in 1990, two years later, McClair and Winterburn got into a tangle which started a brawl that sucked in every player except for the Arsenal 'keeper'.

(*The Irish Times*, 1/12/05)

DISCUSS

1 Why do you think the two clubs would preserve a hatred that began seventeen years previously?
2 Can you think of other examples of how people hate one another simply because they are in some way connected to an earlier feud?
3 In your opinion, does such animosity serve any purpose or make any sense?

the

inner

place

SIN IN THE CATHOLIC TRADITION

ORIGINAL SIN

> It is in Christ, Redeemer and Saviour, that the divine image, disfigured in [the human person] by the first sin, has been restored to its original beauty and ennobled by the grace of God.
>
> *(Catechism of the Catholic Church*, par. 1701)

In the book of Genesis 3:1-21, we read the account of how the first man and woman disobeyed God and were banished from Eden. While this account should not be taken literally, it does provide a profound insight into human nature.

Adam and Eve brought sin into the world, and in the Catholic tradition this is termed original sin. The effects of this original sin have been passed on from generation to generation throughout human history. In paragraph 1707, the Catechism states that, though we still desire what is good, in our nature we still bear 'the wound of original sin'. We are now 'inclined to evil and subject to error'.

Yet Christians believe that Jesus saved us from sin through his death on the cross. The sacraments continue to give us grace, which strengthens us to do good and avoid evil.

MORTAL AND VENIAL SIN

The Catechism defines sin as follows:

> Sin is an offence against reason, truth and right conscience; it is failure in genuine love of God and neighbour caused by a perverse attachment to certain goods. It wounds the nature of [the human person] and injures human solidarity.
>
> *(Catechism of the Catholic Church*, par. 1849)

We noted earlier how in the Christian tradition morality is founded on love. Sin, then, is a failure of love, and it affects our relationship with God and with our neighbour. And as we noted from the stories above, sin destroys human happiness and can only cause hurt and bitterness, along with feelings of revenge or retribution.

The Catholic Church has defined different levels of sin, and, as we know from experience, sin can have different levels of seriousness. In the Catholic tradition, sin has been classified into mortal and venial.

A mortal sin destroys a person's relationship with God in so far as they turn away from God. It is an act deliberately chosen and whereby a person is deliberately aware of the consequences. It is a serious act, committed freely. The Ten Commandments specify serious acts. For example, if a person murders another in full knowledge of what they are doing and of its consequences, then they have committed a mortal sin.

A venial sin is not fully intended and is often carried out without full knowledge of the action or its consequences. It doesn't turn a person away from God, but it can weaken their relationship with God and with others.

THE ACT OF FORGIVENESS

> So if anyone is in Christ, there is a new creation: everything old has passed away; see, everything has become new! All this is from God, who reconciled us to himself through Christ, and has given us the ministry of reconciliation.
>
> (2 Corinthians 5:17–18)

Christians have been given a model of how to behave towards those who cause us pain or hurt. Read the following account of how a mother forgives those who kill her son.

A Mother Forgives

Anthony Walker's mother saw his killers convicted of racially motivated murder yesterday, then declared: 'I forgive them.'

In an astonishing display of compassion, Gee Walker, 49, said: 'I have got to forgive them. My family and I still stand by what I believe – forgiveness. It will be difficult but we have got no choice but to live on for Anthony.'

Michael Barton, the 17-year-old brother of Manchester City footballer Joey Barton, was convicted by a unanimous verdict of murdering 18-year-old Anthony, whom he subjected to appalling racist taunts. Barton's cousin Paul Taylor, 20, had earlier pleaded guilty to murdering the gifted teenager by burying an ice axe in his head after chasing him through a park in Huyton, Merseyside.

Anthony Walker (front) with friends

When the jury returned its guilty verdict on Barton at Liverpool Crown Court yesterday, Anthony's family let out an audible sigh of relief before turning and hugging each other. Barton, who had supplied the murder weapon to Taylor, sank his head in his hands and began to cry when the verdict was announced.

Yesterday Anthony's cousin David Okoro said: 'Anthony was a wonderful young man who had everything to live for and his murder has put my family through a living nightmare. Anthony was a devout Christian and the world was a worse place without him today. Our lives will never be the same again.'

Mrs Walker

Mrs Walker added: 'I think justice has been done. I am pleased with the outcome.' Explaining why she forgave her son's killers, the devout Christian said: 'At the point of death, Jesus said, "I forgive them, for they know not what they do".'

(*Daily Mail*, 1/12/2005)

the

inner

place

DISCUSS

1　Why did Anthony's mother forgive the killers of her son?

2　Why was Anthony killed?

3　What kind of emotions do you think Anthony's mother would have felt as she forgave her son's killers?

'If I was God...'

    ❝ If I was God there are several things that would get my immediate attention. Firstly I would magic a substantial amount of money into my bank account, and I'm talking lottery figures here. Then I'd get the bus down to the BMW garage and walk in and get a BMW 320i coupe. I'd love looking at them check my account details and then apologetically hand over the keys of the motor. If I was God I'd like to start in the morning because I'd have a lot to do. Then I'd drive over to L R's house and, with the motor, check out whether she really fancies me or not. I'd definitely bring me ma out for lunch to a really nice place, but more important things first. But then I'd get down to the business of retribution. Like in the film *Pulp Fiction* where yer man talks about the 'vengeance of the Lord'. I am that Lord. That's me. There's three blokes live over the road and I'd visit them. I'd like to bring them outside and just stand there. They'd laugh and then make their move on me. It would be the last move they'd make. If I was the Lord that is how I would begin my day. The Lord of Vengeance. Day one. And it's only 10.30 in the morning. It's going to be a long day. ❞

(Pat, 16)

Luckily, Pat never made it to be God. Perhaps just as well. Unlike Pat, Jesus didn't talk about vengeance or retribution, but instead he offered one of the most profound challenges to our thinking and acting, which is the act of forgiveness. Forgiveness is one of the most difficult things to do, yet it is the Christian response to hurt and wrongdoing.

Throughout his ministry, Jesus preached forgiveness and constantly welcomed the sinner. In the story of the woman caught in adultery in John 8:1–11, Jesus condemns the sin but not the sinner. Jesus' ministry was one of healing and forgiveness. He also welcomed sinners to his table and ate with the outcast and marginalised of his day. But perhaps Jesus' greatest statement about forgiveness was when he forgave those who executed him on a cross (Luke 23:34). Jesus didn't just talk about forgiveness but he forgave even those who ended his life in a barbaric way. As we saw in the above story of Anthony Walker, Jesus' acts of forgiveness have inspired others to do the same.

When we do consider forgiveness as an option, we are sometimes tempted to hold back a little bit. It's that bit that says, 'I forgive you but I really wouldn't mind if something horrible happens to you. You deserve it, etc.' For Jesus, forgiveness couldn't be compromised. You can't put a limit on it. Peter tried to see if there was a limit to how often you might forgive. Would it be seven times? No. There was no limit.

> **Then Peter came and said to him, 'Lord, if another member of the church sins against me, how often should I forgive? As many as seven times?' Jesus said to him, 'Not seven times, but, I tell you, seventy-seven times.'**
>
> (Matthew 18:21–22)

DISCUSS

1 Why do you think Jesus put no limits on forgiveness?
2 If people adopted Jesus' challenge to forgive in all circumstances, what differences would it make to the world today?
3 What would you do if you were God?

the

inner

place

Imagine this...

A teenage son, sick of being under his father's thumb, approached his father one day.

'Da, let's say you're dead. In such a situation I would be entitled to half of the house and farm. Let's face it, there's no real connection between us two, so let's fast forward. Re-mortgage the property and give me my share. I want to have a life while I'm still young.'

The father agreed.

The young lad headed off to the city, rented a penthouse and lived the high life. The money, though, ran out very fast, and in a space of time that he couldn't measure he found himself on the streets, scratching together enough money for a fix.

Sometimes when he woke up, cold and with a thumping head, he'd think of his family. He'd lean against the reeking walls of the underside of a bridge he'd now called home. He wasn't alone here; there were twenty other down-and-outs, and countless vermin. Images of working the land, big feeds and sound sleep visited his aching head. Surely it was a better option. Surely they would give him a job on the farm. He knew the names of none of the grunting bodies beside him. At least at home they knew who he was.

'Return of the Prodigal Son' by Rembrandt van Rijn (1662)

the inner place

We know the end of the story of the prodigal son. While the son was still a long way from home, his watching father saw him and ran out to meet him. He embraced him and ordered a party. It's a shocking thing to wish your parents to die. Awful, because one day they will. But in this story there is no death, just a father who gives, waits, embraces and forgives.

This is the unconditional love that awaits all who return to God and seek forgiveness.

The good news of this parable is that we are loved by God in this way. You may block the source of love, but God cannot stop loving you, no matter what. If you turn to God, the vigilant parent will see you from a long way off and run to meet you. God will embrace you and celebrate your return with great joy.

(Adapted from *Religious Education and the Comic Sensibility* by Frances Cotter)

MORAL DEVELOPMENT

ASIDE

A theory put forward by Lawrence Kohlberg suggests that we go through six different stages of moral development as follows:

1. Small infants base their moral thinking around reward and punishment. Something is perceived as bad if one is punished for the action, but not because the action is intrinsically bad in itself.
2. In the second stage of moral development, the person's thinking becomes more pragmatic and they view morality as something that is in their own interest. Morality is done in exchange for something that suits their own concerns.
3. In this stage, the person is becoming aware of the expectations of the wider community. They begin to realise that morality is not something that is dependent upon the individual. People now look to their parents and teachers and it becomes important to earn the respect and trust of those in authority by obeying the rules laid down.
4. Now the person looks to the norms and laws of the society to which they belong. A person is moral in so far as they maintain the rules as adopted by the social group.
5. The person now begins to base their morality not on what is socially accepted but on the underlying

the inner place

ethical principles of social norms. People reject a universal application of rules or principles to situations and they realise that morality is complex, demanding different responses to different situations.

6 In this last theoretical stage, moral judgement is based on the ethical principles for which laws are devised. The person realises that the rights of individuals transcend social or cultural boundaries.

In recent years, it has become apparent that we develop not only physically and socially but also morally. The morality of a child, for example, is not the same as that of an adult. Here we will examine the different stages of moral development.

MORAL DEVELOPMENT OF CHILDREN

As we grow, we change dramatically. For example, the way people think as teenagers is radically different from the way they thought as children. The way we think and feel about morality also changes. The small child views morality in terms of reward and punishment – 'If I don't write on the walls, there's a better chance I'll get sweeties!' An older child is more aware of the approval of others and will behave according to rules set down by parents and teachers, not because they are inherently good, but because if the child acts that way they will get approval. A child usually adopts the beliefs of parents. If the parent supports Manchester United, the child will most likely do the same. Children, therefore, are very much influenced in their moral thinking by their parents.

the

inner

place

MORAL DEVELOPMENT OF TEENAGERS

When the child reaches adolescence, everything changes, and so too their moral thinking. The teenager is seeking independence and is more aware of their own identity. Now it's not so cool to agree with parents and teachers. To be seen to disagree with them is a very effective way of saying that I have my own identity now. If the parents are dead against smoking, then smoking, though damaging to one's health, becomes a good way of establishing one's own identity. Not as much willing to listen to parents, teenagers are more influenced by their friends with regard to their moral thinking. For example, if the general consensus amongst teenagers is that the American war on Iraq is bad, then most teenagers will most likely go along with that. If teenagers generally feel that drinking to excess isn't bad at all, then many other teenagers are likely to adopt this value. As teenagers strive to become more independent of their parents and authority figures, they simply become more dependent on their peers.

MORAL MATURITY

Moral maturity is linked to independent thinking. As long as an individual is thinking and acting in accordance with what other people think, then moral maturity cannot be attained. When a person can go beyond reward and punishment, approval and disapproval, they can begin to think in a morally mature way. The person now adopts opinions and beliefs based on their own inner convictions. Of course, these opinions will be influenced by the person's environment, but not solely. The person is willing to be unpopular for their beliefs. The person is willing to look decidedly 'uncool' for what they believe in themselves. This is genuine independence and is a foundation for moral maturity.

DISCUSS

1 Why do you think teenagers are more likely to be influenced by their peers instead of their parents in moral decisions?

2 Give examples of instances where teenagers might be influenced to think in a particular way in regard to morality because of their peer group.

the
inner
place

SOURCES OF MORALITY

HOW DO I KNOW WHAT'S RIGHT AND WRONG?

In chapter 15, we examined the role that conscience plays in making moral decisions. We also noted that it is everyone's duty to inform their conscience in different ways. The different ways we develop and inform our conscience can be viewed as sources of morality. We have already examined the role that religion plays in morality as a source of guidance. Here are some other sources of morality.

Family: The family is a very influential source of morality for children. Children learn their basic moral framework in the home. They learn that stealing and telling lies are wrong. As previously noted, they accept these moral guidelines based on reward and punishment and approval.

Friends: Teenagers are more likely to turn to their friends as a source of morality. Teenagers are more likely to learn the parameters of social behaviour from their friends than from their parents. Teenagers are also influenced by the music they listen to and the television programmes they watch. They may be influenced by the group they associate themselves with as well, for example Grunge, Goth or Indie kids.

the inner place

The State: The State is a powerful source of morality because it has the power to arrest and imprison those who don't accept the moral norms of the land, as enshrined in its Constitution. Killing, stealing and violence towards others are all punishable by the State. The State also has the power to influence and change our moral behaviour. It is now not acceptable to drink and drive, and media campaigns have gone some way to change people's perception of alcohol abuse. Speeding is also now seen as being morally unacceptable. Twenty years ago, it was acceptable to boast openly about how quick a person could drive from A to B. Now it's generally perceived as being idiotic and a danger to others on the road. It was once acceptable to smoke in the workplace, but now information on passive smoking has altered people's perception of this cancer-related activity.

A conflict arises, however, between what the State accepts as morally acceptable and what individuals perceive as justifiable. During the Iraq war, the State deemed it acceptable for American aeroplanes involved in the war to use Shannon airport as a stopover from America to Iraq. However, many people believed the war wasn't justified, and so they protested outside Shannon airport. The State had the power to arrest those who tried to interfere with the planes.

Another area of conflict exists between the State and the Church. The State now allows people who have married to divorce. This is explicitly against the teachings of the Catholic Church. The State allows contraceptives to be sold, whereas the Church does not accept the use of contraceptives. Periodically in Ireland, referendums are held in order to change the Constitution. Referendums have been held with regard to abortion and divorce. These usually occasion heated debates between those who base their morality on Church teaching and those who favour a more liberal agenda.

the

inner

place

Can you think of any examples of where a person's morality came into conflict with the State? Alternatively, can you think of any examples of where a person's religious convictions came into conflict with State laws? Present your findings to the class.

the
inner
place

Chapter Seventeen

INFERTILITY AND
REPRODUCTIVE TECHNOLOGIES

THE DESIRE FOR A CHILD

One of the most basic of human instincts is for a couple to have a child. As a teenager, you may not be overly concerned with the desire to have a child, but in later years it may become a number-one priority for you. In older societies, the lifespan may have been as little as thirty to forty years, so people had to have children in their early teens. Now, with life expectancy at an all-time high, many young women are more inclined to wait until their late twenties or early thirties before they consider starting a family.

There is an inclination to believe that the reproductive process is fairly straightforward and something to be taken for granted. However, the reality is that one-sixth of couples experience fertility problems and have difficulty when it comes to conceiving a child. While this may seem like a cold fact, such couples feel like they are being denied what becomes for them the most important thing in the world. There's a certain carefreeness about teenage life, but eventually many people do want to settle down and have a family. For an infertile couple, it can be agonising to see their friends all produce children, while they face up to the inevitability of a childless marriage.

In response to this, in the last few decades the medical community has devised procedures to help treat infertility. While this is obviously something to be welcomed, many of the treatments have raised serious ethical and moral considerations. Reproductive technologies have allowed many childless couples to have children, but sometimes the technology can facilitate the creation of a child in some extraordinary situations.

Consider the following example from France, where a family decided they quickly needed an heir to their fortune.

An Extraordinary Birth

On 24 June 2001, *The Sunday Times* reported the case of Jeanine Salomone who, at the age of sixty-two, gave birth to a baby boy. Unable to conceive naturally at that age, Jeanine went through a fertility treatment that allowed her to become pregnant. In a normal pregnancy, the egg comes from the mother and the sperm from the father. In this case, the egg came from a young American woman, not Jeanine. What makes the case even stranger is that the sperm didn't come from her husband, but from her brother Robert. Jeanine was counting on Robert to save the family line and have children himself, but after a failed suicide attempt, when he blew off the bottom of his face with a shotgun, Jeanine decided to resort to science in order to protect their two-million-pound fortune.

It is unusual for a fertility doctor to enable a woman so old to become pregnant, but Dr Vicken Sahakian, a Lebanese expert in Los Angeles, treated Jeanine. Because Jeanine and Robert had the same surname, the clinic assumed they were husband and wife, yet it is usually customary for a clinic to ask how long a couple have been trying to have a child and how often they have sexual intercourse.

Jeanine paid nearly two thousand dollars for the procedure, known as IVF or *in vitro* fertilisation. The American donor egg was fertilised, using Robert's sperm, outside of Jeanine's womb in a glass or plastic dish. The fertilised egg was then placed inside Jeanine's womb. Dr Sahakian was unhappy that the

the

inner

place

326   Infertility and
       Reproductive Technologies

egg was fertilised by Jeanine's brother's sperm but he explained that the child would not be born as a result of incest because there was no genetic link between the donor egg and the sperm. Researchers in Switzerland, however, are considering the possibility of 'genetic bleed', whereby it may be possible for some of the host mother's DNA to leak into the donor egg while it is gestating. In that case, the egg would have some of Jeanine's DNA. This would raise critical issues about incest.

Jeanine eventually gave birth to a boy whom she named Benoit-David. But, as back-up, Robert fathered a child in the same clinic with a surrogate mother. In surrogacy, a woman agrees to carry a child for someone else, and hands it over when it is born. The surrogate mother gave birth to a girl named Marie-Cecile. The relationship between Benoit and Marie-Cecile is a little confusing. It would seem that Robert is Benoit-David's uncle and father, while he is Marie-Cecile's father. Neither child knows who their genetic mother is.

DISCUSS

1 At the time, locals were appalled by Jeanine's pregnancy. Why do you think people were so disturbed by the birth of Benoit-David?
2 Do you think Benoit-David was born as a result of incest by *in vitro* fertilisation?
3 Do you think Jeanine should have been allowed to have a child? Give reasons for your answer.

WHAT CAUSES INFERTILITY?

The reproductive years for both men and women begin with the commencement of puberty, but while men can remain reproductive all their lives, a woman ceases to be reproductive at her menopause. During her reproductive years, a woman produces an *ovum* or egg from her ovaries mid-way between her menstrual cycles. The ovum may be fertilised in the fallopian

tube in the event of sexual intercourse, and the resulting embryo travels down to the uterus, where it implants into the uterine wall.

A couple who attempt to have a child will only be treated as infertile if the woman fails to become pregnant after two years. It is usual for pregnancy to occur after six months of regular sexual intercourse. If fertility problems are encountered, they can be attributable to either the male or the female. In the case of the male, infertility is due to poor sperm quality or a low sperm count. Women may experience problems with infertility for a variety of reasons. Around one-third of infertility in women is caused by faulty fallopian tubes, where they may be blocked due to infection. Another cause is endometriosis, where there are problems with the lining of the uterus or uterine wall. A woman may also produce anti-sperm antibodies that attack sperm. However, around forty per cent of cases of infertility in women remain unexplained.

the

inner

place

DISCUSS

1   What effect do you think problems associated with infertility would have on a couple trying to start a family?
2   What kind of pressures are placed on a married couple to have children?

Infertility and
Reproductive Technologies

THE STATUS OF THE EMBRYO

As mentioned above, medical breakthroughs have resulted in a range of treatments for infertility in recent years. The treatments begin when pregnancy through normal sexual intercourse fails. In this chapter, we will examine different ways of treating infertility, along with many reproductive technologies. All seem very attractive, considering that all procedures are orientated towards the birth of a beautiful and healthy child. Yet one particular consideration must be taken into account before we begin our examination, and it concerns the status of the embryo.

An unborn child is an embryo from the moment of conception until two months. From two months until birth, the child is referred to medically as a foetus. Putting this simply, it means that human life begins at conception, and the resulting embryo is a human life. It means that your human life began when you were an embryo, and had that embryo been destroyed, you would not exist. It is important to establish the status of the embryo at this stage because in many reproductive treatments, excess numbers of embryos are created in the hope that one will implant in the womb and reach full maturity. Yet often the 'spare' embryos are sent for experimentation or are discarded. If we believe that human life begins with the embryo, then these procedures have obvious serious moral and ethical implications.

DISCUSS

1 Why do you think some people refuse to grant an embryo the status of human life?

2 In many treatments that we will examine shortly, human embryos are often stored outside the womb. These are known as *cryostored* embryos. That means that they are frozen in liquid nitrogen. At present, there are hundreds of thousands of cryostored embryos in laboratories around the world. What do you think should be the status of these embryos? Should they be regarded as full human beings, with all the rights of a human being? If so, what would be the implications?

the inner place

One line of argument is being put forward here, yet there are plenty of people who would question that the embryo has the status of a human life. We will now briefly examine two different arguments.

In some countries, it is legal to experiment on an embryo up until the fourteenth day. On the fourteenth day, a primitive streak is evident in the embryo and, according to some, it is only at this stage that the embryo should be afforded protection. The primitive streak shows the longitudinal axis along which the embryo will develop. Also, each primitive streak denotes an individual embryo, because up until the fourteenth day the embryo may cleave into two, or twin. According to this argument, before fourteen days the embryo could potentially develop into one or two primitive streaks. Therefore, until we are sure that the embryo is one, it cannot be regarded as an individual human being.

Yet in response to this argument, it must be noted that the majority of embryos do not twin, so therefore the majority of embryos before fourteen days are individual human beings. Even if the embryo is destined to twin, it simply means that there are two presences in the embryo instead of one, and both share the same body mass, just as Siamese twins can share vital organs.

Others accept that human life in theory begins at conception, but that the embryo should not be afforded the same rights as a fully mature human being. It is only as the embryo develops senses such as hearing and feels pain that it should be afforded more respect. Others claim that only when there is evidence of rationality and an awareness of self, should full human rights be recognised.

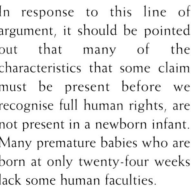
Premature baby

In response to this line of argument, it should be pointed out that many of the characteristics that some claim must be present before we recognise full human rights, are not present in a newborn infant. Many premature babies who are born at only twenty-four weeks lack some human faculties.

the
inner
place

Infertility and
Reproductive Technologies

TREATING INFERTILITY

We will now examine four current technologies.

1 *IN VITRO* FERTILISATION (IVF)

This treatment refers to the process whereby an egg is fertilised outside the body in a glass or plastic dish. It is offered to couples who experience infertility for any of the reasons outlined above. *In vitro* fertilisation, or IVF, however, represents a complicated and emotionally difficult time for any couple. It operates as follows. First the woman's ovaries are stimulated to produce multiple *ova* or eggs. The drugs may have to be injected into the woman daily over a monthly period and can cause some discomfort, and they are not risk-free. The eggs are allowed to ripen and then they are

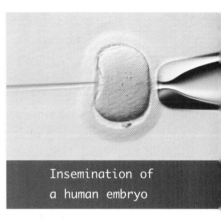

Insemination of a human embryo

removed, during which time sperm is obtained from the man by masturbation. The ova are then fertilised individually and several embryos are created. After a couple of days, two or three embryos are transferred to the uterus using a fine plastic tube. In IVF, there are always excess embryos and they can be stored for future use, used for experimentation or discarded.

ASIDE

Louise Brown was the first child to be born using *in vitro* fertilisation (IVF). She was conceived *in vitro*, which means 'on glass', as opposed to in the womb. She was born on 25 July 1978 in Manchester, England. She was known as the first 'test-tube baby'. The doctors, Steptoe and Edwards, had managed to remove ova or eggs from her mother's womb, and then fertilised them with semen on a culture dish in a medical laboratory.

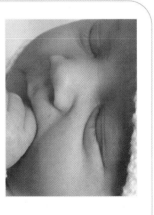

the inner place

DISCUSS

Louise Brown was a celebrity baby and each birthday she was watched with interest by the media. Why do you think she received so much attention? How do you imagine she would have felt about being the first 'test-tube baby'?

IVF gives hope to many childless couples, but less than thirty per cent result in pregnancy. This means that seventy per cent of couples will experience emotional distress and discomfort. Whether the process is successful or not, it entails a very definite trauma for the couple, as the following account by a woman undergoing IVF treatment shows.

> The thing about infertility is that you can't justify it. I couldn't possibly ring up work and announce that I had picked up a bad dose of infertility and that there was no way I would be able to do my job today. And so, although some days I feel worse than if I had the worst possible flu, I get no sympathy because… what do you say? Life goes on. I look fine. Every day I go into work with infertility.
>
> So, I'm sniffing and sniffing. Four times a day. One sniff up each nostril. I am completely mithered. Yesterday, I came downstairs especially to take the 5.30 sniff and an hour later I could not remember whether I had taken it or not. I suspect I may not have, as I had a temporary lapse into good humour around eight o'clock.
>
> I am acutely aware of every little twitch in my body. A spot, yes it's there on the list of side effects. Dry skin, that's there too. Hoarseness, I have it.
>
> On our first IVF attempt, after sniffing for about ten days, my face went all tingly and numb. I was assured by a very nice doctor at the clinic that this was probably temporary and, sure enough, when I stopped sniffing the numbness went away.

the

inner

place

Infertility and
Reproductive Technologies

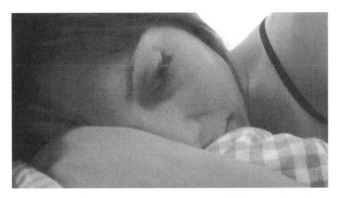

My mind has gone haywire. We can't plan anything. Our lives are on hold. We have to take into account scans, sedation for egg collection, the transfer, resting and the outcome. We are afraid to think too far ahead.

I am in a permanent state of disguise. As far as the outside world is concerned, I'm fine, pleasant, accommodating, helpful, kind. But J bears testimony to my other self. The anti-pleasant, the not-so-helpful, over-emotional wreck.

I find it hard to imagine how anyone gets pregnant by accident. Over the next few weeks my body will be monitored by the experts at the clinic. I will be scanned regularly, blood will be taken, J will inject me with hormones. Hopefully my ovaries will produce sufficient follicles to allow for egg collection. Then the embryologist takes over. The sperms have to be "washed" to remove seminal plasma, which becomes toxic over time and inhibits fertilisation, and then the inseminated eggs are put in an incubator. The thing about being involved in this stage of the cycle is that there is hope. IVF works for some people. I hope it works for us.

(*The Sunday Times*, 9/5/04)

DISCUSS

In your opinion, what kind of trauma does IVF involve for a couple?

the

inner

place

2 ARTIFICIAL INSEMINATION BY HUSBAND (AIH)

In some cases of infertility, the man has a low sperm count or the quality of his sperm is insufficient to achieve conception by normal means. In AIH, the man produces sperm through masturbation and it is then inserted into the woman's uterus in sufficient quantity to improve the chances of conception. AIH is also used if the woman's cervical mucus contains anti-sperm antibodies or the mucus is abnormal or absent. In this case, the procedure places the sperm directly in the uterus, thus bypassing the passage of the sperm through the mucus into the uterus.

3 DONOR INSEMINATION (DI)

If a man has low sperm count or poor sperm quality, then a couple can resort to Donor Insemination, whereby the sperm of a donor is used to achieve pregnancy. Alternatively, a man may have a hereditary condition that he does not want to pass on to his offspring, so donor sperm is used instead, using the same method as Artificial Insemination by Husband.

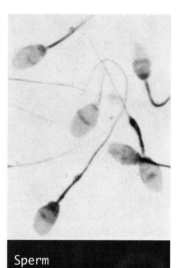

Sperm

Donors are aged between eighteen and fifty-five and are screened for a variety of diseases, including AIDS, syphilis and cystic fibrosis. The sample is stored for six months, and then it is tested again, as some diseases such as AIDS may not show up on the initial sample. The identity of the donor is not provided, but certain characteristics such as skin colour, blood group and occupation may be included so as to provide as close a match as possible to the woman who is the recipient of the sperm. In the UK, if a married couple does choose to use Donor Insemination, the husband can register himself as the child's father on the birth certificate. This raises serious issues with regard to the child's right to know who their father was.

the

inner

place

Infertility and
Reproductive Technologies

4   GAMETE INTRAFALLOPIAN TRANSFER (GIFT)
ZYGOTE INTRAFALLOPIAN TRANSFER (ZIFT)

In the first procedure (GIFT), a special instrument is used to place eggs and sperm into the woman's fallopian tubes, where fertilisation normally occurs. In the second procedure (ZIFT), the same instrument is used to place a fertilised egg or *zygote* (single-cell embryo) into the fallopian tubes.

In each procedure, either spouses or donors may provide the sperms or eggs. In the latter procedure, excess embryos may be frozen and used in later procedures if other children are wanted. In comparison to natural reproduction methods, around thirty to seventy per cent of zygotes fail to implant, or the pregnancy results in spontaneous abortion or miscarriage.

THE STATUS OF THE EMBRYO IN CATHOLIC CHURCH TEACHING

Everyone started out life in embryonic form. Everyone reading this was a cluster of cells only a few days old. Yet if an embryo that is only a few days old has no rights, then there was a time when all of us could have had our lives experimented on or discarded. It is tempting to view a cluster of cells as simply that, but Pope John Paul II in his encyclical letter *Evangelium vitae* in 1995 reminded all that to interfere with human life at any stage is to interfere with what God has planned for that life; 'the dignity of this life is linked not only to its beginning, to the fact that it comes from God, but also to its

final end, to its destiny of fellowship with God in knowledge and love of God' (par. 38). The status of the human embryo then is based on the fact that its origins are in God and its destiny is ultimately to share in God's absolute love for that life. The

human journey starts with God at the moment of conception and, despite its primitive form, the embryo is loved by God and destined to journey with God into the promise of eternal life.

According to Catholic tradition, the embryo must be granted the same rights as any human being and must not be discriminated against. In *Donum vitae*, the Catholic Church outlines the following points with regard to the status of the human embryo:

- The Church defends the right to life of the human being from the moment of conception: 'The human being is to be respected and treated as a person from the moment of conception; and therefore from that same moment his [or her] rights as a person must be recognised, among which in the first place is the inviolable right of every innocent human being to life' (chap. 1, par. 1). It is unacceptable, therefore, that any embryo should be disposed of in any reproductive treatments, including IVF and ZIFT.

- The Church defends the right of the embryo not to be subjected to experimentation unless it is for the sole benefit of the embryo in terms of some therapeutic procedure: 'If embryos are living, whether viable or not, they must be respected like any other human person; experimentation on human embryos which is not directly therapeutic is illicit' (chap. 1, par. 1).

- In certain reproductive therapies, embryos that are created but not used are frozen and stored. This procedure, however, exposes the embryo to unnecessary risk and damage: 'The freezing of embryos, even when carried out to preserve the life of an embryo – cryopreservation – constitutes an offence against the respect due to human beings by exposing them to grave risks of death or harm to their physical integrity and depriving them, at least temporarily, of maternal shelter and gestation, thus placing them in a situation in which further offences and manipulation are possible' (chap. 1, par. 6).

Many couples experience genuine problems when it comes to trying to have a child. As noted, there are now various treatments that can treat infertility, yet many seriously infringe on the rights of the embryo. However, it must be noted that the Church does

Infertility and
Reproductive Technologies

not object to the use of technology in aiding a couple to become pregnant. The Church does not object to hormonal treatment to increase fertility, nor to the use of procedures that make sexual intercourse more effective. What the Church does object to are reproductive technologies that include the donation of sperm or eggs, technologies that bypass sexual intercourse and procedures that undermine marriage as the proper context for procreation.

DISCUSS

1 In Catholic Church teaching, on what is the status of the embryo based?
2 Why does the Catholic Church object to IVF?
3 What forms of fertility treatment does the Catholic Church not object to?

PROCREATION AND MARRIAGE IN CATHOLIC CHURCH TEACHING

Some of the medical procedures used when treating infertility involve the donation of *gametes* or the egg or sperm. If a child is created in such a manner, then a third part has been added to the spousal relationship of a husband and wife. The child that is born has a genetic link to only one of its parents. According to Catholic teaching, the child that is born should be genetically linked to both its father and its mother. The reason for this is that the child is created in the love of God, and its creation must reflect the love that exists between both its

the inner place

Infertility and Reproductive Technologies

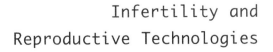

parents. The child that is born becomes a sign of their love: 'The procreation of a new person, whereby man and woman collaborate with the power of the Creator, must be the fruit and the sign of the mutual self-giving of the spouses, of their love and their fidelity' (*Donum vitae*, chap. 2, par. 1).

PROCREATION AND THE PROCREATIVE ACT IN CATHOLIC TEACHING

According to Catholic teaching, procreation is not simply a human act. Instead, it must be understood in the context of a husband and wife being co-creators with God. Our relationship with God is one of love, and so a child must be created within the loving act of

sexual intercourse between its parents: 'The human person must be accepted in his[/her] parents' act of union and love; the generation of a child must therefore be the fruit of that mutual giving which is realised in the conjugal act wherein the spouses co-operate as servants and not as masters in the work of the creator who is Love' (*Donum vitae*, chap. 2, par. 4).

Human procreation should be the result of the physical union between a husband and wife. If a human life is created using medical technologies in the place of sexual intercourse, then the child is a product of technology and is reduced to a scientific object:

The one conceived must be the fruit of his[/her] parents' love. He[/she] cannot be desired or conceived as the product of an intervention of medical or biological techniques; that would be the equivalent to reducing him[/her] to an object of scientific technology.

(*Donum vitae*, chap. 2, par. 4)

338

Infertility and
Reproductive Technologies

TREATING INFERTILITY: A MORAL DILEMMA

In chapter 15 we examined the process involved in making a morally mature decision. We will now apply this process to the moral dilemma of treating infertility.

A Moral Situation: Morality concerns itself with actions that are right or wrong, and the treatment of infertility is a moral dilemma because it raises the issue of whether the treatment is right or wrong.

Applying Values: A moral dilemma can arise when there emerges a conflict of values with regard to a particular situation. Here we will take the example of a married couple who want to have a family but are unable to do so using natural means. They value having children and bringing them up in a caring and loving environment. Unable to have children by natural means, they look to reproductive technologies.

Informing Conscience: The couple become aware that some technologies raise serious ethical questions regarding the treatment of embryos. Some technologies also involve sperm or egg donation. For whatever reason, the couple may value the life of the embryo. The dilemma arises because of a conflict of values: between the value they place on having children and the value they place on the life of the embryo.

The Religious Perspective: If the couple are Catholic, they will be aware of Church teaching, which raises serious questions regarding the status of the embryo in reproductive technologies. The Church also objects to technologies that include the donation of sperm or eggs, or to technologies that bypass sexual intercourse as the proper context for procreation.

Doing the Right Thing: Having informed their conscience, the couple then must decide what is the right thing to do. If they are religious, they will also take into consideration the teachings of their religion.

the

inner

place

Infertility and
Reproductive Technologies

REPRODUCTIVE TECHNOLOGIES

So far in this chapter, we have examined methods whereby medical procedures can treat infertility for couples who experience difficulties. Yet some of these same technologies, and others, can be used not simply to overcome infertility for couples but, in instances, to assist individuals or same-sex partners to have children. Read the following account outlining how a single woman got pregnant using donor insemination after buying sperm online.

The morning I found out I was pregnant I ran out of my gynaecologist's office, whipped out my mobile and dialed my therapist's number. I didn't know who else to call. After leaving the news on his voicemail, I decided to tell my friend Amy, my friend Linda and then the clerk at Whole Foods, who directed me to the prenatal vitamins. By the end of the day I'd told everyone from my mother to my postman.

I didn't, however, tell the baby's father. I wanted to, but I have no idea who he is. I'm not married, don't have a boyfriend, and hadn't recently returned from a drunken one-night stand. Instead I got knocked up by half a cubic centimetre of defrosted sperm that had been posted in a nitrogen tank from an east-coast donor facility to my doctor in Los Angeles. Now, if all goes well, my dream will become a reality: I'll be a single mum...

I guess you could say I was cheating on my boyfriend back in 2003 when I logged on and typed out a sperm bank's URL. Or maybe it was more like viewing internet porn: I wasn't scouring dating sites for actual boyfriends, but I was certainly fantasising about what was out there. Could I find someone younger, taller, more athletic-looking and mathematically gifted – but who also wasn't 'real', and therefore wouldn't shoot icy stares at me across the dinner table?

the inner place

Infertility and Reproductive Technologies

Many of the guys sounded like men I'd want to date. Maybe, I thought, the sperm banks should just have a big singles party and cut out the middleman. Then I remembered my boyfriend – I'd met him through an online dating site where I'd selected him, too, based on a written profile. On some level I must have been attracted to the same Darwinian characteristics.

The thought saddened me. Whatever happened to love? Or was believing in love today akin to believing in Santa Claus, the Easter Bunny and age-defying cosmetics?

At the same time it felt liberating. Without the emotional context, finding the donor seemed less like the intimate act of finding the child's father and more like buying a car. One could select a basic model (tall, good-looking, healthy) and then accessorise with options (musical, adventurous, likes museums).

The irony wasn't lost on me: I was considering spending all that money when I had my boyfriend's good sperm at the ready. One friend suggested that I let him get me pregnant 'accidentally' and then

the
inner
place

break up and ask for custody in exchange for releasing him from all financial obligations. Another friend suggested I get pregnant, break up, and not tell him at all. But what kind of mum would I be, duping an innocent boyfriend into having a baby? Hard as it might be to tell my child about a sperm donor, I figured it would be far easier than trying to explain that Mommy was a conniving liar...

Some sperm banks claim to restrict donors to 10 or even 25 births each, with an exemption for siblings (which, I suppose, could theoretically mean as many as 40 to 50 kids per donor, especially given the high rate of twins and triplets with artificial-insemination treatments). But since there's no formal system of reporting births to the banks, and since a high percentage of women who postpone marriage live in big cities such as New York or Los Angeles, a high percentage of our children will live in the same communities. What if my future child falls in love with a classmate in high school, and unbeknown to them their half siblings?

And yet there was a silver lining. By bypassing the uncontrollable world of romance, I was able to choose a man to father my child who might be completely out of my league in the real world. Instead of marrying a schlubby but lovable man and thinking, I hope our kid doesn't get his crooked nose or bad eyesight or thin hair, I could pick from cold hard DNA.

(*The Sunday Times*, 21/8/05)

the

inner

place

Infertility and
Reproductive Technologies

1. The author ponders what has happened to love in the context of bringing a child into the world. How do you react to the way she creates her child in the complete absence of a loving and physical relationship between a man and a woman?

2. 'Buying sperm online was a bit like buying a car.' What is your reaction to children being treated as commodities that can be bought online?

3. How do you think this child will react to the news that his or her father's sperm was bought online? Should she tell the child? Give reasons for your answer.

4. One consequence of reproductive technologies is that, given the anonymity of the donors, half siblings could well form relationships with each other without realising they are half sisters and brothers. Can you identify other consequences of the above procedure that might have negative effects on the child?

the

inner

place

Chapter Eighteen
THE GENETICS DEBATE

The desire to live a long and healthy life preoccupies most cultures and modern societies. To be human is to fear sickness and the inevitability of death. It's not surprising then that so much scientific and medical effort goes into creating new treatments for disease and new therapies, thus preventing the proximity of death. The questions we pose in this chapter are: just how far will medicine and science go in order to deliver our biological and medical needs, and, more importantly, what are the ethical and moral concerns for such advances?

The Pigoon Project
Often we are given a glimpse into the future through fiction or film. In her book *Oryx and Crake*, Margaret Atwood creates a vision of a future world that is host to the 'pigoon project', where pigs are genetically manipulated to grow human tissue and organs. As we will see in this chapter, however, science fiction can sometimes become medical fact.

The goal of the pigoon project was to grow an assortment of foolproof human-tissue organs in a transgenic knockout pig host – organs that would transplant smoothly and avoid rejection, but would also be able to fend off attacks by opportunistic microbes and viruses, of which there were more strains every year. A rapid-maturity gene was spliced in so the pigoon kidneys and livers and hearts would be ready sooner, and now they were perfecting a pigoon that could grow five or six kidneys at a time.

Such a host animal could be reaped of its extra kidneys then, rather than being destroyed, and it could keep on living and grow more organs, much as a lobster could grow another claw to replace a missing one. That would be less wasteful, as it took a lot of food and care to grow a pigoon. A great deal of investment money had gone into OrganInc Farms...

The pigoon organs could be customised, using cells from individual human donors, and the organs were frozen until needed. It was much cheaper than getting yourself cloned for spare parts – or keeping a for-harvest child or two stashed away in some illegal baby orchard. In the OrganInc brochures and promotional materials, glossy and discreetly worded, stress was laid on the efficacy and comparative health benefits of the pigoon procedure. Also, to set the queasy at ease, it was claimed that none of the defunct pigoons ended up as bacon and sausages: no one would want to eat an animal whose cells might be identical with at least some of their own.

Still, as time went on and the coastal aquifers turned salty and the northern permafrost melted and the vast tundra bubbled with methane and the drought in the midcontinental plains regions went on and on, and the Asian steppes turned to sand dunes, and meat became harder to come by, some people had their doubts. Within OrganInc Farms itself it was noticeable how often back bacon and ham sandwiches and pork pies turned up on the staff café menu.

(Margaret Atwood, *Oryx and Crake*)

the

inner

place

1   The vision of the future given in the extract above includes human organ-growing pigs and baby orchards where people hide their illegal clones in case they might need to transplant an organ or two in the future. Though fictional, do you think such a world might some day exist? Do you think it is something we should welcome or fear? Explain your answer.

2   In what ways do you think morality and ethical concerns might challenge such a world?

THE HUMAN GENOME PROJECT

In 1990, one of the most ambitious scientific projects began. It promised to have far-reaching consequences for our understanding of the genetic structure of human beings. It was called The Human Genome Project. Its objective was to map all the genes that determine human life.

ASIDE

In 1953, James Watson and Francis Crick discovered human DNA in the nucleus of each human cell. It had long remained a secret as to how human life reproduced itself. Crick and Watson discovered a DNA molecule which comprised of a double-helix-like structure. This structure was quite like a twisted ladder with two strips of twisted strands. The ladder acts like a zipper, and when it is unzipped each strand bears the identical information of the other. Now with two identical strands a cell can divide, and this ability for exact replication of a cell is essential to human life.

James Watson

Francis Crick

the inner place

Every living organism has a genetic code on its DNA. The twenty-three rungs on the DNA ladder each have 30,000 genes. Each gene has a specific function in determining the production of a protein that guides the growth and development of the organism. So, for example, there is a gene that determines hair colour and height. There is also a gene that causes the colour of eyes and skin. What was really fascinating for those involved in the project was the possibility of discovering the genes that could be attributed to cancer and other diseases.

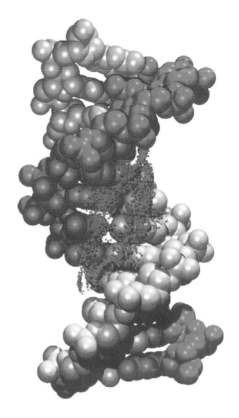

For years, cancer treatment has relied on three options: surgery, radiotherapy and chemotherapy. Progress has been slow. Yet the Human Genome Project sought to identify all 30,000 genes and their function. If the genes that caused certain diseases could be identified, then medicine would be less concerned with treatment of symptoms and more concerned with the fundamental causes of the disease. To date, the genes that cause many diseases, including cancers, have been identified, and new discoveries of genes and their functions continue.

the

inner

place

DISCUSS

1 Do you think the ability to predict disease is a good thing? What if life insurance companies decided that you had to send in your genetic sequence before they would cover you?

2 If the genes responsible for violence or criminality were discovered, what might be the implications? Would every human born have to be screened? What do you think civil authorities might do with that kind of information?

3 In the future, if you went on a date, do you think it's possible you might be asked for a copy of your genetic sequence before it went any further? What would that do to romance?

GENE THERAPY

The breakthroughs in the Genome Project obviously lead to the question as to whether it is possible to remove a defective gene that causes some disease. Would it then be possible to replace it with one that creates proteins that do not contribute to that disorder? Scientists have discovered that there are two possible types of gene therapy.

1   Somatic-cell gene therapy: Here cells that are not egg or sperm cells are targeted. Defective cells belonging to organs like the lungs or liver are targeted. This form of therapy would only affect the person who receives the therapy and would most probably not be passed on to future generations.

2   Germ-line therapy: This form of gene therapy tries to eradicate a disease that is being inherited from parent to child. In this therapy, egg and sperm cells are targeted. Here, future generations would be affected and defective genes would not be passed on to offspring. To date, this type of therapy has not been tested on humans.

Gene therapy is proving to be difficult to achieve and is dependent on other IVF technological breakthroughs. So far,

the

inner

place

gene surgery is proving elusive, but types of gene addition are progressing. In the case of gene addition, special viruses, known as retroviruses, are designed so as to infiltrate the human cell in order to replace some defective DNA with its own specially harvested DNA. The difficulty is to persuade the body to accept and adopt the new genes without rejecting them through its own immune system. Unfortunately, in 1999, Jesse Geslinger, a volunteer at the University of Pennsylvania, died as a result of gene therapy, due to the reaction of her own immune system. Safe gene therapy would appear to be a long way off.

> **DISCUSS**
>
> What are your own fears about a world where we can tamper with a person's genetic make-up? What do you think might be possible adverse consequences of interfering with human genes?

PRE-IMPLANTATION GENETIC DIAGNOSIS (PGD)

Advancements in genetic technology have presented the possibility of actively determining the genetic make-up of a child before it is born. The technologies obviously exist because of the perceived advantages of selecting one embryo over another. Yet what would it be like for a person to have been selected or created for a specific purpose? In her novel *My Sister's Keeper*, Jodi Picoult tells the story of Anna, who was created 'because a scientist managed to hook up my mother's eggs and my father's sperm to create a specific combination of precious genetic material'. Anna was created to serve a particular purpose; to be a perfect genetic match to save her sister's life.

> Kate has acute promyelocytic leukaemia. Actually, that's not quite true – right now she doesn't have it, but it's hibernating under her skin like a bear, until it

decides to roar again. She was diagnosed when she was two; she's sixteen now. Molecular relapse and granulocyte and portacath – these words are part of my vocabulary, even though I'll never find them on any SAT. I'm an allogeneic donor – a perfect sibling match. When Kate needs leukocytes or stem cells or bone marrow to fool her body into thinking it's healthy, I'm the one who provides them. Nearly every time Kate's hospitalised, I wind up there, too…

There is way too much to explain – my own blood seeping into my sister's veins; the nurses holding me down to stick me for white cells Kate might borrow; the doctor saying they didn't get enough the first time around. The bruises and the deep bone ache after I gave up my marrow; the shots that sparked more stem cells in me, so that there'd be extra for my sister. The fact that I'm not sick, but I might as well be. The fact that the only reason I was born was as a harvest crop for Kate. The fact that even now, a major decision about me is being made, and no one's bothered to ask the one person who most deserves it to speak her opinion.

There's way too much to explain, and so I do the best I can. 'It's not God. Just my parents,' I say. 'I want to sue them for the rights to my own body.'

(Jodi Picoult, *My Sister's Keeper*)

the
inner
place

DISCUSS

1 'I wouldn't be alive if it wasn't for Kate being sick.' Do you think Kate's parents made the right decision when they decided to create another baby to save their daughter's life? Give reasons for your answer.

2 Do you think Anna was right to want to sue her parents? Give reasons for your answer.

The Genetics Debate

3   What are the ethical implications if embryos were discarded before Anna was born? Is it right to destroy other embryos so as to find the right one in order to help a sick child? What moral principles could be applied here that we studied in earlier chapters?

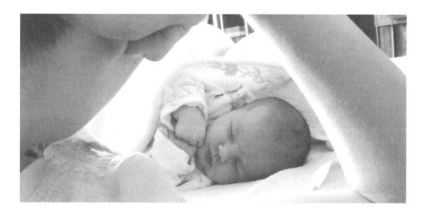

In chapter 17, we examined the process and moral implications of *in vitro* fertilisation (IVF). Pre-implantation genetic diagnosis, or PGD, is a combination of the reproductive procedures associated with IVF and genetic technologies. In PGD, embryos created outside the body through IVF can be screened in the laboratory for possible genetic defects before the embryos are implanted into the womb. Sometimes the screening is done to establish the sex of the embryo, because some diseases that are passed on from parents are passed only through a particular sex. PGD is used, for example, to screen for cystic fibrosis and Down's syndrome amongst others.

PGD is dependent upon the ethical and physical unpleasantness of IVF. For the parents, there is the stress of the uncertainty surrounding this type of procedure, where nothing is guaranteed. This emotional burden is coupled with a considerable financial one. The process involves removing one or two cells from the developing embryo around two or three days after fertilisation. Due to the advances in science, the cells can then be screened for their genetic material to see if there are defective genes present.

the
inner
place

DISCUSS

1 What do you think would be the possible implications for society if PGD became widely available? For example, would parents be under pressure to avail of the treatment in case their child was disabled or seriously ill?

2 Do you think PGD brings with it the suggestion that disabled or sick children are no longer welcome in a modern society? How do you feel about that?

3 What would be your own reservations about the possible availability of PGD?

Ethical Concerns

PGD seems to have found favour amongst those who are against abortion and the destruction of an embryo after it implants in the womb. These same people, however, do not consider the pre-implantation embryo to be a person. In chapter 17, we considered the ethical issues around the status of the embryo, and these obviously apply here with regard to the pre-implantation embryo. There are also the ethical and moral consequences of IVF and, even though there would appear to be no adverse effect from IVF on children born through this procedure, the effect of removing cells from a three-day-old embryo, approximately one-eighth of its total cells, is still far from certain.

If PGD eventually became used quite extensively in a society, there might emerge social pressure to avail of the procedure. If parents are known to carry defective genes and their offspring also have them, some might accuse them of being irresponsible for not using PGD so as to ensure that their offspring wouldn't suffer the consequences of genetic defects. Parents might be made feel guilty for having children who are disabled.

In this environment, children might become commodities that are manufactured and loved on condition that they possess the desired requirements. PGD offers a future where parents might create multiple amounts of embryos, select the best, modify it and then give birth to a 'perfect baby'. The child then becomes 'a thing' that is bought in the PGD clinic. Some parents would no doubt sue and complain if everything didn't work out according to plan; 'We like the colour of the eyes but they were definitely brighter in the brochure.' Can such children be brought back for a refund?

HUMAN CLONING

Science Fiction Nightmare

For years, cloning was the stuff of pure science fiction. Cloning refers to the process of creating an identical organism from a living one. An unfertilised egg has its genetic material in its nucleus. In cloning, this material is removed and replaced with the genetic material of the donor. The egg is then activated and  begins to divide to become the genetically identical replica of the donor. Cloning offers the possibility of creating genetically identical humans.

ASIDE

When cloning belonged to the realms of science fiction, a world was envisaged whereby genetically superior humans would be cloned so that the world would be full of identically superior humans. It was a world where individuality was of no value. It was also a world that was heading for extensive civil disorder, where the cloned ones would begin to dominate those who were genetically inferior. A world of the genetically 'haves' and 'have nots' would descend into anarchy and chaos. Alternatively, a Hitler-type character would decide to clone himself many times to ensure that his 'vision' for the world would continue after his death. For obvious reasons, this was never desirable.

the inner place

On 24 February 1997, a team of scientists from the Roslin Institute in Edinburgh successfully cloned a sheep named Dolly. It achieved worldwide attention, yet only for the reason that it heralded the very real prospect of human cloning. Immediately, human cloning was banned in most countries, yet despite this, various groups have claimed to have produced the first human clone. To date, none has been verified.

It is generally accepted that there are two types of cloning: reproductive and therapeutic.

REPRODUCTIVE CLONING

Reproductive cloning refers to the process of creating new and identical human beings. It involves the use of IVF, whereby the genetic material from one parent only is used. The child born would be genetically identical to the donor parent. (Therapeutic cloning creates cloned embryos that are not implanted in the womb. These embryos would be used to treat the original cloned human.)

Reproductive cloning has not yet been achieved and the procedure presents many challenges. In total, 277 sheep eggs had to be used before the cloning procedure for 'Dolly' the sheep was successful, and so to clone a human would also require the use of many eggs. In addition, there are also doubts regarding the wellbeing of the clone. Cloned sheep have developed medical problems, and so the process is by no means problem-free.

The Possibilities
In theory, cloning offers the following possibilities:

- As fertility treatment for couples. If all other treatments fail, the DNA from the father or mother would be inserted into the mother's egg. The fertilised egg would then be implanted, and the woman would give birth to a baby which would be the clone of either the father or the mother.

- As part of fertility treatment, DNA could be taken from the mother and put into a donor egg taken from another woman. The fertilised egg could then be implanted into a

third woman, who would act as a donor womb. In effect, the child would have three 'mothers'.

- Two homosexual men could clone one partner and, using a donor egg, could then implant the clone in a donor womb. The child would have two 'mothers' and its 'father' would be its own clone.

- Two lesbian women could clone one partner and, using one of their eggs, they could implant the egg in one of their wombs. This procedure would require donor sperm. The child would not know its father, and its mother would be its own clone.

- A single person could clone themselves using the above procedures, and then bring up their clone as their offspring, a situation whereby 'you' would mean 'you'.

- In cases where organ donors were needed for a sick child, a clone of the child could be created. The clone could then provide, for example, bone marrow for the sick child. (See *My Sister's Keeper* above.)

- A couple who lost a child in some tragedy could create a clone of the child so as to replace a dead sibling. The child would be loved for who they are and who they were, which really seems very strange.

- Eventually people could make clones of themselves in laboratories. These clones could be created without any form of consciousness, and simply exist on life-support machines, to be used whenever the original donor needed a replacement organ. If a vital organ were needed, it could be removed from the clone, who would then be switched off. (Remember the 'baby orchards' in *Oryx and Crake* above?)

- Using the above procedure, and given that brain transplants became possible, a person could have their brain transplanted into their clone. A sixty-year-old could then continue living in a much younger cloned body. (Take a moment to consider this last surgical procedure. Do you think he or she would still be the same person? What would happen to their mnd or their soul? What would happen to their personality?)

the

inner

place

Some of the above options might seem like they belong to the realm of science fiction, but cloning itself belonged to science fiction up until the end of the last century.

Ethical Concerns

People who favour cloning as a reproductive technique argue that couples have the right to have children in any way they want, as long as it doesn't harm the cloned child and as long as everyone gives their consent and nobody is forced into the procedure. But how exactly you get the consent of an embryo is far from certain and, as we noticed above in *My Sister's Keeper*, it's quite possible that the cloned child will be vulnerable to exploitation.

So far, animal cloning experiences a very high failure rate, and sometimes the 'failure' is only detected after birth. What would be done with clones who are deemed to be a 'failure'? As mentioned already, if a clone were created simply as a donor to a sibling, this would raise serious issues with regard to consent.

ASSIGNMENT

In terms of the cloned child, there are obvious ethical concerns around identity and relationships. Consider trying to answer some of the following questions to a cloned child.

- If a male child is cloned from his father, then does the child relate to its father as father or as twin brother?
- Is the child's father really his grandfather?
- What is the child's relationship to his siblings and to his mother?
- If the child is cloned from his father, then is the woman he lives with his mother or his wife?

These seem bizarre questions, but they are totally relevant nonetheless. Also, as mentioned above, if a clone was created to replace a dead sibling, then there are obvious psychological issues, such as 'Why am I loved? Is it because of who I am or because I am my dead sibling's replacement?'

the

inner

place

DISCUSS

1 If cloning became readily available for humans, who do you think might use it?
2 What are your fears about cloning? Consider, for example, if a tyrannical dictator cloned himself or herself over and over. What are the moral issues for you concerning cloning?

THERAPEUTIC CLONING: STEM-CELL RESEARCH

When an organ is damaged in a human being, traditional treatment has been to replace the organ from a donor. When a person dies, organs can be harvested from the body once consent has been given prior to death. Alternatively, siblings can become donors. The problem with transplants is that they can be rejected by the body's own immune system. The body can fight the new organ because it is a foreign tissue. An obvious way around this problem is for the body to grow its own replacement organs through cloning.

Genetic research has discovered that special cells in the developing embryo have the ability to become any type of tissue or organ. These special cells are called stem cells and, if they are cultivated, they could replace diseased organs. These cells could be used to create new heart, spinal or lung tissue. Theoretically, then, they could be used to heal damaged spinal cords or to provide sheets of skin for burn victims. They could also be used to create neurons or brain cells for victims of Parkinson's or Alzheimer's disease.

Yet stem-cell research is dependent upon cloning, and once the cells are removed from the embryo it is destroyed. If one accepts that the embryo is a human person, then this leads to obvious moral and ethical objections.

the

inner

place

Another serious objection to embryonic stem-cell research is that it may not be needed. Research has shown that stem cells can be obtained from the body itself without recourse to cloning. Adult stem cells can be taken from the body and cultivated for diseased areas. They can also be taken from umbilical cord blood. Blood stem cells can be cultivated to treat leukaemia, and stem cells taken from leg muscles have been used to treat damaged heart tissue. There are no moral objections to this procedure.

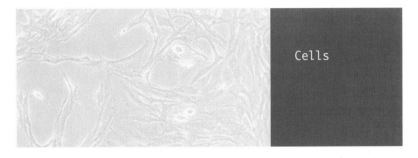

Cells

Yet scientists are not convinced by the use of adult stem cells and they maintain that while they have their uses, embryonic cells are far more flexible and adaptable. In accordance with Catholic teaching, their stance is morally objectionable.

DISCUSS

1 Some commentators believe that therapeutic cloning, for example, to treat burns or heart disease, would eventually lead to reproductive cloning for children. Do you agree with their stance? Give reasons for your answer.

2 Some researchers believe that because of the shortage of human donor eggs, it may be necessary to create embryos for stem-cell research using rabbit eggs that have had their genetic material removed and replaced with human DNA. In your opinion, what are the dangers associated with this type of research, where rabbit–human hybrids are created?

the

inner

place

GENETIC ENHANCEMENT: A GLIMPSE OF THE FUTURE?

The process of genetic enhancement has often been referred to as 'designer babies'. Whilst gene therapy attempts to remove defective genes from a person's genetic make-up, genetic enhancement is an attempt to improve the otherwise normal genetic make-up of the person. To date, this process is not available, but given the cultural obsession with plastic surgery and physical makeovers, it would be no surprise to see a steady demand develop for a genetically engineered baby. Parents might argue that they are only doing what's best for their child and that they want to give them the best chance in life. So, instead of paying out money on plastic surgery to make their daughter absolutely beautiful, parents could have it sorted before birth by inserting genes that are attributed to physical beauty. Instead of paying out for fees to private collages and grind schools, parents could genetically engineer their child to be intelligent.

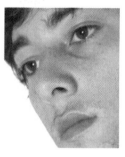

Genetic enhancement faces many challenges. First, there are the ethical and moral issues which a discerning public might be too well aware of. For example, what happens if the child does not turn out as planned? What are the consequences if mistakes happen? Will embryos be used during research and how will they be treated? Scientifically, we are still a long way from genetic enhancement because there is no trustworthy means to insert or remove genes from an embryo. Scientists still have to unravel the role of each gene, and it is thought that there may be up to three thousand responsible for intelligence. Interfering with that many genes would be prohibitively risky. Would parents really be willing to take that kind of risk with their child? Finally, scientists do not yet know what effect genes have on one another. Inserting genes to increase musical intelligence, for example, may have a devastating effect on some other characteristic, which may not become evident until the child reaches nine or ten years of age. What happens then? Can a nine-year-old be sent back to the clinic for a refund?

the inner place

DISCUSS

1   Along with the attributes mentioned above, what other attributes might parents want in their genetically enhanced child? (Perhaps create a list here of things like sport and kindness. Why do we pick some and not others? Why do we value some and not others? What are the implications for very intelligent people with no kindness?)

2   Do you think parents are within their rights to use whatever means possible to give their child the best genetic make-up.

3   Do you think that genetic enhancement is giving a child 'the best chance in life'?

Social Disintegration?

There is another consequence of genetic enhancement that could potentially have disastrous consequences for society as we know it. Read the following account of the likely consequences of a world that might embrace genetic enhancement in the future.

The year is 2350. A secret, high-level commission reports to the Health and Human Services Secretary in Washington DC on their findings. Developments in genetic enhancement technology, the eminent academics have concluded, are leading inexorably to a situation that had often been predicted by alarmists but had never been taken seriously by policy-makers. Genetic modifications had been routinely available for three hundred years, after some decades of initial research. At first they had been confined to replacing genes for obvious disorders, but pretty quickly enhancements for various athletic and cognitive traits had come on the market, as it was argued that distinctions between gene therapy and gene enhancement were fundamentally arbitrary. Those who were sufficiently wealthy had increasingly taken the use of genetic improvements for granted as part of giving their children a good start in life. Over time a class of people came to be identified who had benefited from several generations of genomic enhancements, and who typically married people of the same class and had children with them. A new biologically based class system had evolved. Despite the obvious new inequities that had arisen, no one had been able to stop the process. The right to reproduce using whatever means individuals could afford had long been accepted as fundamental to their way of life.

The corporations which had researched, produced and marketed the procedures collectively accounted for a large part of the American economy. Other countries had banned the use of genetic enhancements, and had suffered economically as a result. Politicians, business leaders and opinion-formers in the media and the universities were all from the genetically enriched class, as were those at the forefront of every area of society; inevitably they were reluctant to make changes which would call things into question too radically. Those who had not benefited from generations of engineering had rarely managed to achieve positions of power, and were too disunited and distracted by other concerns to mount any effective protest about the situation, beyond some occasional rioting.

the
inner
place

The alarming new situation described in the recent government report suggested that by the end of the third millennium the growing division between the two classes would lead to sharply decreased fertility rates whenever a genetically enriched person attempted to have children with a 'natural'. The implication was stark: as the report put it, there would be 'entirely separate species with no ability to cross-breed, and with as much romantic interest in each other as a current human would have for a chimpanzee'. It was not clear how this result could be avoided. Even if the political will was there for it to be banned in the US, biotechnology companies and their customers would simply move to poorer countries that needed the revenue. Moral appeals to the enhanced class would probably not work either: given that it was in each individual's interest to continue to give their children a better genetic inheritance, and nobody was being directly harmed by their actions, it was going to be virtually impossible to persuade more than a few to change their behaviour. The free choices of individuals had inexorably led to a situation that could not be regarded as best for the population as a whole.

(Robert Song, *Human Genetics*)

DISCUSS

The above is a fictional account of how the world might look in three hundred years' time if genetic enhancement becomes a reality. Is the above account likely to remain science fiction, or do you think it could become a reality? Give reasons for your answer.

the

inner

place

ACKNOWLEDGEMENTS

Scripture quotations from the *New Revised Standard Version Bible*, 1993 and 1998 by the Division of Christian Education of the National Council of the Churches of Christ in the United States of America, used with permission. Extracts from *Catechism of the Catholic Church* (pp.283/285/300–1/306/307/313), Libreria Editrice Vaticana. 'A Failed Execution' (pp.9/10) from *True Tales of American Life* (ed. by Paul Auster), courtesy of Faber and Faber, 2002. Quote from *After Religion: Generation X and the Search for Meaning* (p.16) by Gordon Lynch, courtesy of Darton, Longman & Todd, 2002. Extract from *The Invention of Solitude: A Memoir* (pp.23/70) by Paul Auster, courtesy of Penguin Ltd., 1988. Extract from *Stand Up and Fight* (pp.30–1) by Alan English, published by Yellow Jersey Press, used with permission of The Random House Group Ltd, 2005. Extract from *The Guardian* (p.32) by Bernard O'Riordan, 15 September 2005, used with permission of Guardian Newspapers Limited 2005. Extract from *Keane: The Autobiography* (pp.41–2) by Roy Keane, courtesy of Penguin Ltd., 2003. Extract from *The Power of Intention* (pp.45/50–1) by Wayne Dyer, Hay House, Inc., 2004, used with permission. Extract from *Timeless Healing* (p.47) by Herbert Benson, courtesy of Simon & Schuster, Inc., 1997. Extract from *The Tenth Circle of Hell* (pp.54–7) by Rezak Hukanovic, courtesy of Abacus / Time Warner, 1996. Article from *The Sunday Times* (pp.61–2) by John Harlow, 4 September 2005, courtesy of *The Sunday Times*. Extracts from *Heavier than Heaven: The Biography of Kurt Cobain* (pp.64–5/175) by Charles R. Cross, courtesy of Sarah Lazin Books, New York, 2002. Extract from *Smashed* (p.106) by Koren Zailckas, published by Ebury Press, courtesy of The Random House Group Ltd., 2006. Extract from *Night* (pp.108–10) by Elie Wiesel, courtesy of Bantam Press, 1982. *Borderlands 1996: A Story of Transcendence* (pp.118–19) by Denis Walsh, *The Sunday Times*, 9 October 2005, used with permission. 'The Dark Destroyer' (p.121) by Brian Doogan, *The Sunday Times*, 15 May 2005, used with permission. 'McDonald's' (pp.128–9) by Shelly Millar from *Chicken Soup for the Teenage Soul* (ed. by Jack Canfield, Mark Victor Hansen and Deborah Reber), HCI Teens, 1991, used with permission. Extract from *The Da Vinci Code* (pp.170–2) by Dan Brown, published by Doubleday, used with permission of The Random House Group Ltd., 2003. Adapted material from *A Marginal Jew: Rethinking the Historical Jesus* (p.184) by John Meier, published by Doubleday, courtesy of The Random House Group Ltd., 1991. Extract (p.210) from *Disturbing the Peace: The Way of Disciples* by Eamonn Bredin, Columba Press, 1985, used with permission. Extracts from *The Human Mind* (pp.228–9/295) by Robert Winston, published by Bantam Press, used with permission of The Random House Group Ltd., 2004. Adapted material from *Enneagram 2: A Spirituality of Brokenness* (pp.232–6) by Eilis Bergin and Eddie Fitzgerald, SDB Media, Salesian College, Celbridge, Co. Kildare, 1993, used with permission. Extract from *Urban Legends* (pp.278–9) by N.E. Genge, courtesy of The Random House Group Ltd., 2000. 'The Shipwreck' (pp.290–2) from *A History of the World in 10 1/2 Chapters* by Julian Barnes, Cambridge University Press, 1995, used with permission. Article from the *Irish Independent* (pp.296–7) by John Meagher, 12 August 2005, used with permission. Article from *The Sunday Times* (pp.303–4) by Mark Franchetti, used with permission. 'A Mother Forgives' (p.315) by Gordon Rayner and Charlotte Gill from the *Daily Mail*, 1 December 2005, courtesy of the *Daily Mail*. Extract (pp.332–3) by Anne McMahon from *The Sunday Times*, 9 May 2004, used with permission. Extract (pp.340–2) by Corri Gottlieb from *The Sunday Times*, 21 August 2005, used with permission. Extract from *Oryx and Crake* (pp.344–5) by Margaret Atwood, courtesy of Nan A. Talese/Doubleday, 2003. Extract from *My Sister's Keeper* (pp.349–50) by Jodi Picoult, Atria Books, 2004, used with permission. Extract from *Human Genetics* (pp.360–2) by Robert Song, Darton, Longman & Todd, 2002, used with permission.

Stock photography courtesy of www.sxc.hu; student art by Jane Beale, Rachel Clancy, Claire Doyle, Natasha O'Malley Moore, Diane Rice, Kim Rowe,

O'Malley Moore, Diane Rice, Kim Rowe, Diana Wilson; images supplied by Getty Images (p.30, 42, 121, 218, 312, 315, 354); cartoons by Paul Young (p.6, 21, 31, 45, 65, 88, 179, 204, 269, 275, 279, 294, 298); 'The Scream', c.1893 (engraving) (b/w photo), Munch, Edvard (1863–1944)/Private Collection, Roger-Viollet, Paris/The Bridgeman Art Library (p.13); image of Auschwitz rail tracks courtesy of Poczta Muzeum (p.58); image supplied by Paul Young/Cartoon Saloon (p.70); photograph courtesy of Brian O'Gorman (p.90); images of sculptures courtesy of Jim Cogley (pp.91,93); photograph of Elie Wiesel courtesy of Georges Borchardt (p.110); 'The Nightmare', 1781 (oil on canvas), Fuseli, Henry (Fussli, Johann Heinrich) (1741–1825)/© The Detroit Institute of Arts, USA, Founders Society purchase with Mr and Mrs Bert L. Smokler/The Bridgeman Art Library (p.160); 'St Mary Magdalene', 1576–1578 (oil on canvas), Greco, El (Domenico Theotocopuli) (1541–1614)/Museum of Fine Arts, Budapest, Hungary, Interfoto/The Bridgeman Art Library (p.173); image of 'Madonna and Child' by Vitale da Bologna appears courtesy of www.biblepicturegallery.com (p.184); image of 'St Paul' by Bernardo Daddi appears courtesy of www.biblepicturegallery.com (p.185); photograph of Sea of Galilee appears courtesy of www.biblepicturegallery.com (p.187); image of crucifixion appears courtesy of www.biblepicturegallery.com (p.189); image of Denarius appears courtesy of www.biblepicturegallery.com (p.190); photograph of Judaea appears courtesy of www.biblepicturegallery.com (p.191); photograph of Jericho appears courtesy of www.biblepicturegallery.com

(p.198); 'Jesus talking to the teacher in the Temple' courtesy of www.biblepicturegallery.com (p.219); image of inscription of Pontius Pilate found at Caesarea appears courtesy of www.biblepicturegallery.com (p.237); photograph of Jesus' tomb appears courtesy of www.freestockphotos.com (p.244); image of 'The Meal in Emmaus' by Rembrandt appears courtesy of www.biblepicturegallery.com (p.245); photograph of Appian Way courtesy of www.greatcommission.com, Rex Geissler (p.246); image of the Shroud of Turin courtesy of the Fortean Picture Gallery (p.247); photograph of St Peter's Basilica appears courtesy of www.freestockphotos.com (p.250); Coptic painting appears courtesy of www.freestockphotos.com (p.252); photograph of the catacombs appears courtesy of www.freestockphotos.com (p.253); image of early Christian mosaics appear courtesy of www.freestockphotos.com (p.254); image of dove appears courtesy of www.freestockphotos.com (p.254); image of shipwreck supplied by Mary Evans (p.290); image of shipwreck supplied by Mary Evans (p.291); photograph of New York courtesy of Nihan Aydin (p.296); image of Mount Sinai appears courtesy of www.biblepicturegallery.com (p.301); 'Return of the Prodigal Son', c.1668–1669 (oil on canvas), Rembrandt Harmensz van Rijn (1606–1669)/Hermitage, St Petersburg, Russia/The Bridgeman Art Library (p.318); photograph of couple courtesy of Paconavarro, www.ohestudio.com, Pro Photo Studio (p.328); photograph of James Watson supplied by Mary Evans (p.346); photograph of Francis Crick supplied by Mary Evans (p.346).